Volume 1

Blood and magic.

Originally published as *Wolf* #1–4

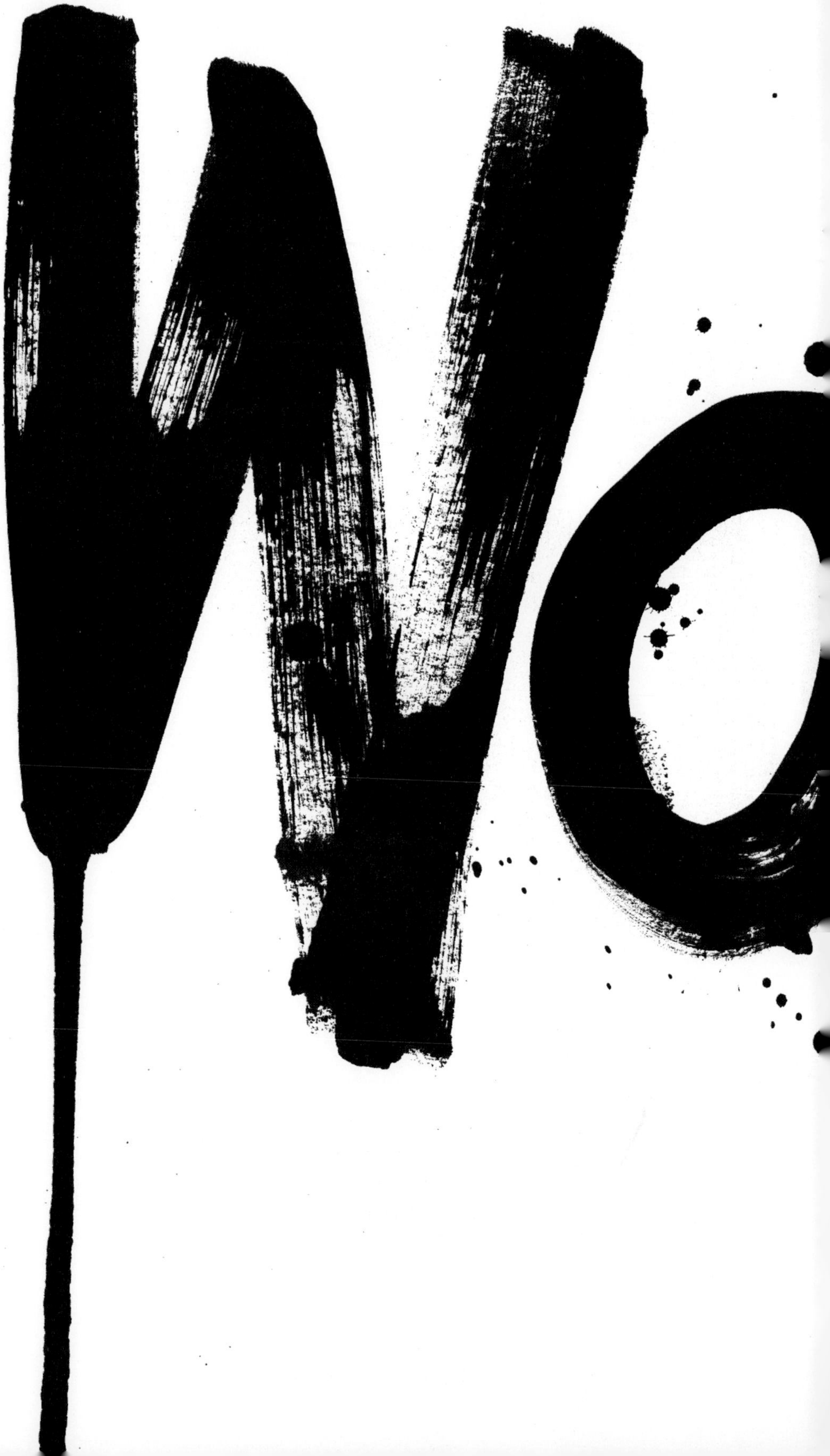

Volume 1

Blood and magic.

Writer	**Ales Kot**
Artist	**Matt Taylor**
Colorist	**Lee Loughridge**
Letterer	**Clayton Cowles**
Designer	**Tom Muller**

Chapter 1

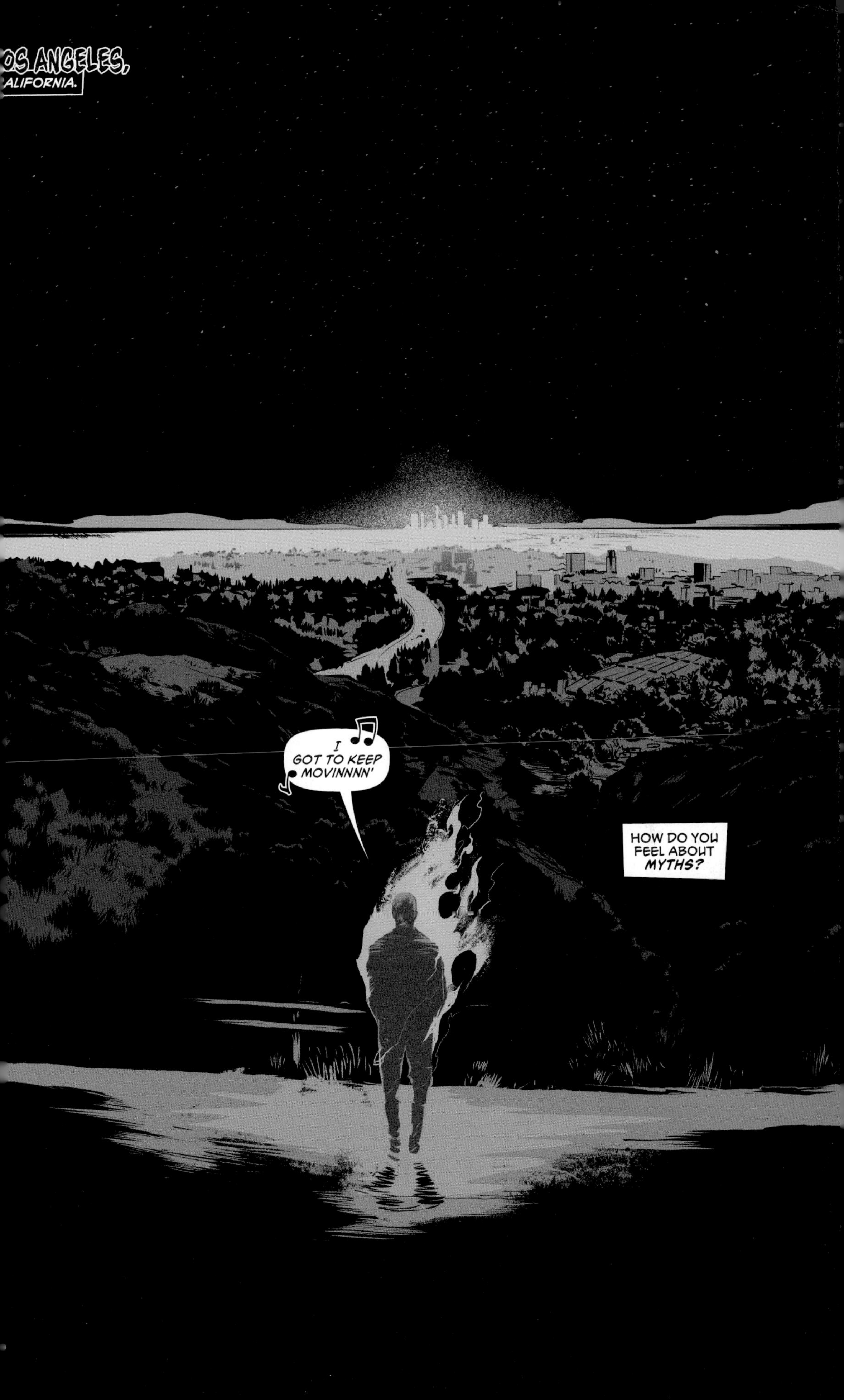
OS ANGELES,
ALIFORNIA.
I GOT TO KEEP MOVINNNN'
HOW DO YOU FEEL ABOUT MYTHS?

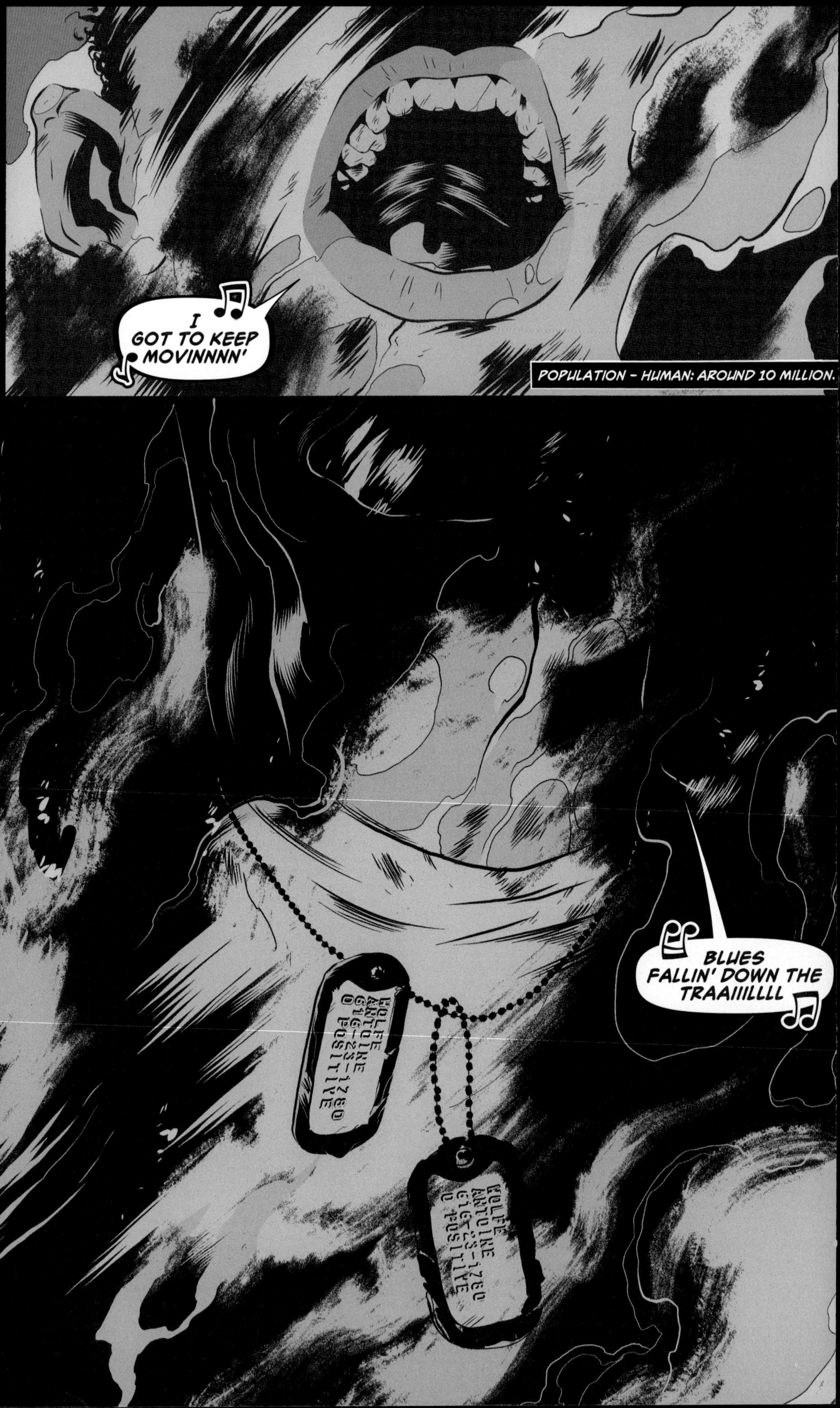
I GOT TO KEEP MOVINNN'
POPULATION - HUMAN: AROUND 10 MILLION.
WOLFE
ANTOINE
616-23-1760
O POSITIVE
BLUES FALLIN' DOWN THE TRAAIIILLLL

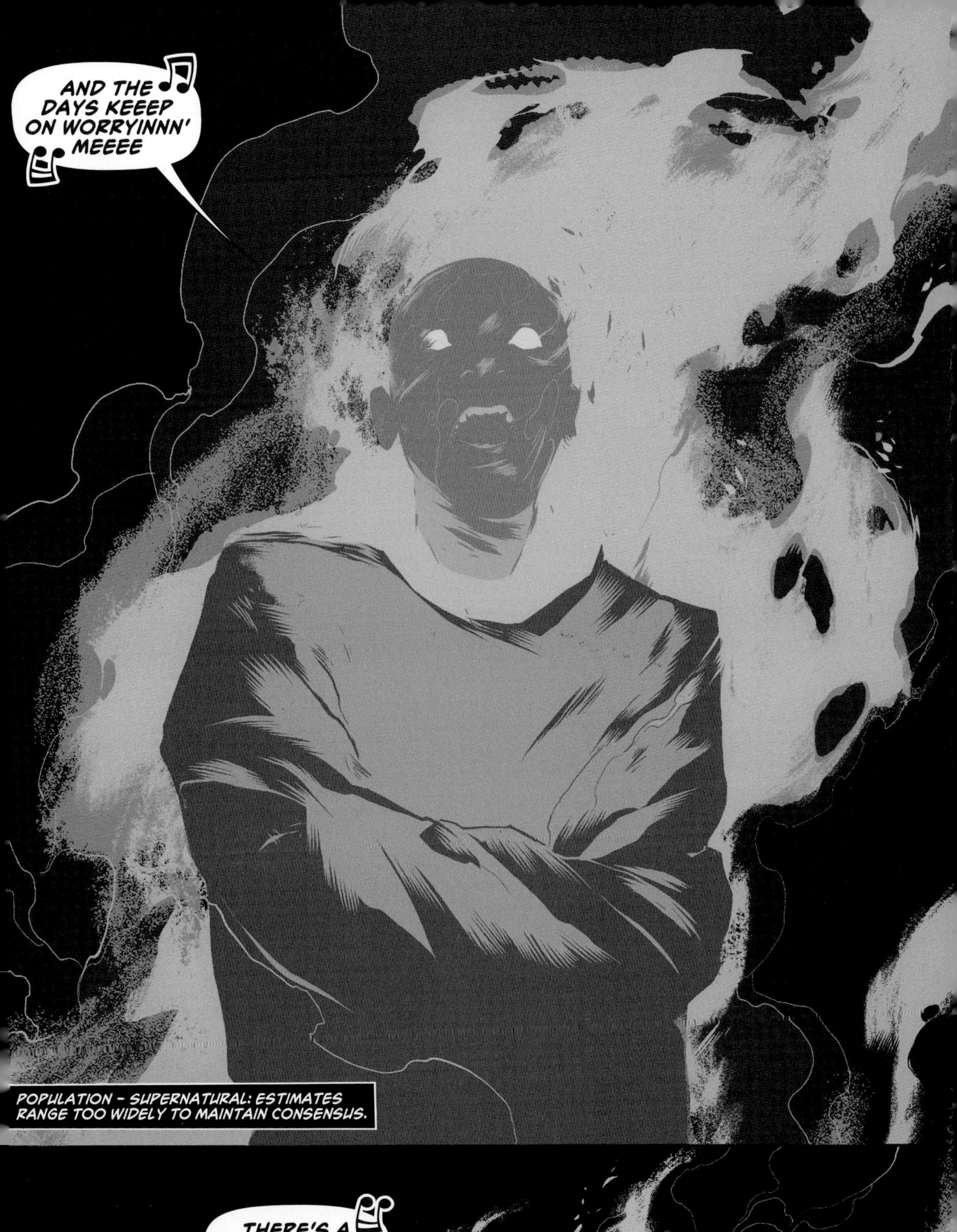
AND THE DAYS KEEEP ON WORRYINNN' MEEEE
POPULATION - SUPERNATURAL: ESTIMATES RANGE TOO WIDELY TO MAINTAIN CONSENSUS.

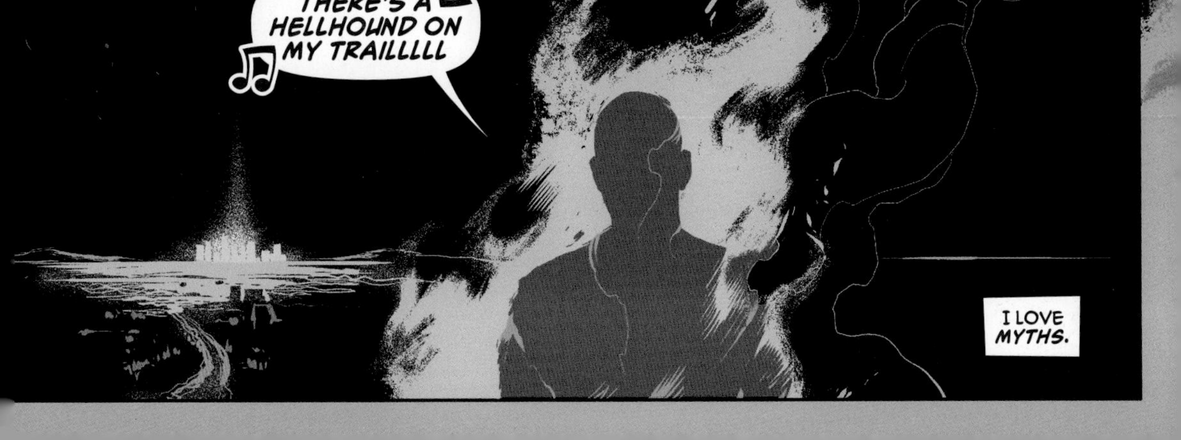
THERE'S A HELLHOUND ON MY TRAILLLLL
I LOVE MYTHS.

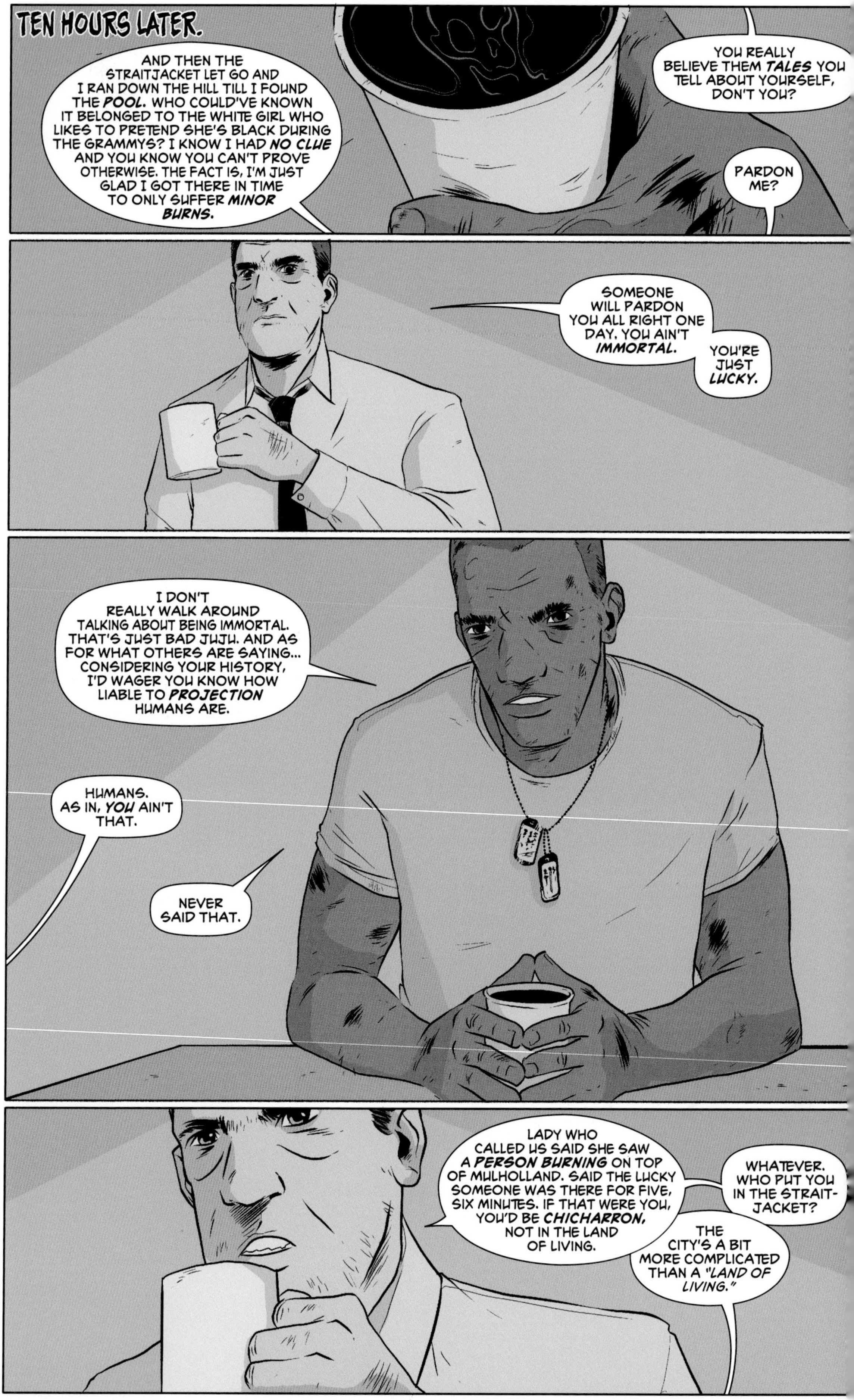
TEN HOURS LATER.
AND THEN THE STRAITJACKET LET GO AND I RAN DOWN THE HILL TILL I FOUND THE POOL. WHO COULD'VE KNOWN IT BELONGED TO THE WHITE GIRL WHO LIKES TO PRETEND SHE'S BLACK DURING THE GRAMMYS? I KNOW I HAD NO CLUE AND YOU KNOW YOU CAN'T PROVE OTHERWISE. THE FACT IS, I'M JUST GLAD I GOT THERE IN TIME TO ONLY SUFFER MINOR BURNS.
YOU REALLY BELIEVE THEM TALES YOU TELL ABOUT YOURSELF, DON'T YOU?
PARDON ME?
SOMEONE WILL PARDON YOU ALL RIGHT ONE DAY. YOU AIN'T IMMORTAL.
YOU'RE JUST LUCKY.
I DON'T REALLY WALK AROUND TALKING ABOUT BEING IMMORTAL. THAT'S JUST BAD JUJU. AND AS FOR WHAT OTHERS ARE SAYING... CONSIDERING YOUR HISTORY, I'D WAGER YOU KNOW HOW LIABLE TO PROJECTION HUMANS ARE.
HUMANS. AS IN, YOU AIN'T THAT.
NEVER SAID THAT.
LADY WHO CALLED US SAID SHE SAW A PERSON BURNING ON TOP OF MULHOLLAND. SAID THE LUCKY SOMEONE WAS THERE FOR FIVE, SIX MINUTES. IF THAT WERE YOU, YOU'D BE CHICHARRON, NOT IN THE LAND OF LIVING.
WHATEVER. WHO PUT YOU IN THE STRAIT-JACKET?
THE CITY'S A BIT MORE COMPLICATED THAN A "LAND OF LIVING."

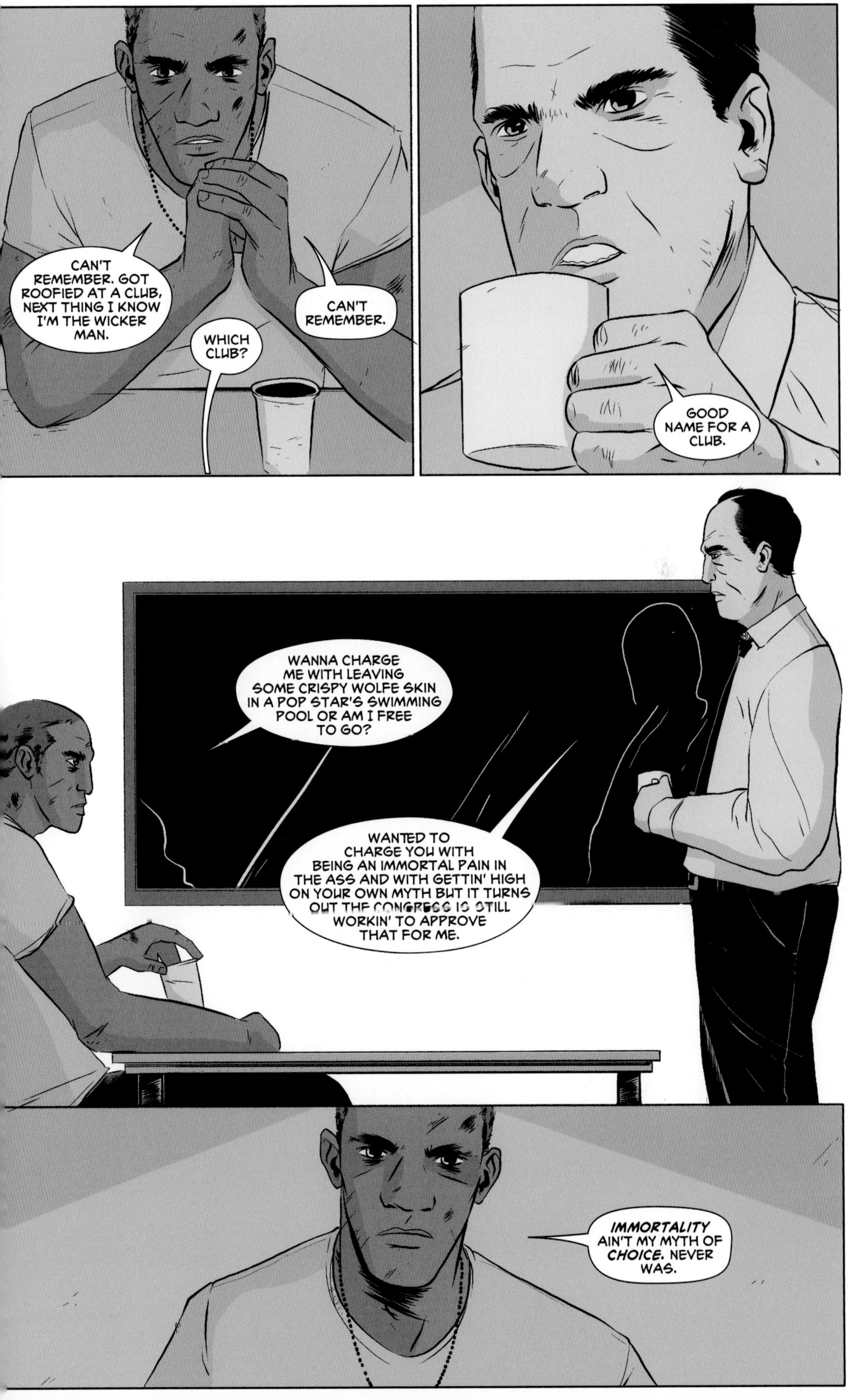
CAN'T REMEMBER. GOT ROOFIED AT A CLUB, NEXT THING I KNOW I'M THE WICKER MAN.
WHICH CLUB?
CAN'T REMEMBER.
GOOD NAME FOR A CLUB.
WANNA CHARGE ME WITH LEAVING SOME CRISPY WOLFE SKIN IN A POP STAR'S SWIMMING POOL OR AM I FREE TO GO?
WANTED TO CHARGE YOU WITH BEING AN IMMORTAL PAIN IN THE ASS AND WITH GETTIN' HIGH ON YOUR OWN MYTH BUT IT TURNS OUT THE CONGRESS IS STILL WORKIN' TO APPROVE THAT FOR ME.
IMMORTALITY AIN'T MY MYTH OF *CHOICE*. NEVER WAS.

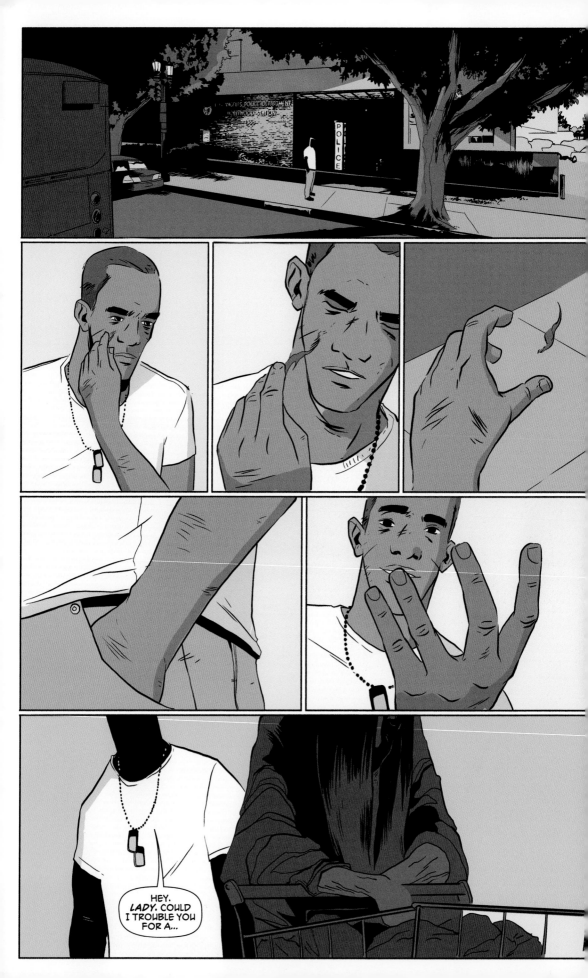

HEY. *LADY.* COULD I TROUBLE YOU FOR A...

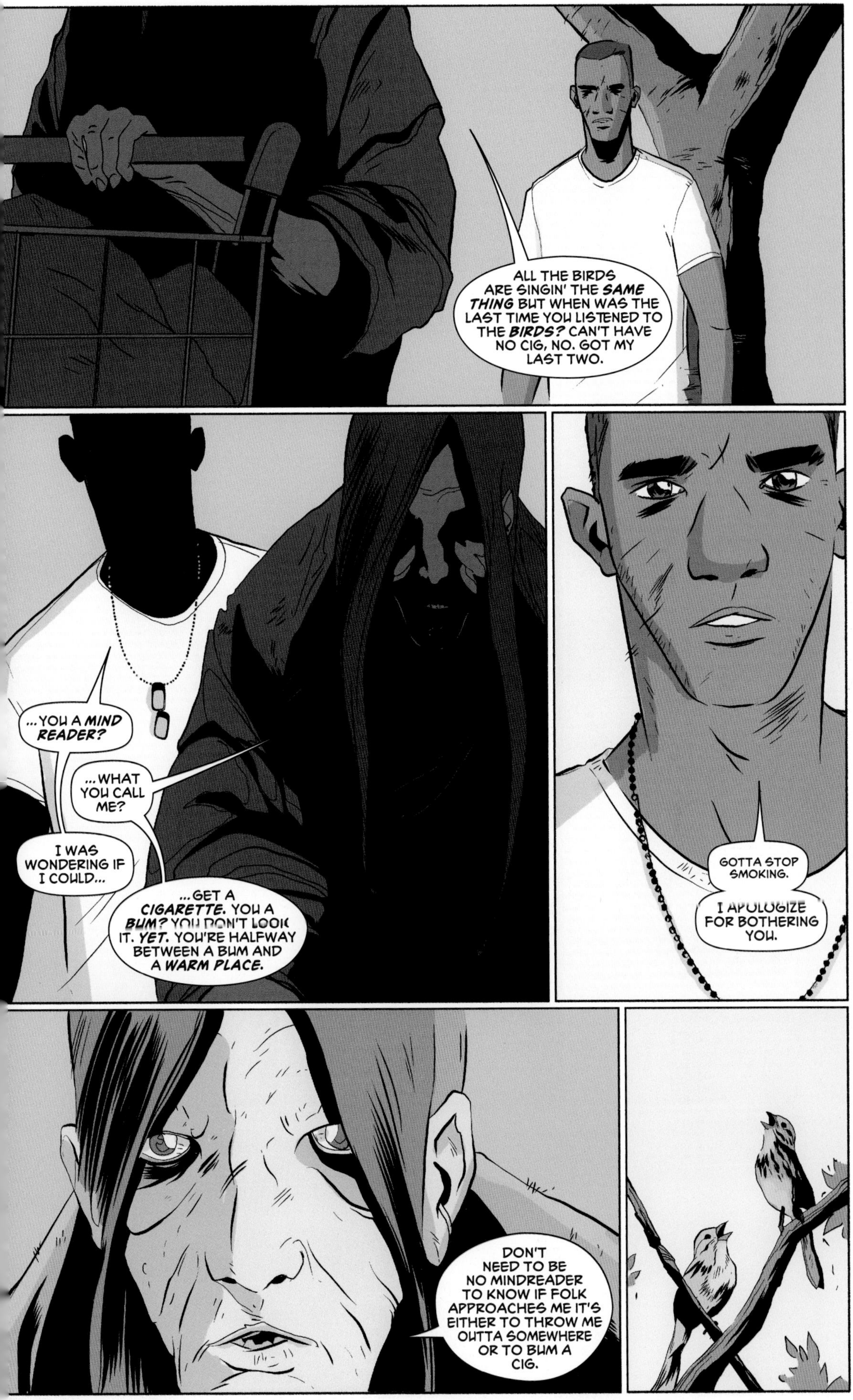
ALL THE BIRDS ARE SINGIN' THE SAME THING BUT WHEN WAS THE LAST TIME YOU LISTENED TO THE BIRDS? CAN'T HAVE NO CIG, NO. GOT MY LAST TWO.
...YOU A MIND READER?
...WHAT YOU CALL ME?
I WAS WONDERING IF I COULD...
...GET A CIGARETTE. YOU A BUM? YOU DON'T LOOK IT. YET. YOU'RE HALFWAY BETWEEN A BUM AND A WARM PLACE.
GOTTA STOP SMOKING.
I APOLOGIZE FOR BOTHERING YOU.
DON'T NEED TO BE NO MINDREADER TO KNOW IF FOLK APPROACHES ME IT'S EITHER TO THROW ME OUTTA SOMEWHERE OR TO BUM A CIG.

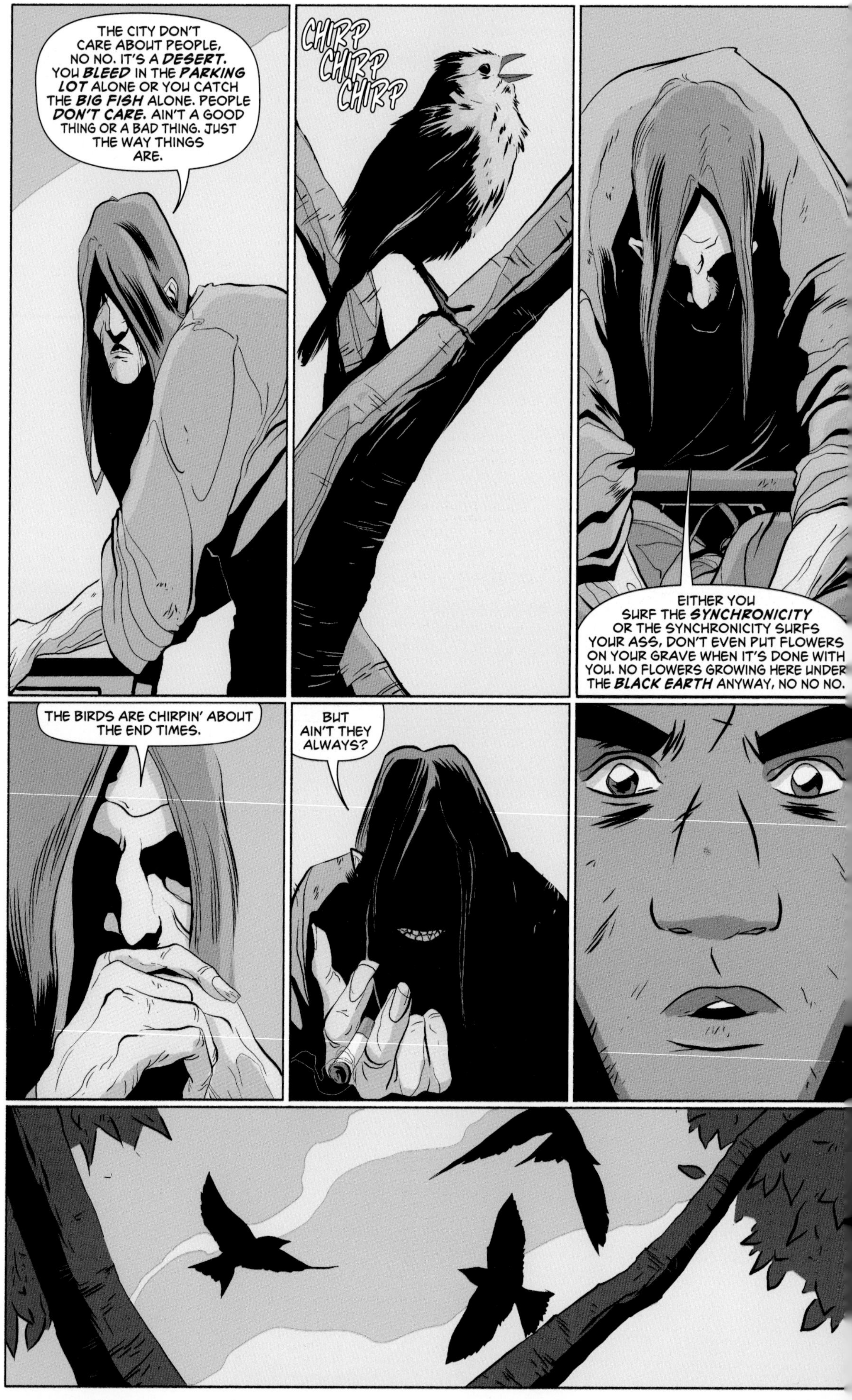

THE CITY DON'T CARE ABOUT PEOPLE, NO NO. IT'S A DESERT. YOU BLEED IN THE PARKING LOT ALONE OR YOU CATCH THE BIG FISH ALONE. PEOPLE DON'T CARE. AIN'T A GOOD THING OR A BAD THING. JUST THE WAY THINGS ARE.
CHIRP CHIRP CHIRP
EITHER YOU SURF THE SYNCHRONICITY OR THE SYNCHRONICITY SURFS YOUR ASS, DON'T EVEN PUT FLOWERS ON YOUR GRAVE WHEN IT'S DONE WITH YOU. NO FLOWERS GROWING HERE UNDER THE BLACK EARTH ANYWAY, NO NO NO.
THE BIRDS ARE CHIRPIN' ABOUT THE END TIMES.
BUT AIN'T THEY ALWAYS?

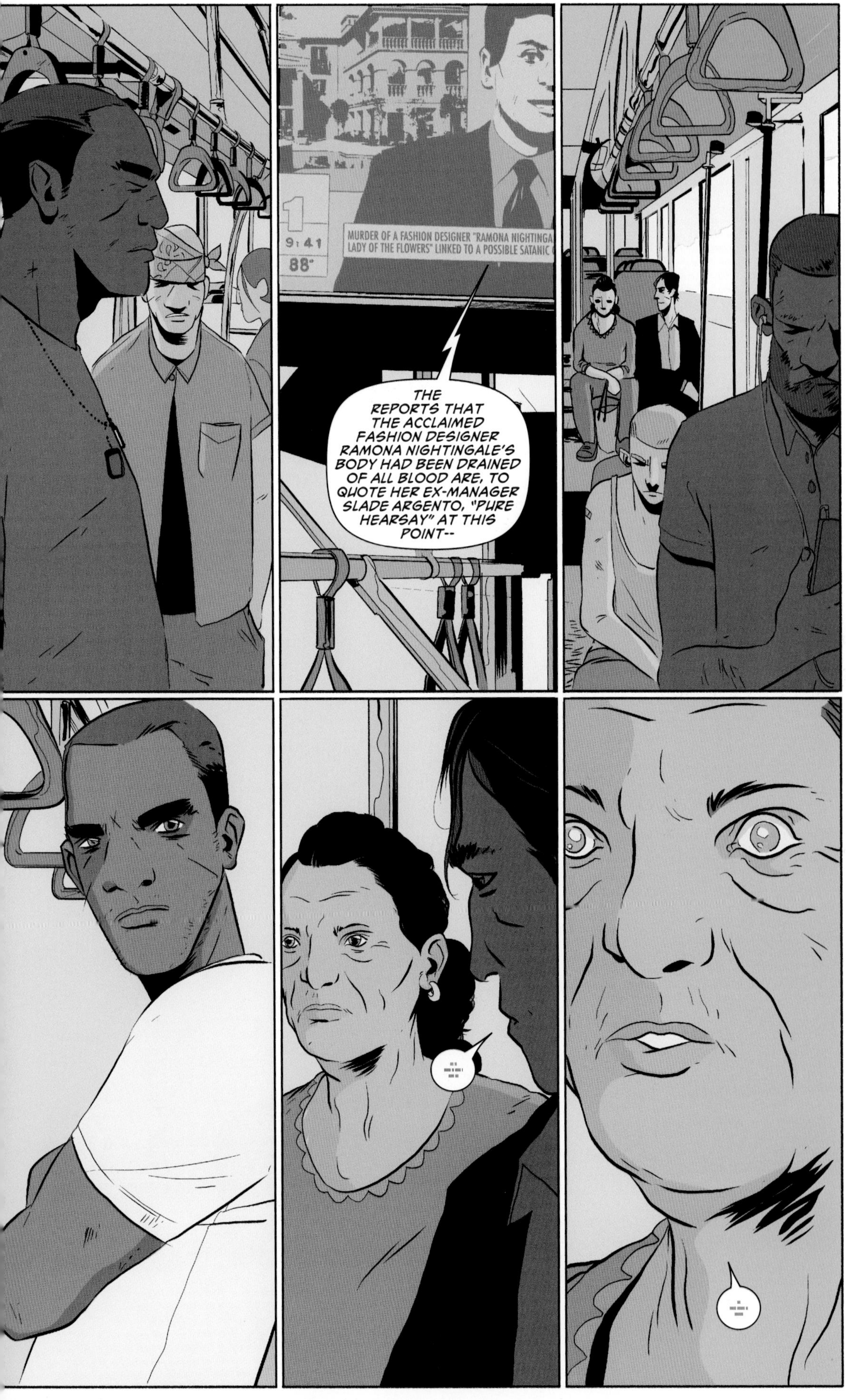

MURDER OF A FASHION DESIGNER "RAMONA NIGHTINGA
LADY OF THE FLOWERS" LINKED TO A POSSIBLE SATANIC
9:41
88°
THE REPORTS THAT THE ACCLAIMED FASHION DESIGNER RAMONA NIGHTINGALE'S BODY HAD BEEN DRAINED OF ALL BLOOD ARE, TO QUOTE HER EX-MANAGER SLADE ARGENTO, "PURE HEARSAY" AT THIS POINT--

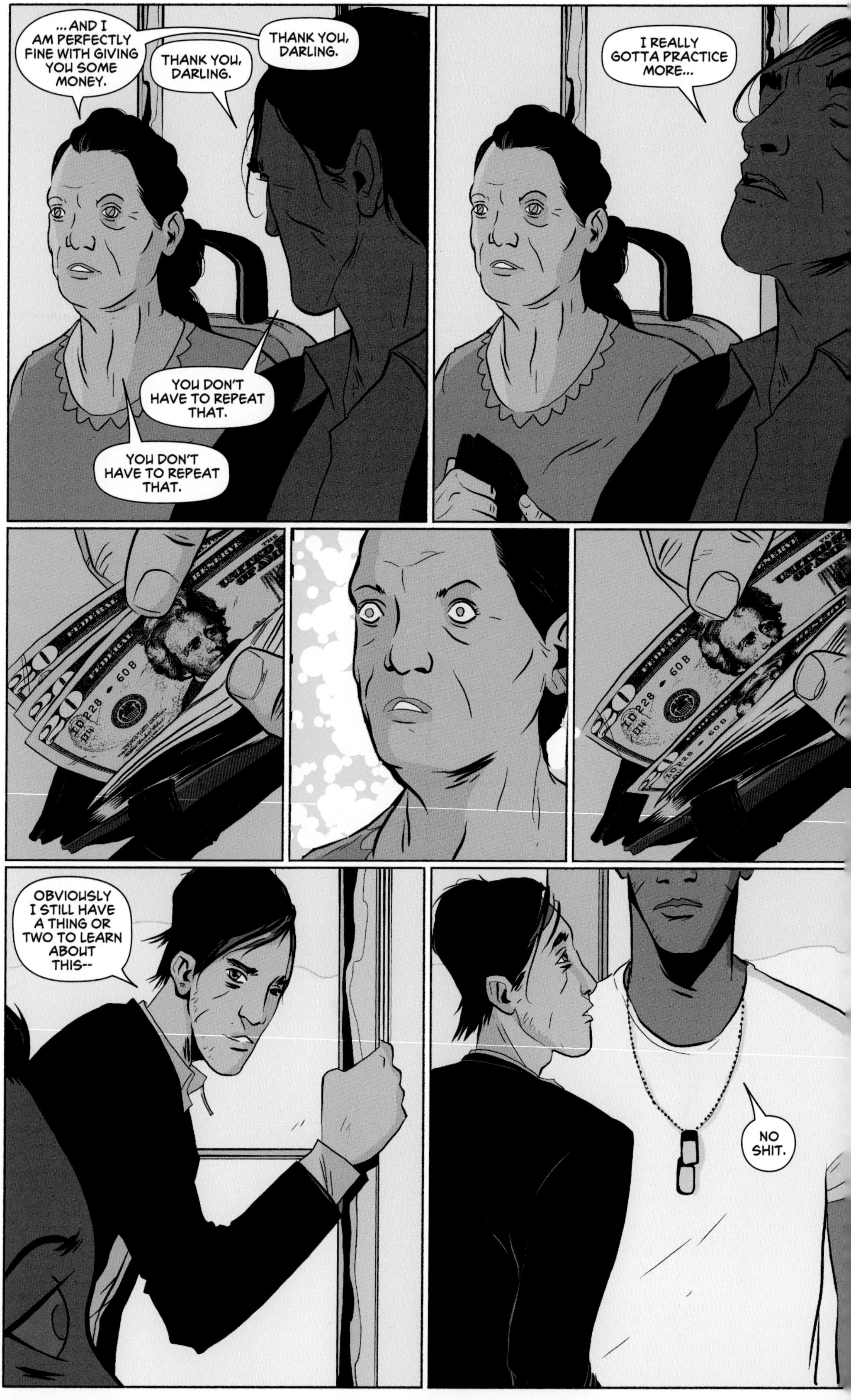
...AND I AM PERFECTLY FINE WITH GIVING YOU SOME MONEY.
THANK YOU, DARLING.
THANK YOU, DARLING.
YOU DON'T HAVE TO REPEAT THAT.
YOU DON'T HAVE TO REPEAT THAT.
I REALLY GOTTA PRACTICE MORE...
OBVIOUSLY I STILL HAVE A THING OR TWO TO LEARN ABOUT THIS--
NO SHIT.

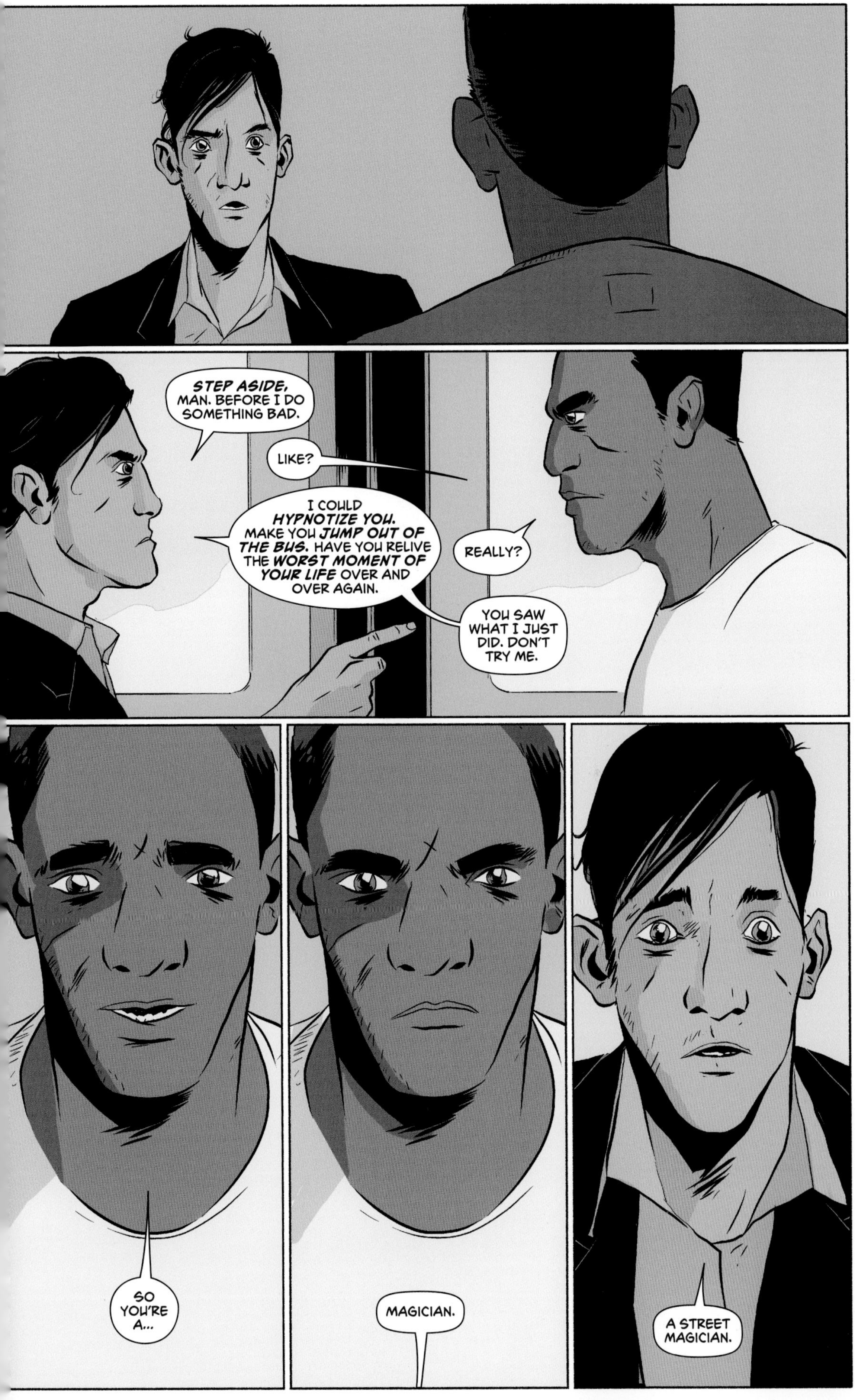
STEP ASIDE, MAN. BEFORE I DO SOMETHING BAD.
LIKE?
I COULD HYPNOTIZE YOU. MAKE YOU JUMP OUT OF THE BUS. HAVE YOU RELIVE THE WORST MOMENT OF YOUR LIFE OVER AND OVER AGAIN.
REALLY?
YOU SAW WHAT I JUST DID. DON'T TRY ME.
SO YOU'RE A...
MAGICIAN.
A STREET MAGICIAN.

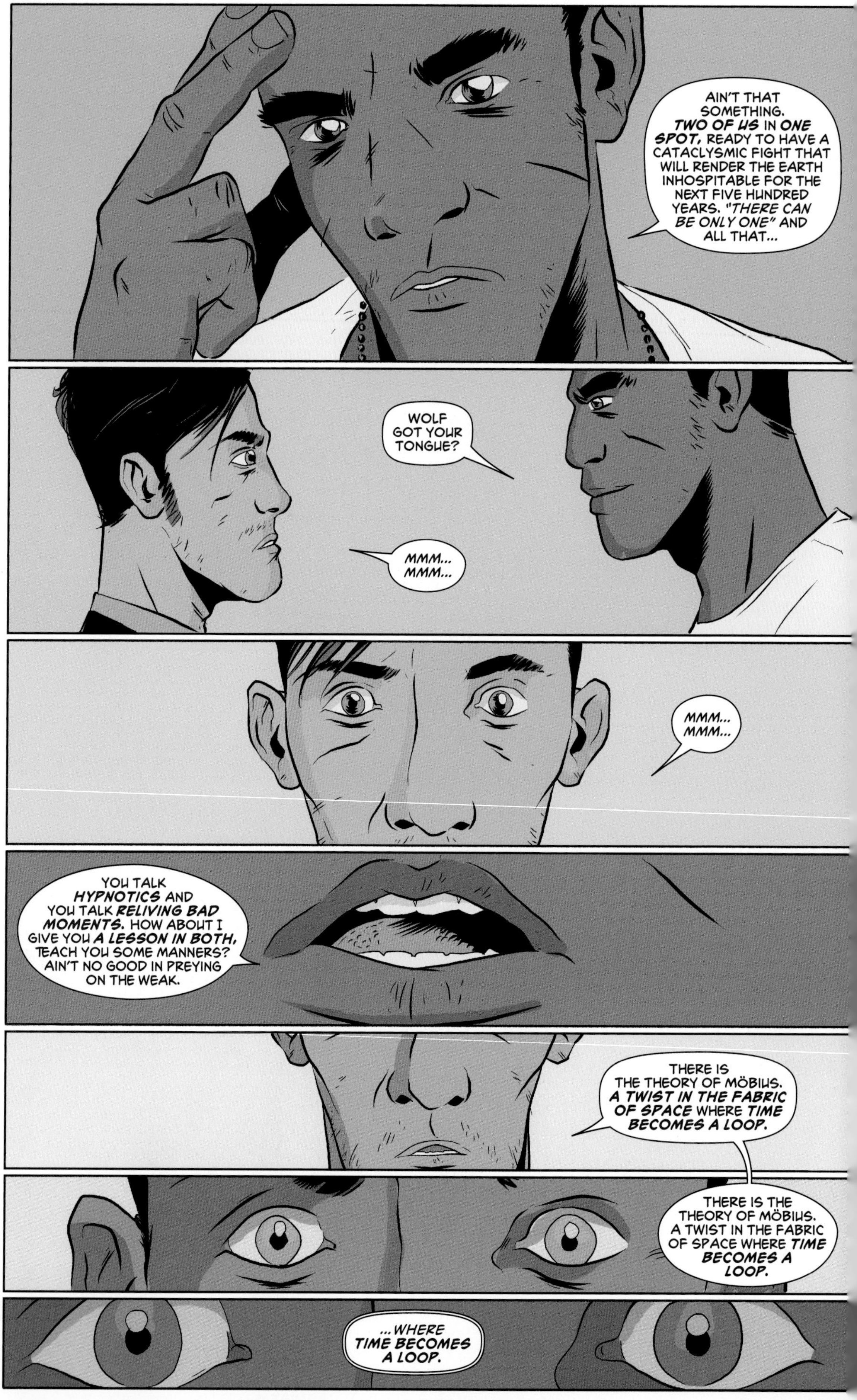

AIN'T THAT SOMETHING. TWO OF US IN ONE SPOT, READY TO HAVE A CATACLYSMIC FIGHT THAT WILL RENDER THE EARTH INHOSPITABLE FOR THE NEXT FIVE HUNDRED YEARS. "THERE CAN BE ONLY ONE" AND ALL THAT...
WOLF GOT YOUR TONGUE?
MMM... MMM...
MMM... MMM...
YOU TALK HYPNOTICS AND YOU TALK RELIVING BAD MOMENTS. HOW ABOUT I GIVE YOU A LESSON IN BOTH, TEACH YOU SOME MANNERS? AIN'T NO GOOD IN PREYING ON THE WEAK.
THERE IS THE THEORY OF MÖBIUS. A TWIST IN THE FABRIC OF SPACE WHERE TIME BECOMES A LOOP.
THERE IS THE THEORY OF MÖBIUS. A TWIST IN THE FABRIC OF SPACE WHERE TIME BECOMES A LOOP.
...WHERE TIME BECOMES A LOOP.

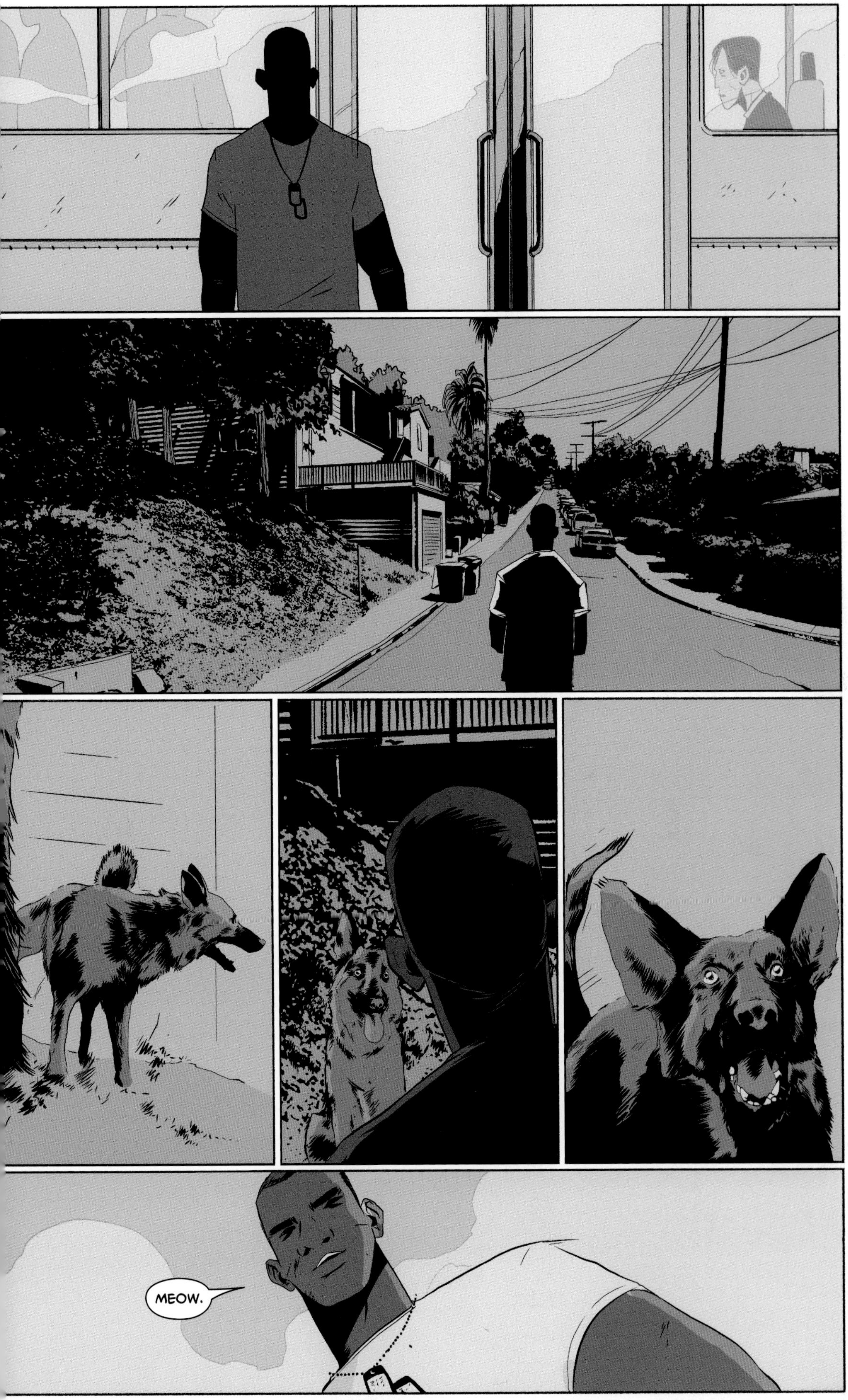
MEOW.

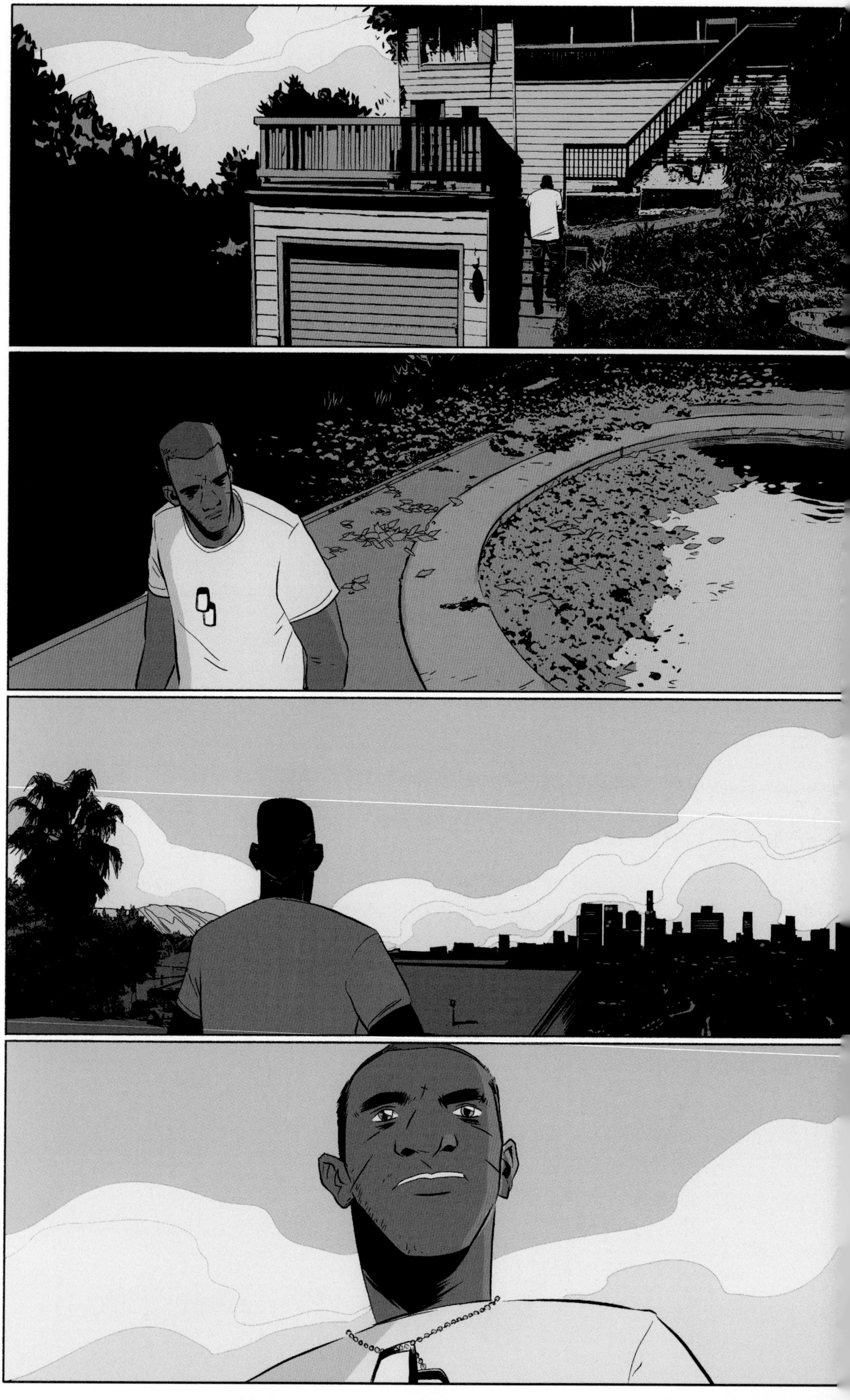

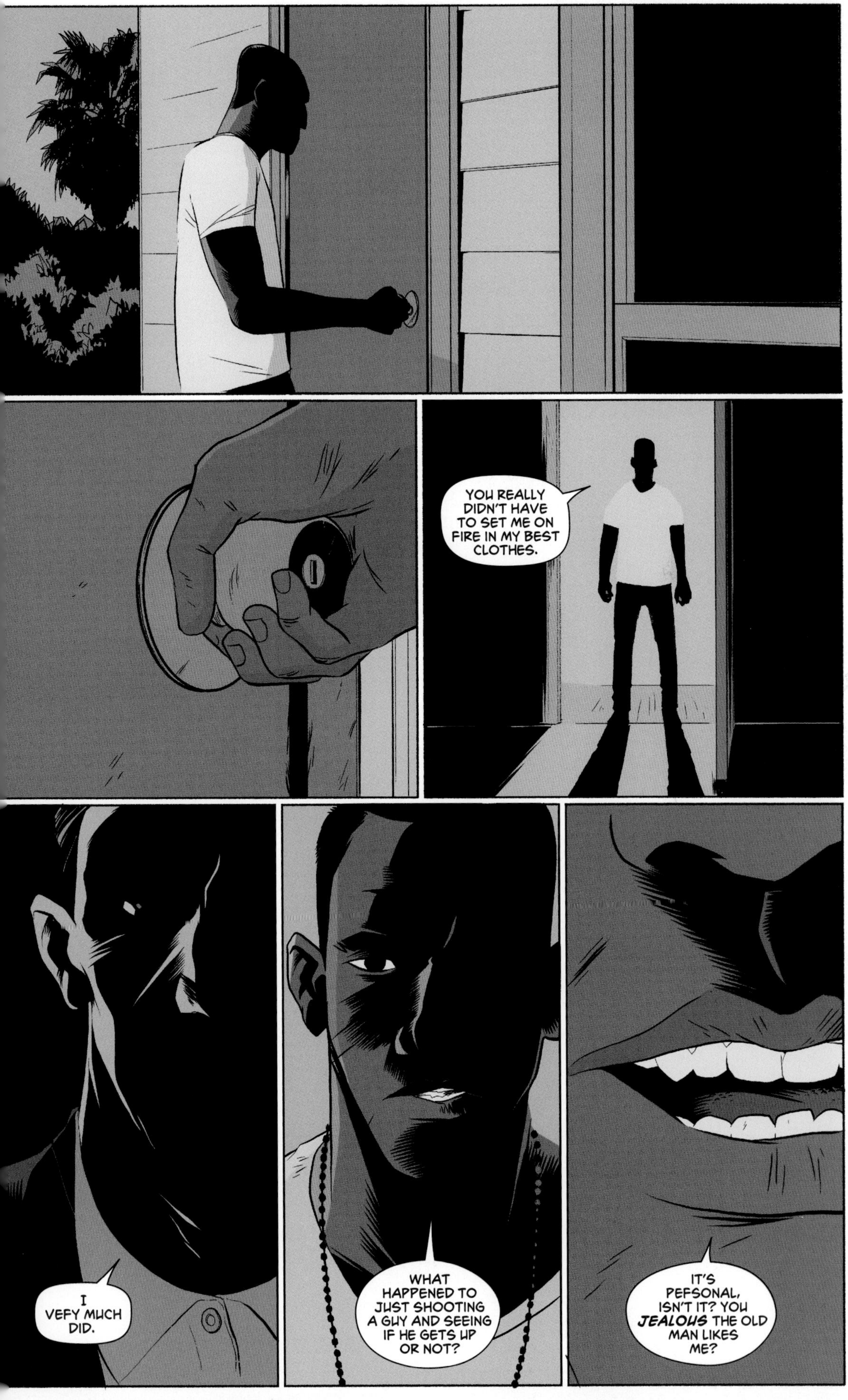
YOU REALLY DIDN'T HAVE TO SET ME ON FIRE IN MY BEST CLOTHES.
I VEFY MUCH DID.
WHAT HAPPENED TO JUST SHOOTING A GUY AND SEEING IF HE GETS UP OR NOT?
IT'S PEFSONAL, ISN'T IT? YOU *JEALOUS* THE OLD MAN LIKES ME?

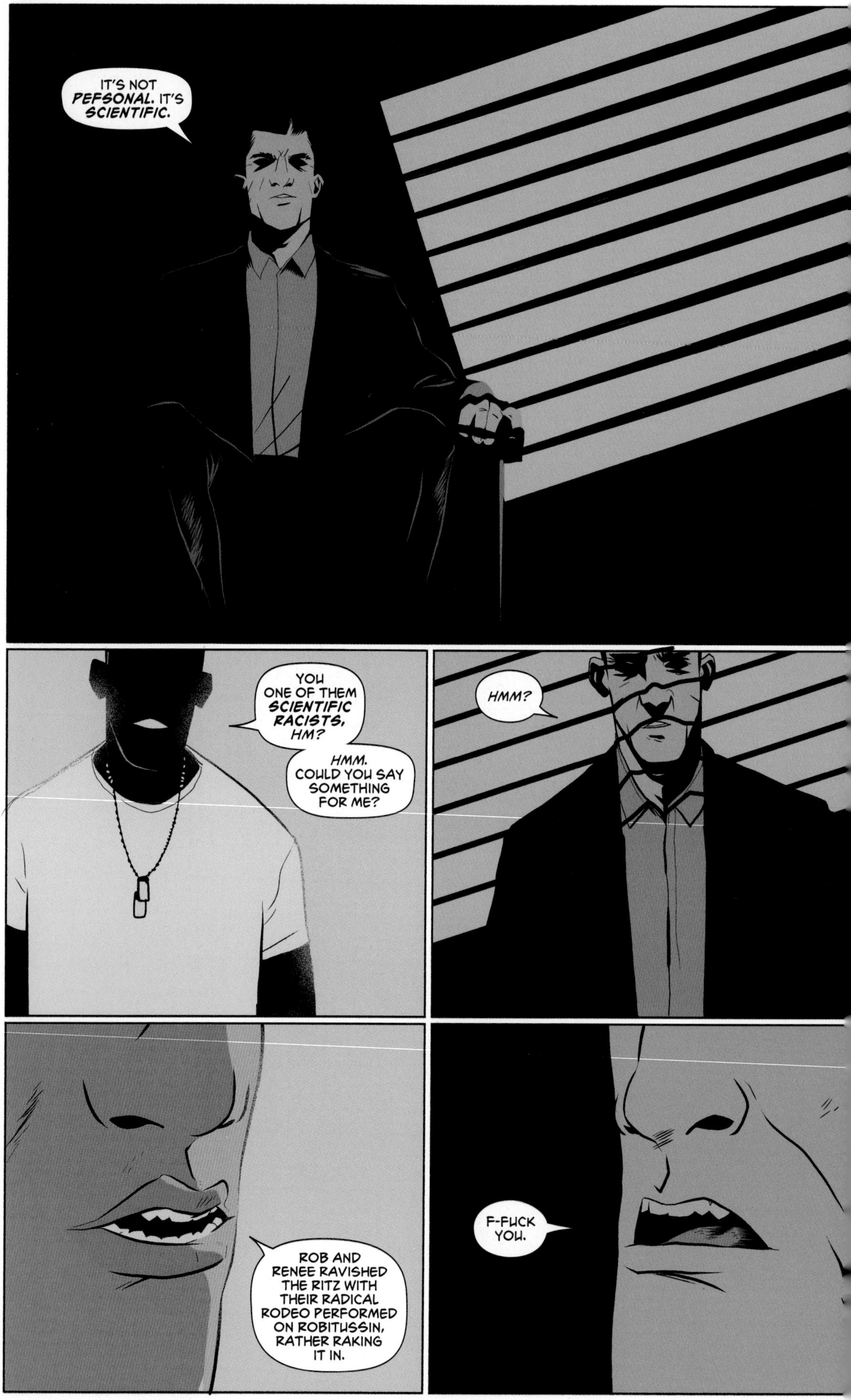
IT'S NOT PEFSONAL. IT'S SCIENTIFIC.
YOU ONE OF THEM SCIENTIFIC RACISTS, HM?
HMM. COULD YOU SAY SOMETHING FOR ME?
HMM?
ROB AND RENEE RAVISHED THE RITZ WITH THEIR RADICAL RODEO PERFORMED ON ROBITUSSIN, RATHER RAKING IT IN.
F-FUCK YOU.

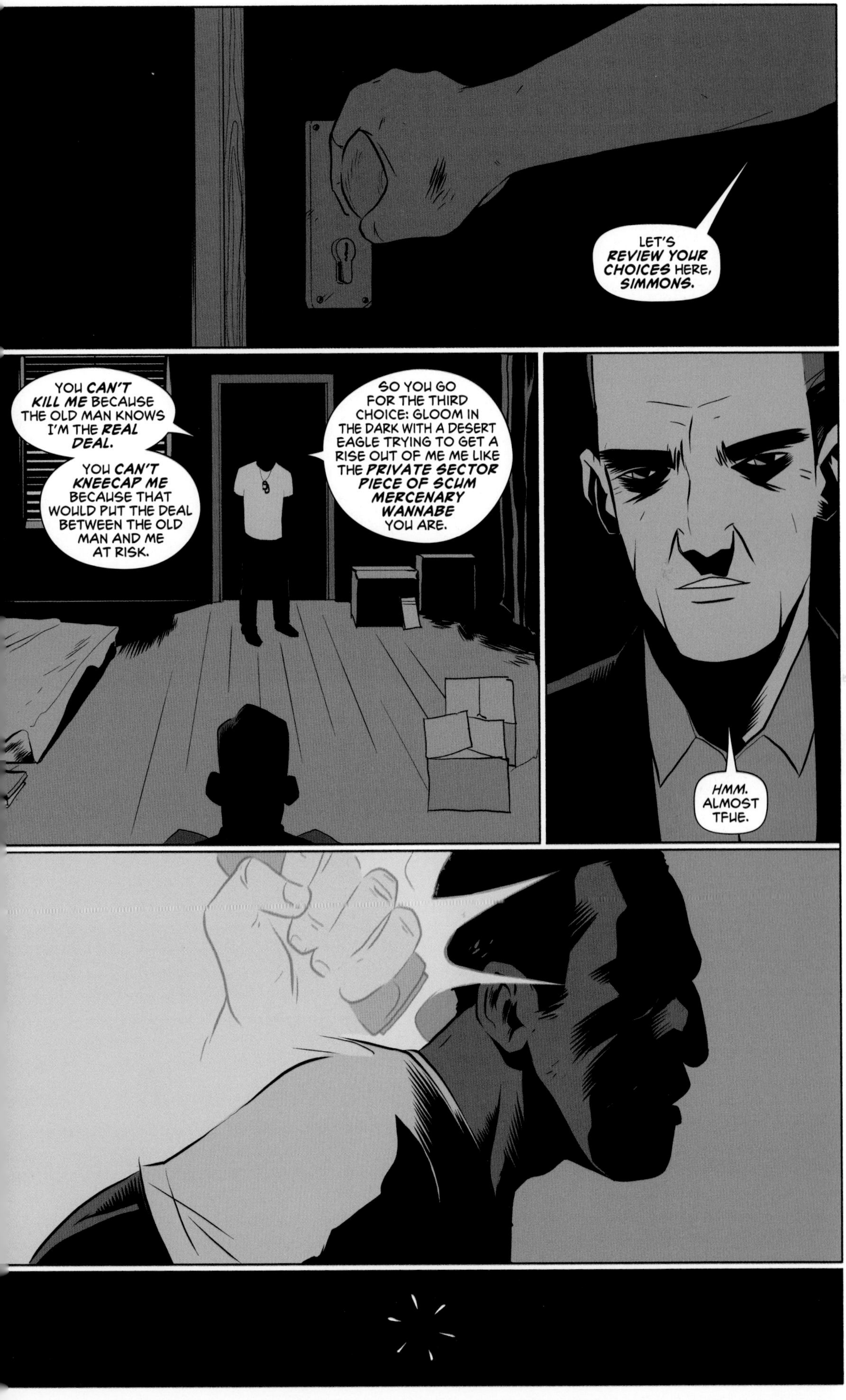
LET'S REVIEW YOUR CHOICES HERE, SIMMONS.
YOU CAN'T KILL ME BECAUSE THE OLD MAN KNOWS I'M THE REAL DEAL.
YOU CAN'T KNEECAP ME BECAUSE THAT WOULD PUT THE DEAL BETWEEN THE OLD MAN AND ME AT RISK.
SO YOU GO FOR THE THIRD CHOICE: GLOOM IN THE DARK WITH A DESERT EAGLE TRYING TO GET A RISE OUT OF ME ME LIKE THE PRIVATE SECTOR PIECE OF SCUM MERCENARY WANNABE YOU ARE.
HMM. ALMOST TFUE.

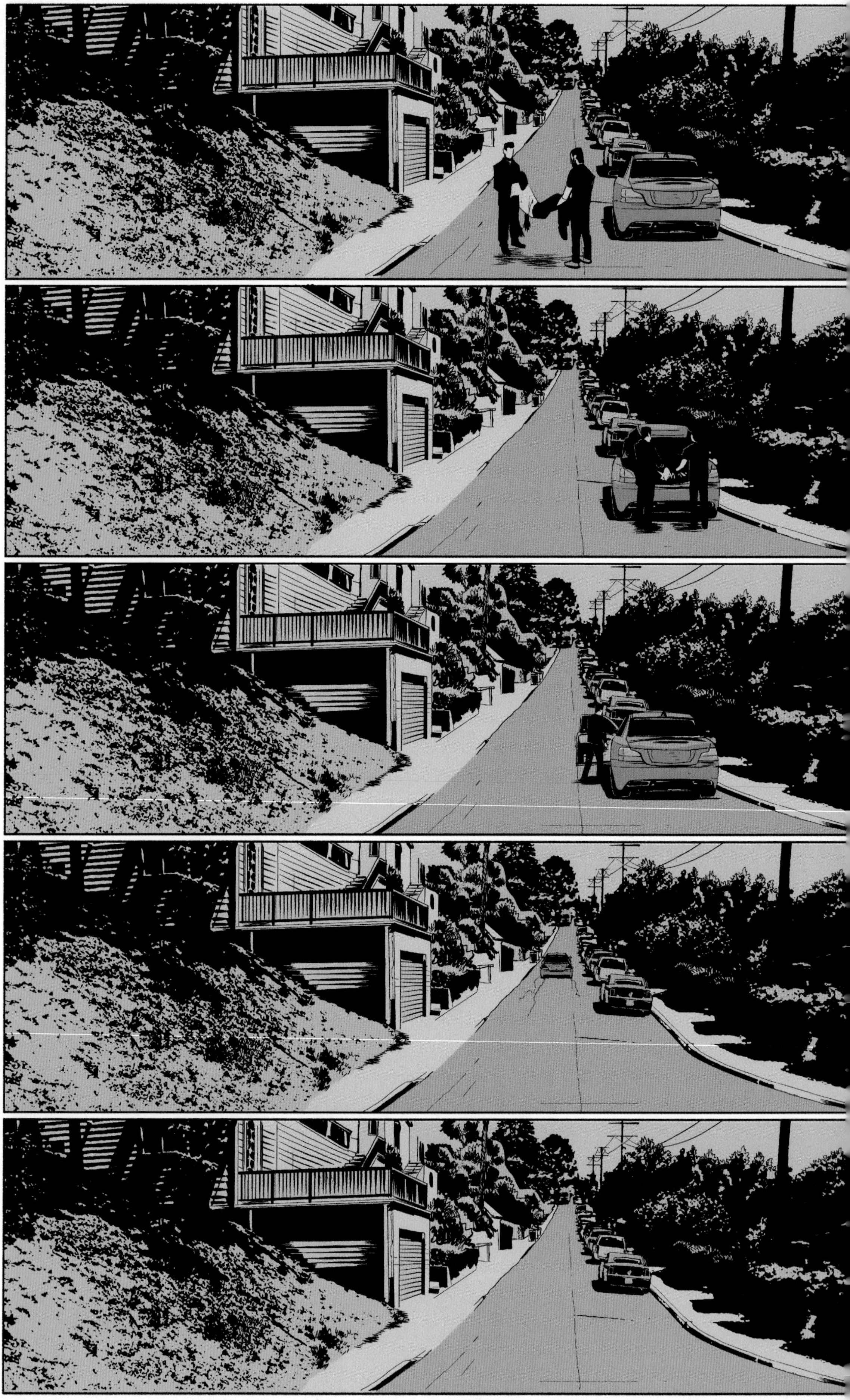

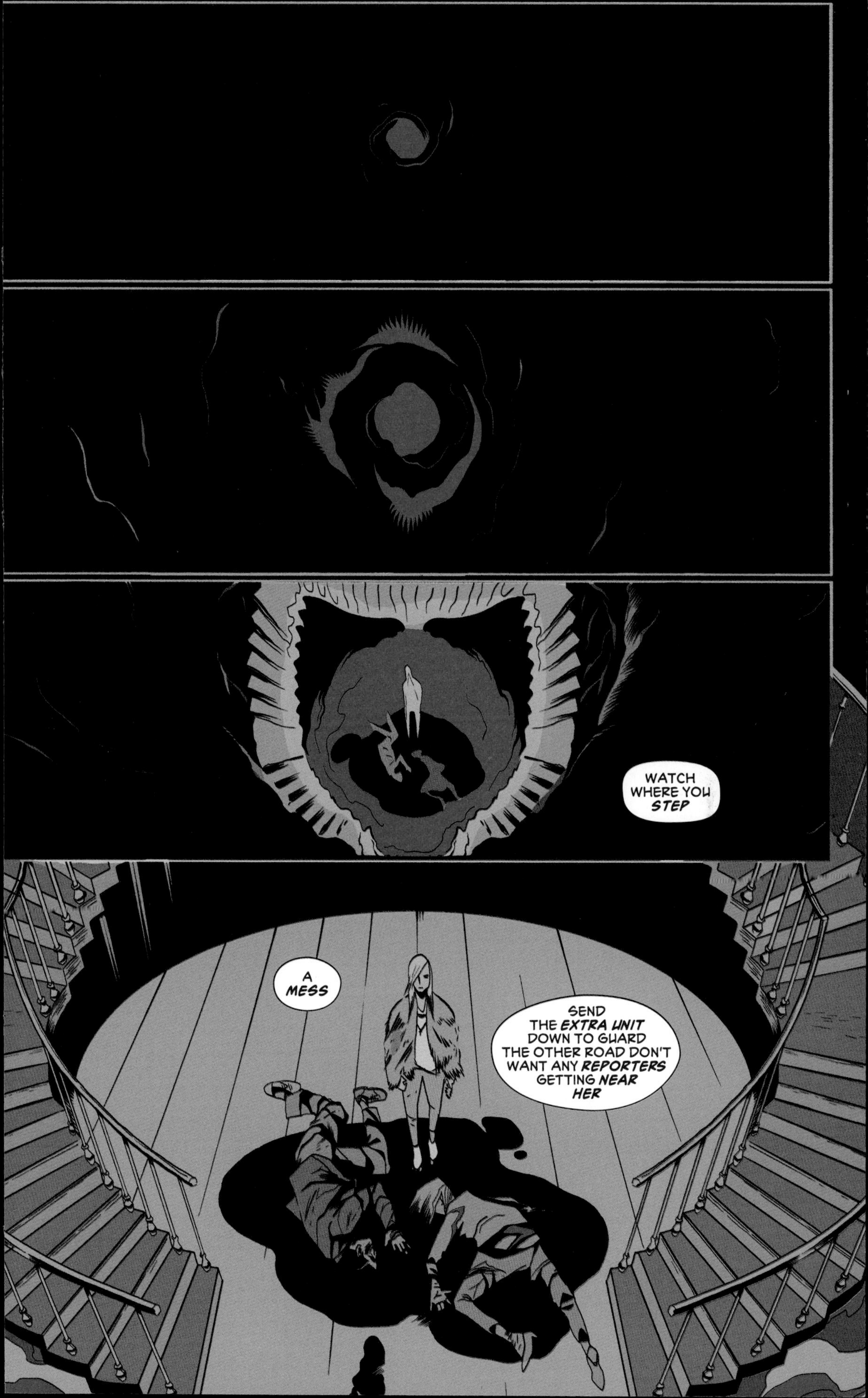
WATCH WHERE YOU *STEP*
A *MESS*
SEND THE *EXTRA UNIT* DOWN TO GUARD THE OTHER ROAD DON'T WANT ANY *REPORTERS* GETTING *NEAR HER*

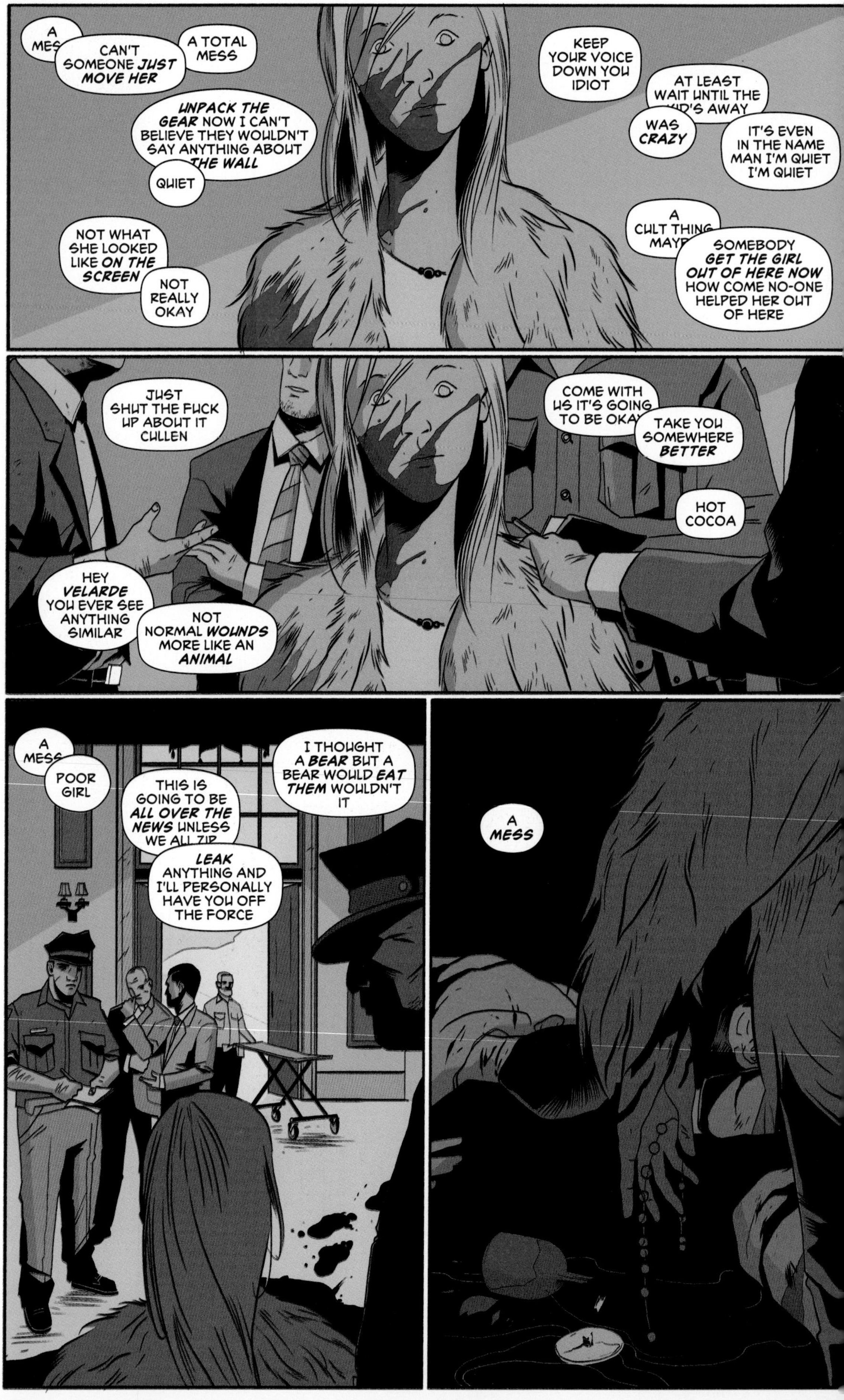
A MESS
CAN'T SOMEONE JUST MOVE HER
A TOTAL MESS
UNPACK THE GEAR NOW I CAN'T BELIEVE THEY WOULDN'T SAY ANYTHING ABOUT THE WALL
QUIET
NOT WHAT SHE LOOKED LIKE ON THE SCREEN
NOT REALLY OKAY
KEEP YOUR VOICE DOWN YOU IDIOT
AT LEAST WAIT UNTIL THE KID'S AWAY
WAS CRAZY
IT'S EVEN IN THE NAME MAN I'M QUIET I'M QUIET
A CULT THING MAYBE
SOMEBODY GET THE GIRL OUT OF HERE NOW HOW COME NO-ONE HELPED HER OUT OF HERE
JUST SHUT THE FUCK UP ABOUT IT CULLEN
COME WITH US IT'S GOING TO BE OKAY
TAKE YOU SOMEWHERE BETTER
HOT COCOA
HEY VELARDE YOU EVER SEE ANYTHING SIMILAR
NOT NORMAL WOUNDS MORE LIKE AN ANIMAL
A MESS
POOR GIRL
THIS IS GOING TO BE ALL OVER THE NEWS UNLESS WE ALL ZIP
I THOUGHT A BEAR BUT A BEAR WOULD EAT THEM WOULDN'T IT
LEAK ANYTHING AND I'LL PERSONALLY HAVE YOU OFF THE FORCE
A MESS

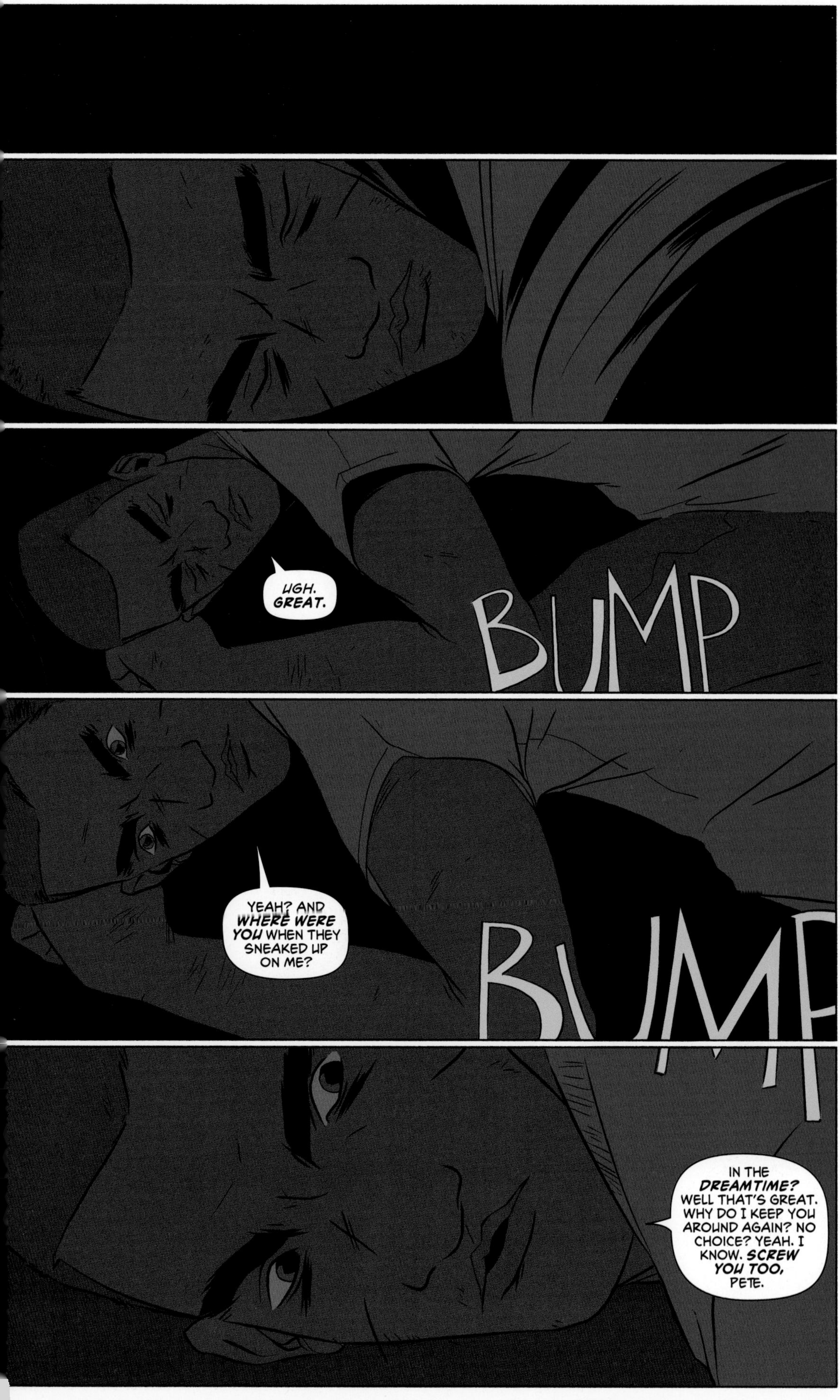
UGH. GREAT.
BUMP
YEAH? AND WHERE WERE YOU WHEN THEY SNEAKED UP ON ME?
BUMP
IN THE DREAMTIME? WELL THAT'S GREAT. WHY DO I KEEP YOU AROUND AGAIN? NO CHOICE? YEAH. I KNOW. SCREW YOU TOO, PETE.

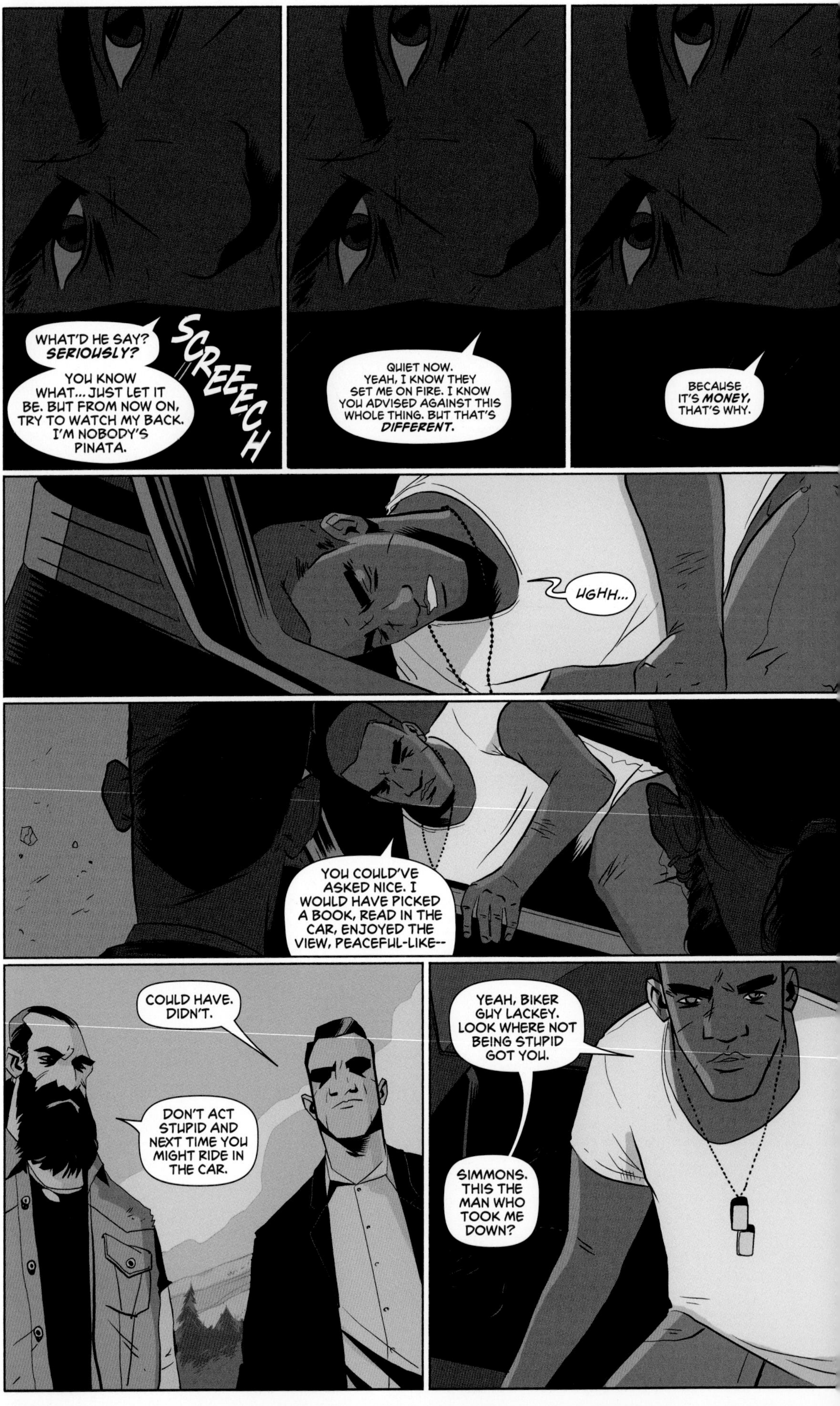
WHAT'D HE SAY? SERIOUSLY?
YOU KNOW WHAT... JUST LET IT BE. BUT FROM NOW ON, TRY TO WATCH MY BACK. I'M NOBODY'S PINATA.
SCREEECH
QUIET NOW. YEAH, I KNOW THEY SET ME ON FIRE. I KNOW YOU ADVISED AGAINST THIS WHOLE THING. BUT THAT'S DIFFERENT.
BECAUSE IT'S MONEY, THAT'S WHY.
UGHH...
YOU COULD'VE ASKED NICE. I WOULD HAVE PICKED A BOOK, READ IN THE CAR, ENJOYED THE VIEW, PEACEFUL-LIKE--
COULD HAVE. DIDN'T.
DON'T ACT STUPID AND NEXT TIME YOU MIGHT RIDE IN THE CAR.
YEAH, BIKER GUY LACKEY. LOOK WHERE NOT BEING STUPID GOT YOU.
SIMMONS. THIS THE MAN WHO TOOK ME DOWN?

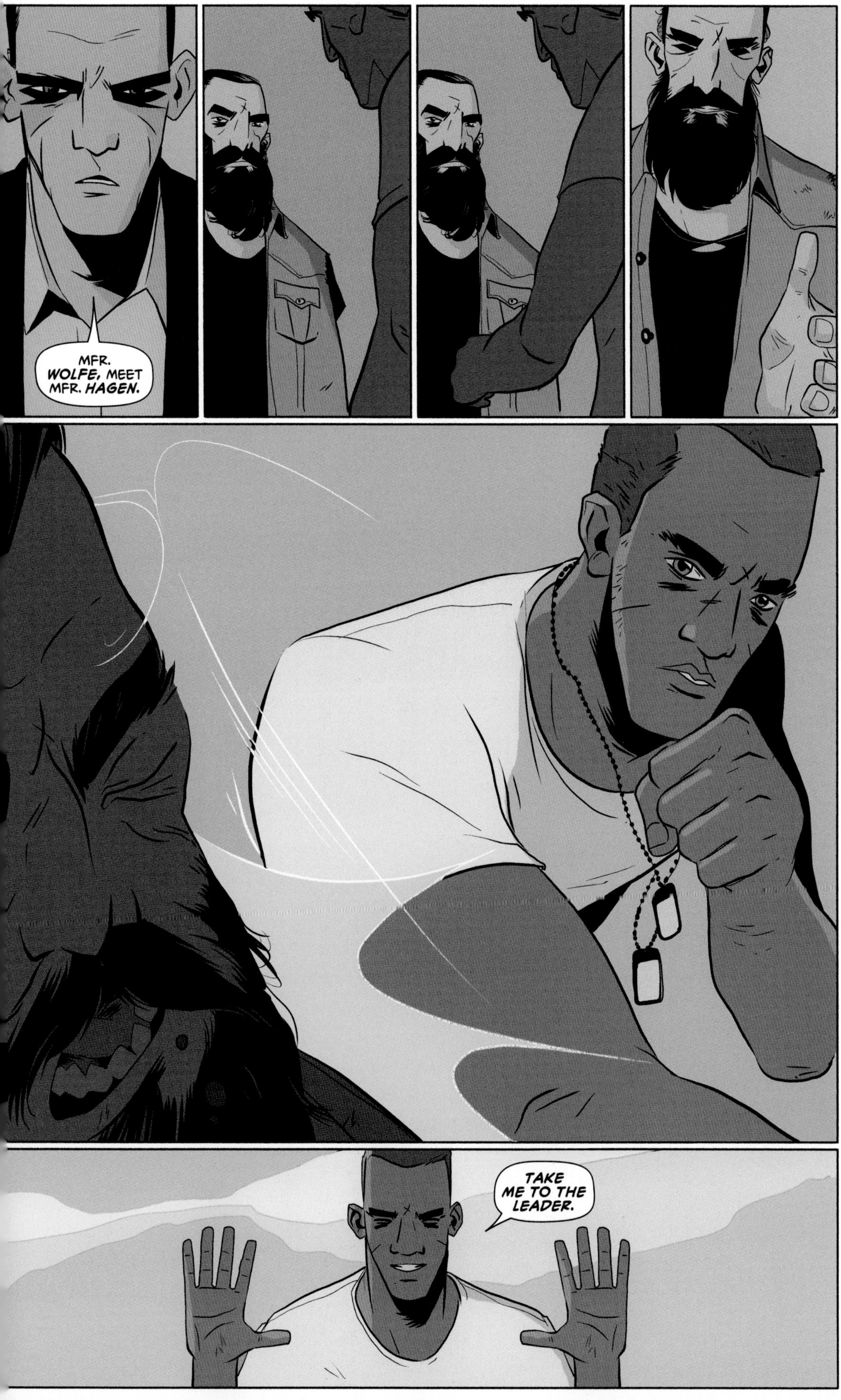
MFR. WOLFE, MEET MFR. HAGEN.
TAKE ME TO THE LEADER.

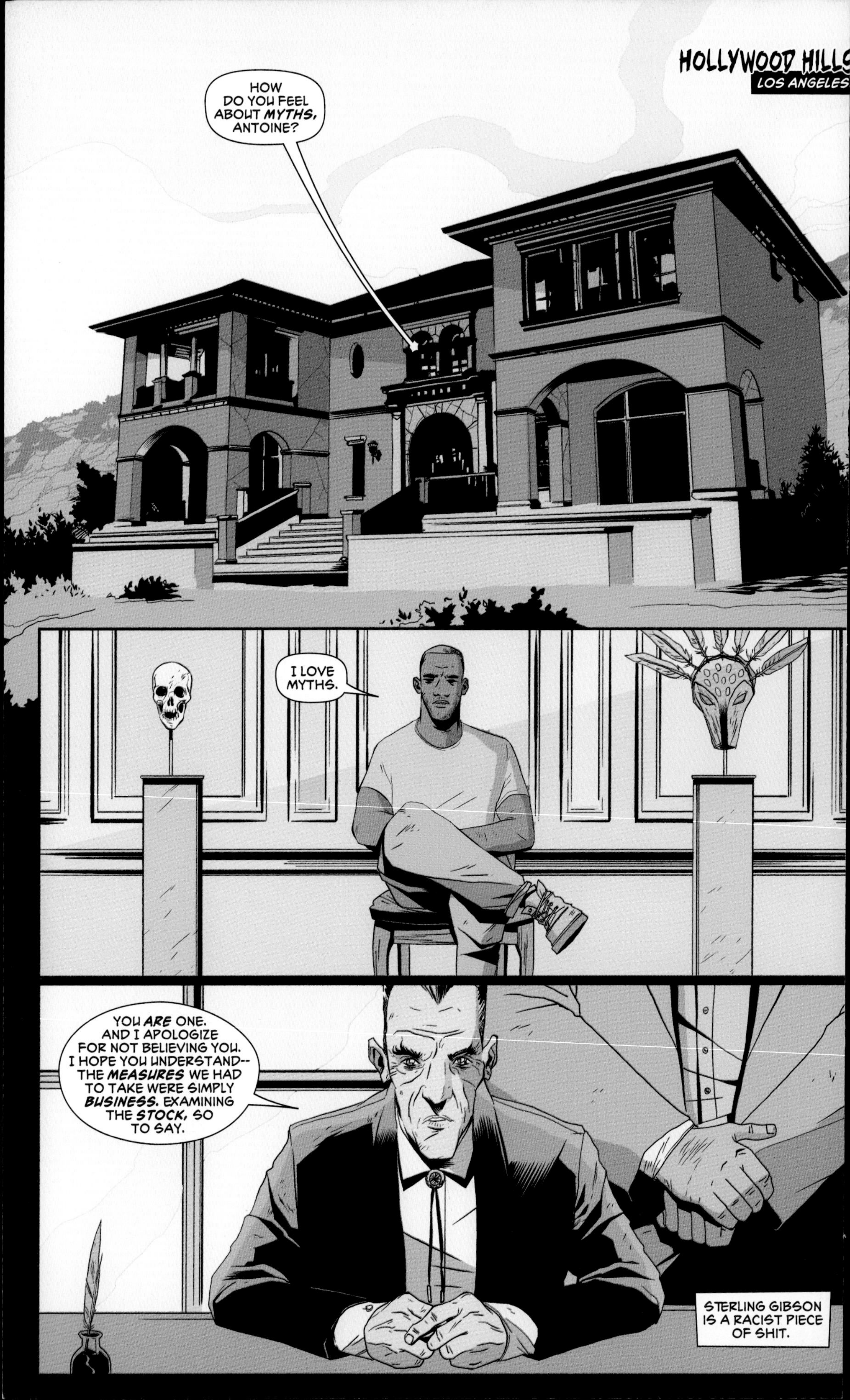
HOLLYWOOD HILLS
LOS ANGELES
HOW DO YOU FEEL ABOUT MYTHS, ANTOINE?
I LOVE MYTHS.
YOU ARE ONE. AND I APOLOGIZE FOR NOT BELIEVING YOU. I HOPE YOU UNDERSTAND-- THE MEASURES WE HAD TO TAKE WERE SIMPLY BUSINESS. EXAMINING THE STOCK, SO TO SAY.
STERLING GIBSON IS A RACIST PIECE OF SHIT.

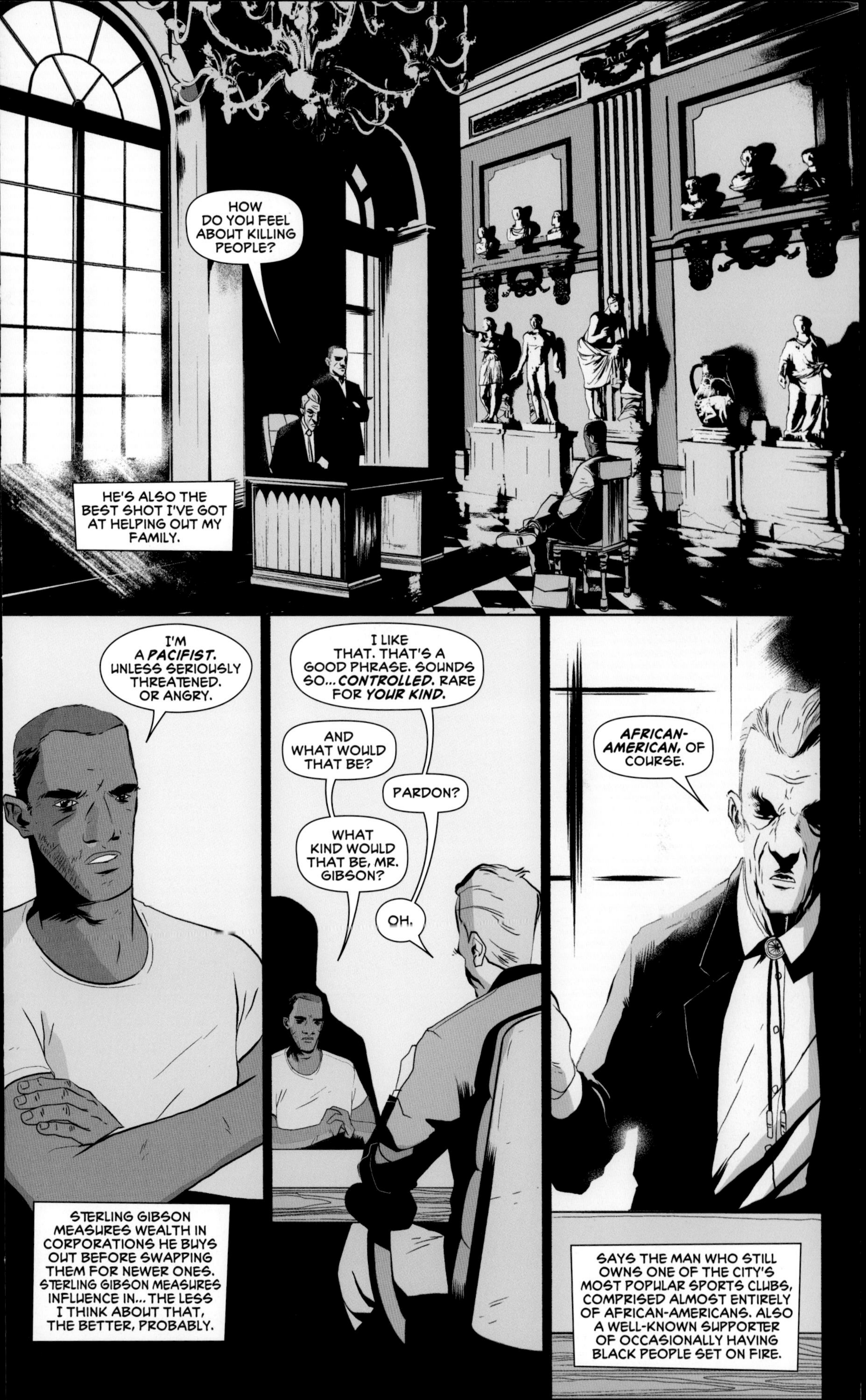
HOW DO YOU FEEL ABOUT KILLING PEOPLE?
HE'S ALSO THE BEST SHOT I'VE GOT AT HELPING OUT MY FAMILY.
I'M A *PACIFIST.* UNLESS SERIOUSLY THREATENED. OR ANGRY.
STERLING GIBSON MEASURES WEALTH IN CORPORATIONS HE BUYS OUT BEFORE SWAPPING THEM FOR NEWER ONES. STERLING GIBSON MEASURES INFLUENCE IN... THE LESS I THINK ABOUT THAT, THE BETTER, PROBABLY.
I LIKE THAT. THAT'S A GOOD PHRASE. SOUNDS SO... *CONTROLLED.* RARE FOR *YOUR KIND.*
AND WHAT WOULD THAT BE?
PARDON?
WHAT KIND WOULD THAT BE, MR. GIBSON?
OH.
AFRICAN-AMERICAN, OF COURSE.
SAYS THE MAN WHO STILL OWNS ONE OF THE CITY'S MOST POPULAR SPORTS CLUBS, COMPRISED ALMOST ENTIRELY OF AFRICAN-AMERICANS. ALSO A WELL-KNOWN SUPPORTER OF OCCASIONALLY HAVING BLACK PEOPLE SET ON FIRE.

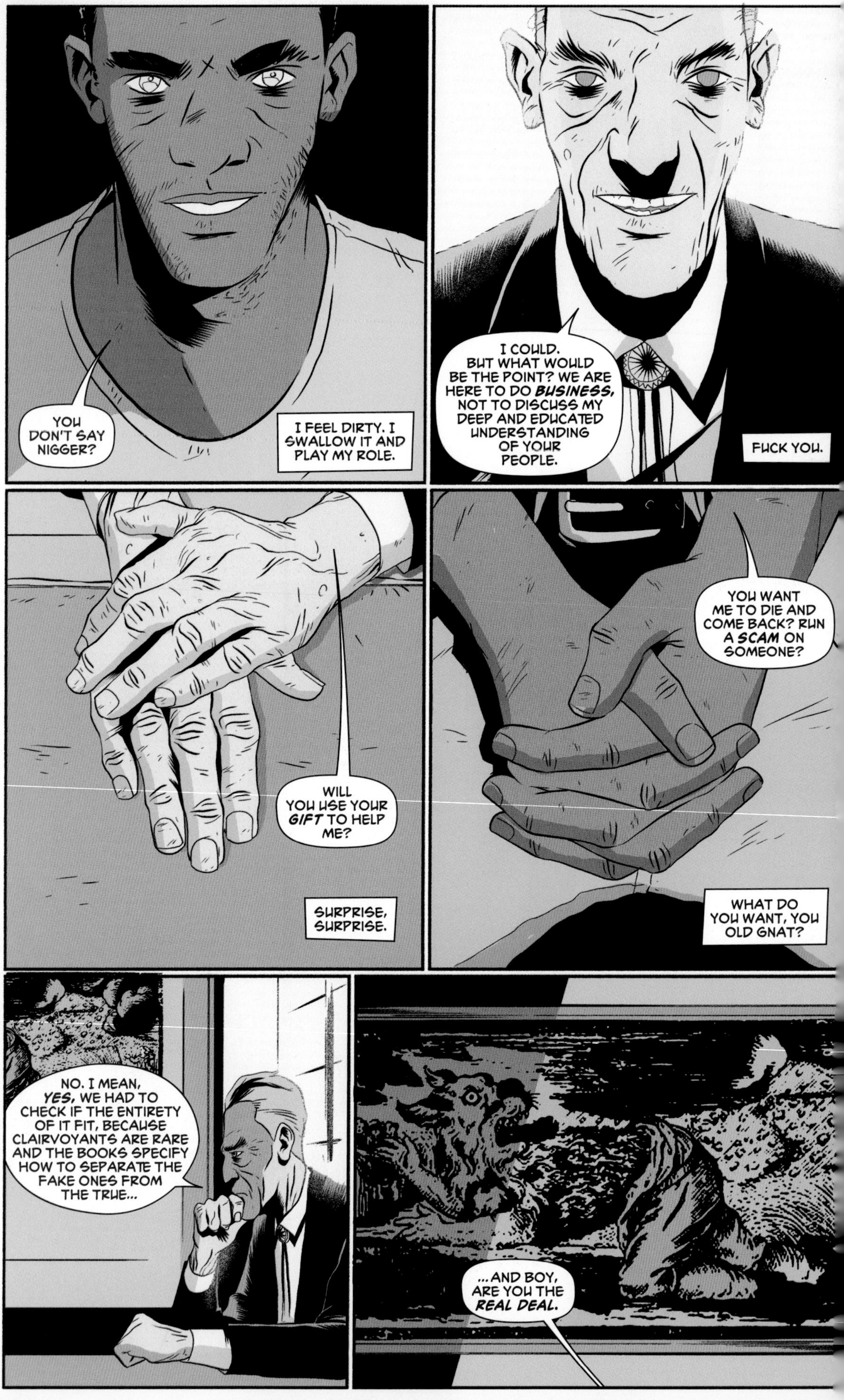
YOU DON'T SAY NIGGER?
I FEEL DIRTY. I SWALLOW IT AND PLAY MY ROLE.
I COULD. BUT WHAT WOULD BE THE POINT? WE ARE HERE TO DO BUSINESS, NOT TO DISCUSS MY DEEP AND EDUCATED UNDERSTANDING OF YOUR PEOPLE.
FUCK YOU.
WILL YOU USE YOUR GIFT TO HELP ME?
SURPRISE, SURPRISE.
YOU WANT ME TO DIE AND COME BACK? RUN A SCAM ON SOMEONE?
WHAT DO YOU WANT, YOU OLD GNAT?
NO. I MEAN, YES, WE HAD TO CHECK IF THE ENTIRETY OF IT FIT, BECAUSE CLAIRVOYANTS ARE RARE AND THE BOOKS SPECIFY HOW TO SEPARATE THE FAKE ONES FROM THE TRUE...
...AND BOY, ARE YOU THE REAL DEAL.

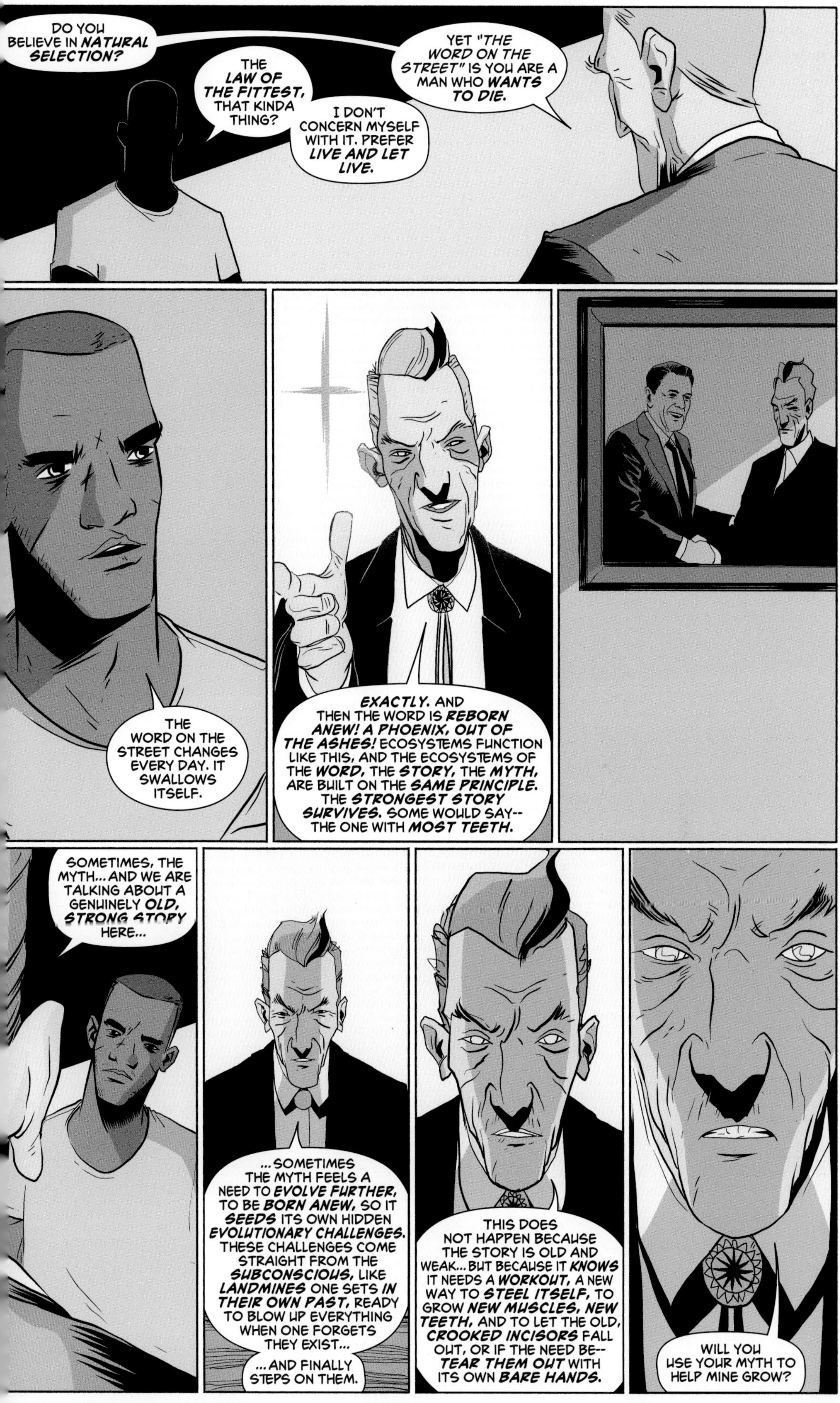
DO YOU BELIEVE IN NATURAL SELECTION?
THE LAW OF THE FITTEST, THAT KINDA THING?
I DON'T CONCERN MYSELF WITH IT. PREFER LIVE AND LET LIVE.
YET "THE WORD ON THE STREET" IS YOU ARE A MAN WHO WANTS TO DIE.
THE WORD ON THE STREET CHANGES EVERY DAY. IT SWALLOWS ITSELF.
EXACTLY. AND THEN THE WORD IS REBORN ANEW! A PHOENIX, OUT OF THE ASHES! ECOSYSTEMS FUNCTION LIKE THIS, AND THE ECOSYSTEMS OF THE WORD, THE STORY, THE MYTH, ARE BUILT ON THE SAME PRINCIPLE. THE STRONGEST STORY SURVIVES. SOME WOULD SAY-- THE ONE WITH MOST TEETH.
SOMETIMES, THE MYTH... AND WE ARE TALKING ABOUT A GENUINELY OLD, STRONG STORY HERE...
...SOMETIMES THE MYTH FEELS A NEED TO EVOLVE FURTHER, TO BE BORN ANEW, SO IT SEEDS ITS OWN HIDDEN EVOLUTIONARY CHALLENGES. THESE CHALLENGES COME STRAIGHT FROM THE SUBCONSCIOUS, LIKE LANDMINES ONE SETS IN THEIR OWN PAST, READY TO BLOW UP EVERYTHING WHEN ONE FORGETS THEY EXIST...
...AND FINALLY STEPS ON THEM.
THIS DOES NOT HAPPEN BECAUSE THE STORY IS OLD AND WEAK... BUT BECAUSE IT KNOWS IT NEEDS A WORKOUT, A NEW WAY TO STEEL ITSELF, TO GROW NEW MUSCLES, NEW TEETH, AND TO LET THE OLD, CROOKED INCISORS FALL OUT, OR IF THE NEED BE-- TEAR THEM OUT WITH ITS OWN BARE HANDS.
WILL YOU USE YOUR MYTH TO HELP MINE GROW?

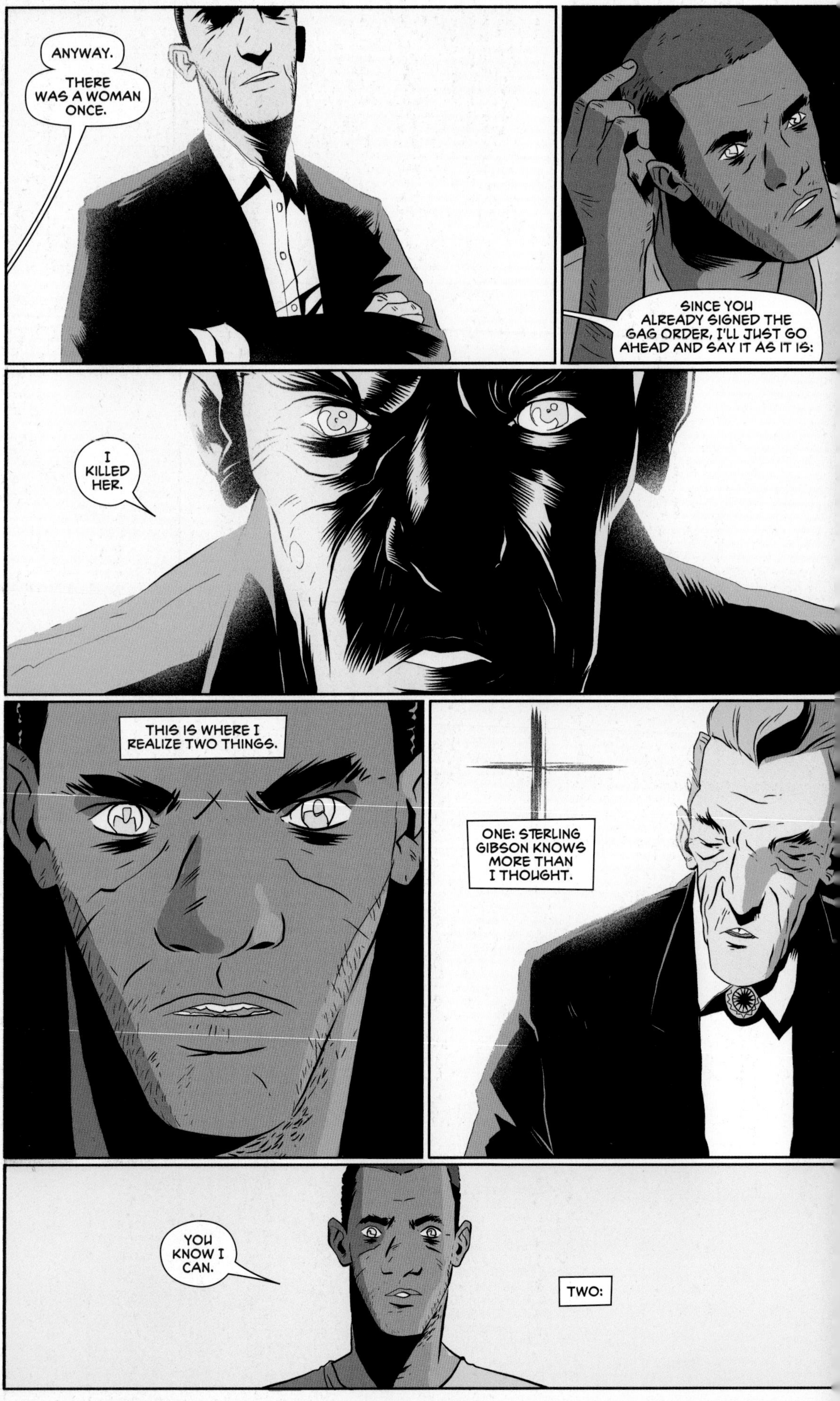
ANYWAY.
THERE WAS A WOMAN ONCE.
SINCE YOU ALREADY SIGNED THE GAG ORDER, I'LL JUST GO AHEAD AND SAY IT AS IT IS:
I KILLED HER.
THIS IS WHERE I REALIZE TWO THINGS.
ONE: STERLING GIBSON KNOWS MORE THAN I THOUGHT.
YOU KNOW I CAN.
TWO:

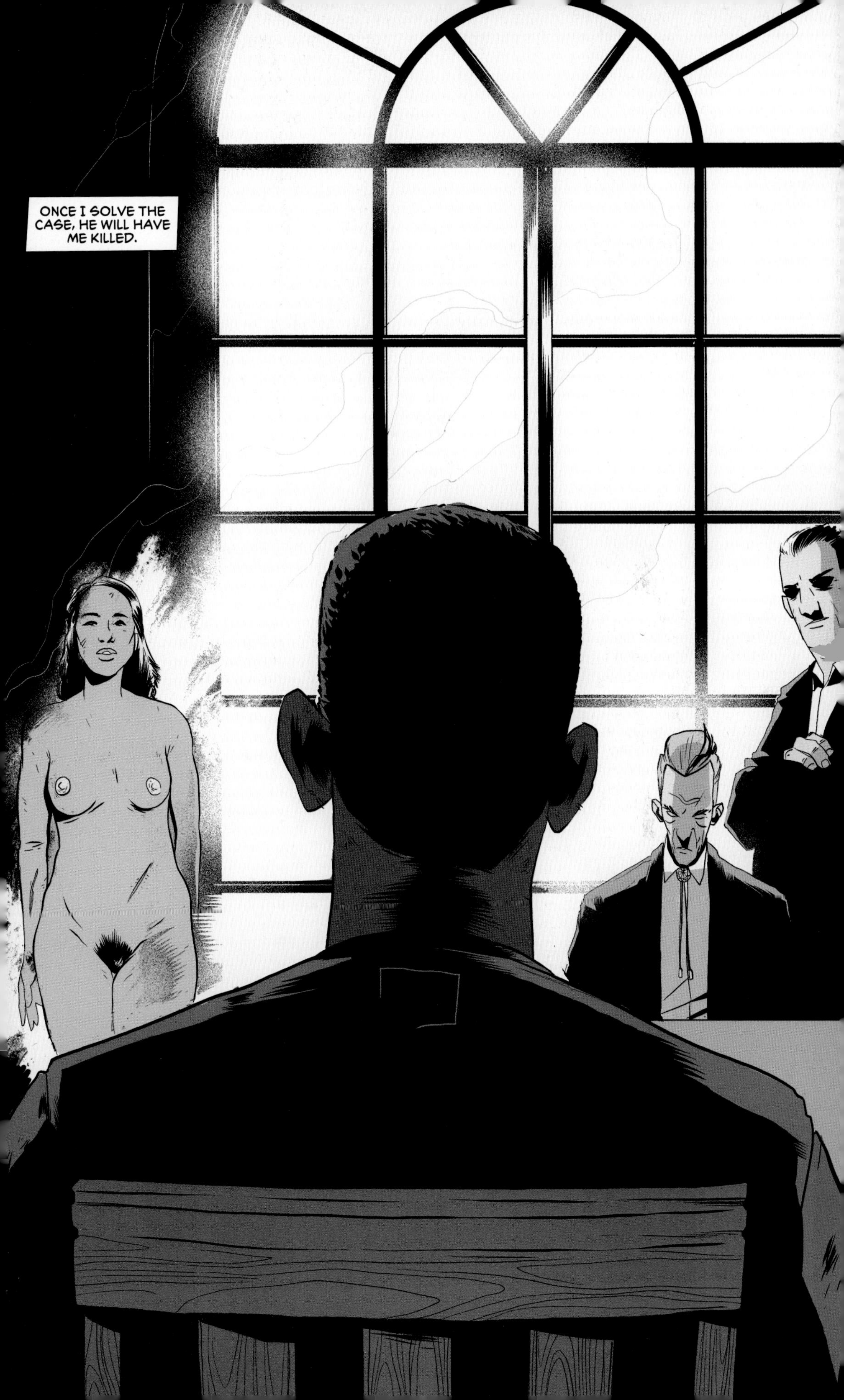
ONCE I SOLVE THE CASE, HE WILL HAVE ME KILLED.

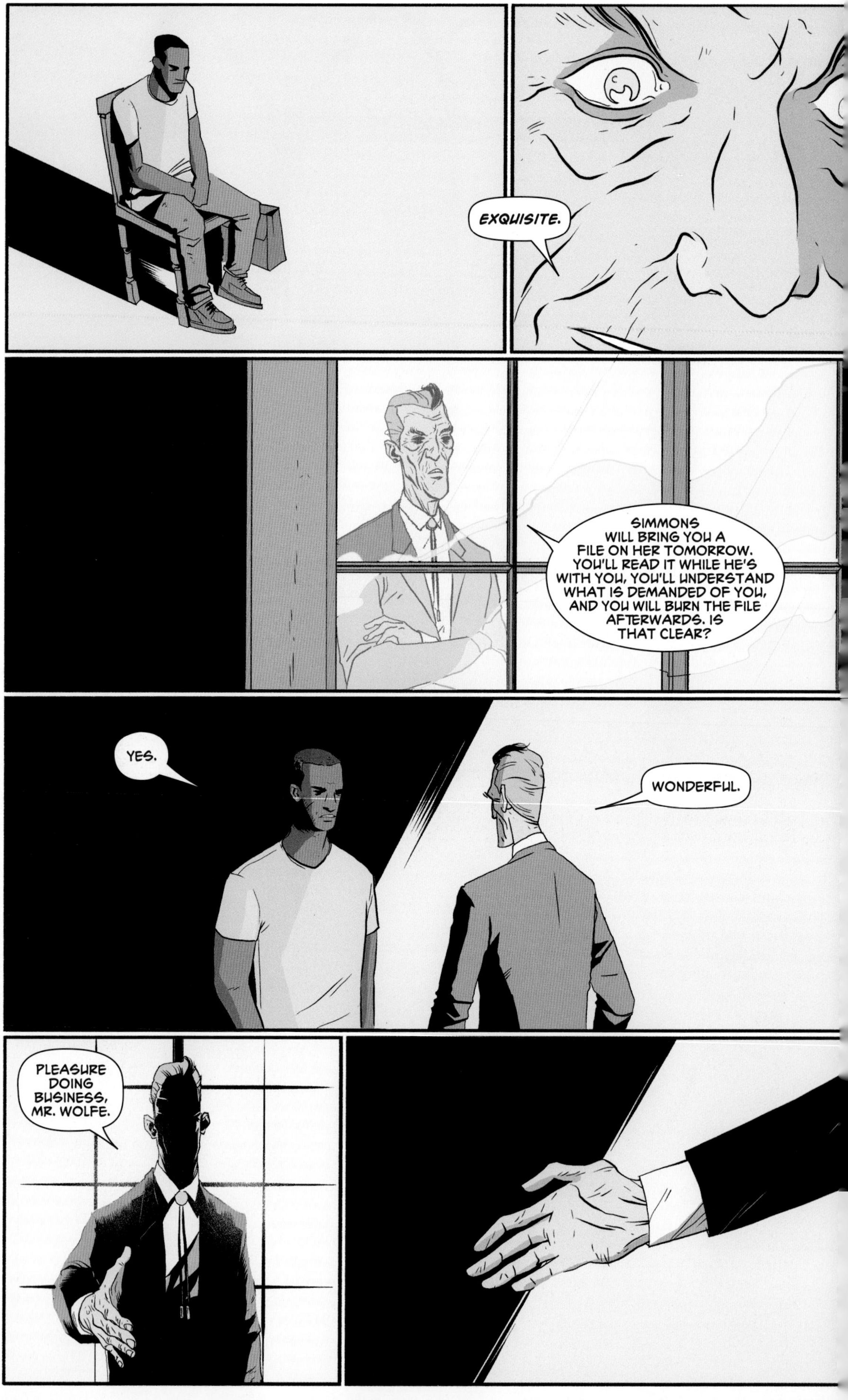
EXQUISITE.
SIMMONS WILL BRING YOU A FILE ON HER TOMORROW. YOU'LL READ IT WHILE HE'S WITH YOU, YOU'LL UNDERSTAND WHAT IS DEMANDED OF YOU, AND YOU WILL BURN THE FILE AFTERWARDS. IS THAT CLEAR?
YES.
WONDERFUL.
PLEASURE DOING BUSINESS, MR. WOLFE.

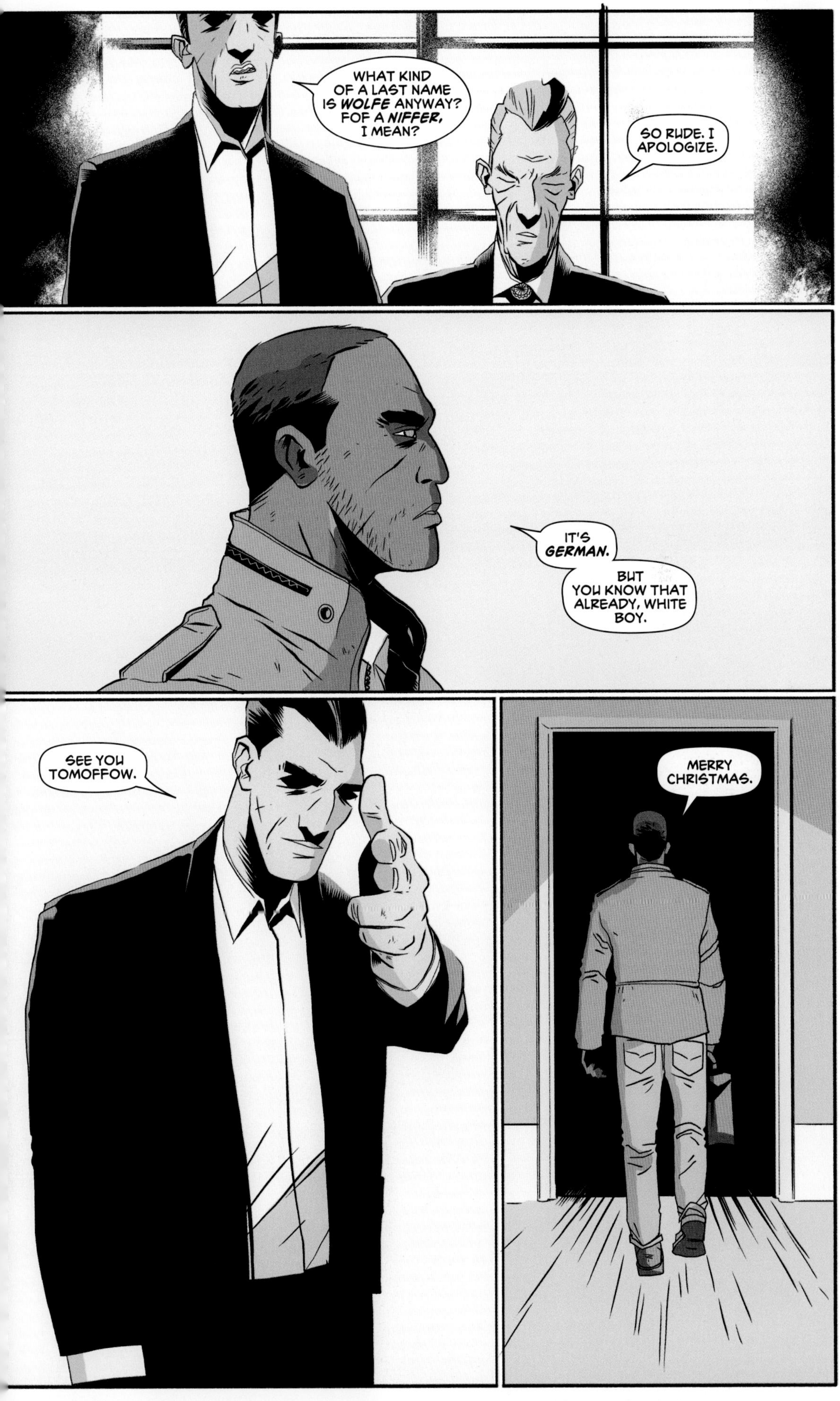
WHAT KIND OF A LAST NAME IS *WOLFE* ANYWAY? FOF A *NIFFER,* I MEAN?
SO RUDE. I APOLOGIZE.
IT'S *GERMAN.*
BUT YOU KNOW THAT ALREADY, WHITE BOY.
SEE YOU TOMOFFOW.
MERRY CHRISTMAS.

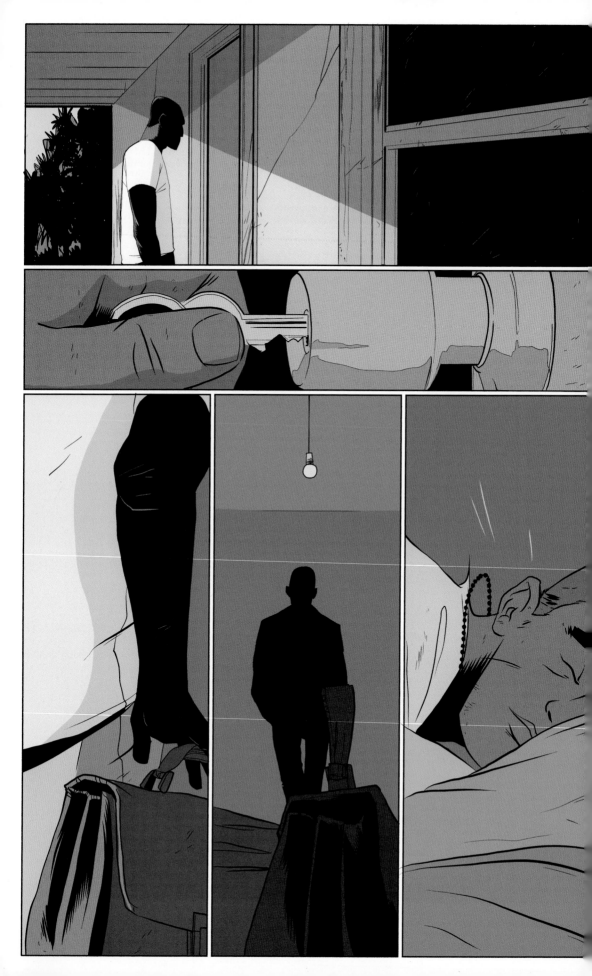

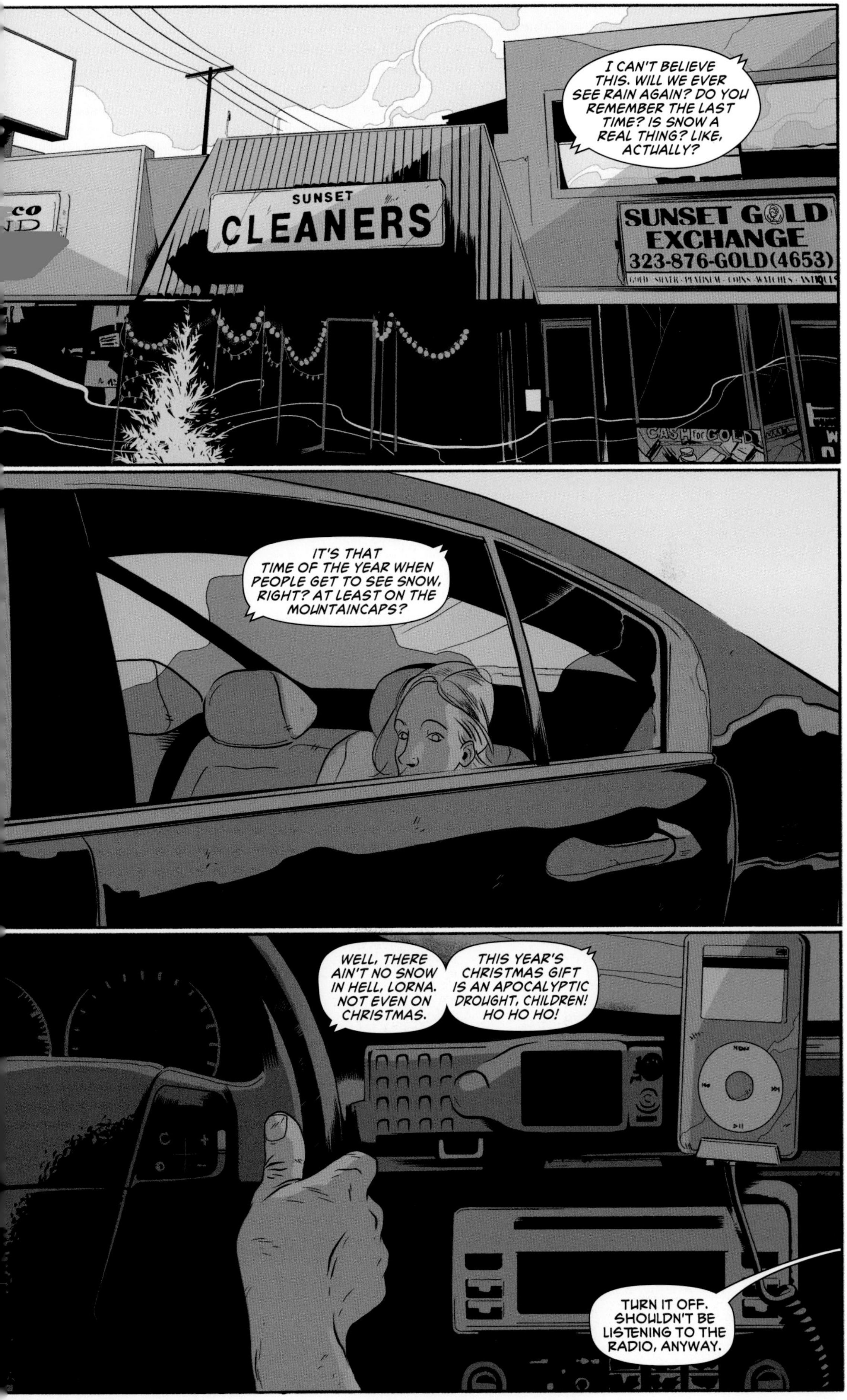
SUNSET
CLEANERS
SUNSET GOLD
EXCHANGE
323-876-GOLD(4653)
I CAN'T BELIEVE THIS. WILL WE EVER SEE RAIN AGAIN? DO YOU REMEMBER THE LAST TIME? IS SNOW A REAL THING? LIKE, ACTUALLY?
CASH for GOLD
IT'S THAT TIME OF THE YEAR WHEN PEOPLE GET TO SEE SNOW, RIGHT? AT LEAST ON THE MOUNTAINCAPS?
WELL, THERE AIN'T NO SNOW IN HELL, LORNA. NOT EVEN ON CHRISTMAS.
THIS YEAR'S CHRISTMAS GIFT IS AN APOCALYPTIC DROUGHT, CHILDREN! HO HO HO!
TURN IT OFF. SHOULDN'T BE LISTENING TO THE RADIO, ANYWAY.

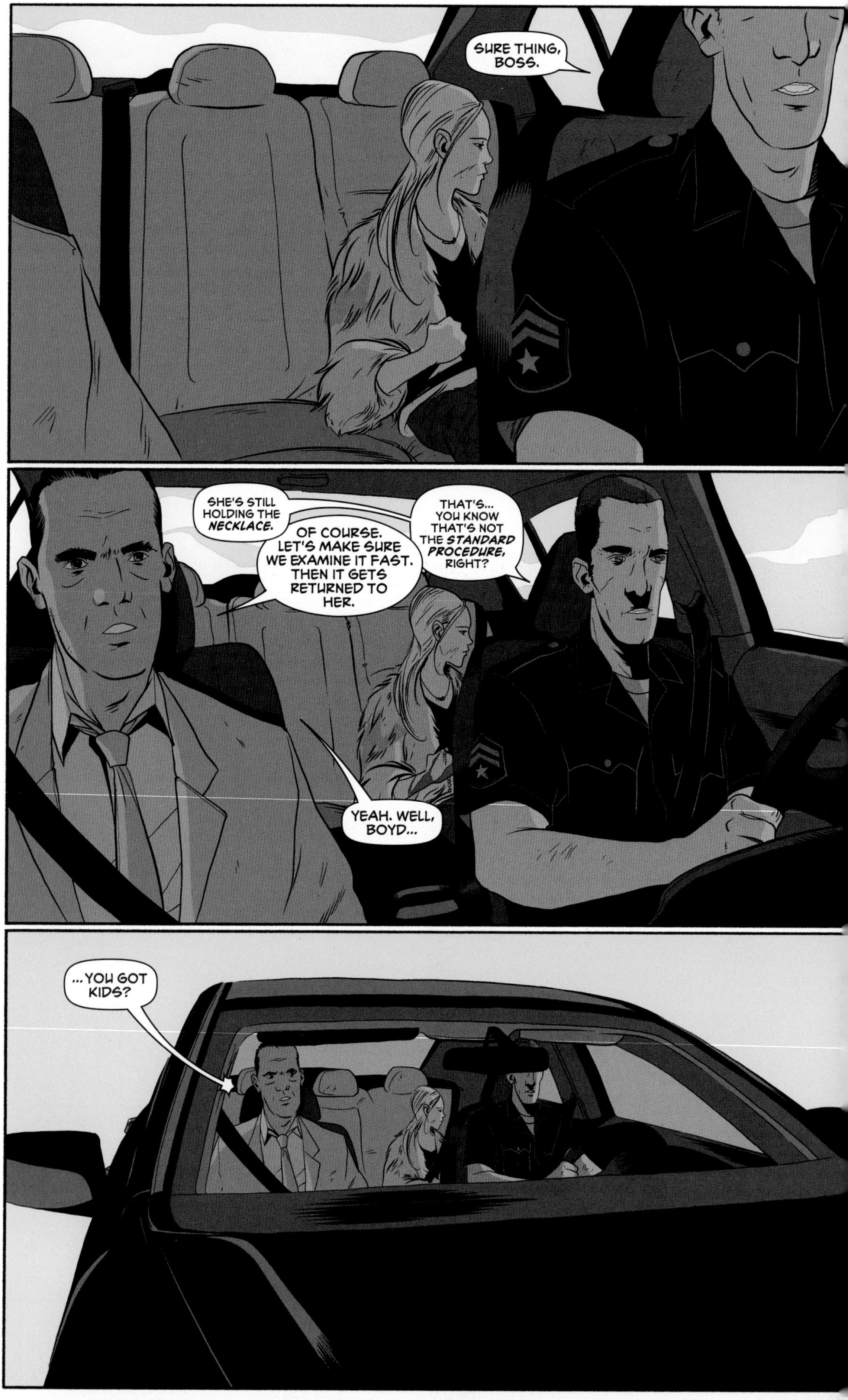
SURE THING, BOSS.
SHE'S STILL HOLDING THE *NECKLACE.*
OF COURSE. LET'S MAKE SURE WE EXAMINE IT FAST. THEN IT GETS RETURNED TO HER.
THAT'S... YOU KNOW THAT'S NOT THE *STANDARD PROCEDURE,* RIGHT?
YEAH. WELL, BOYD...
...YOU GOT KIDS?

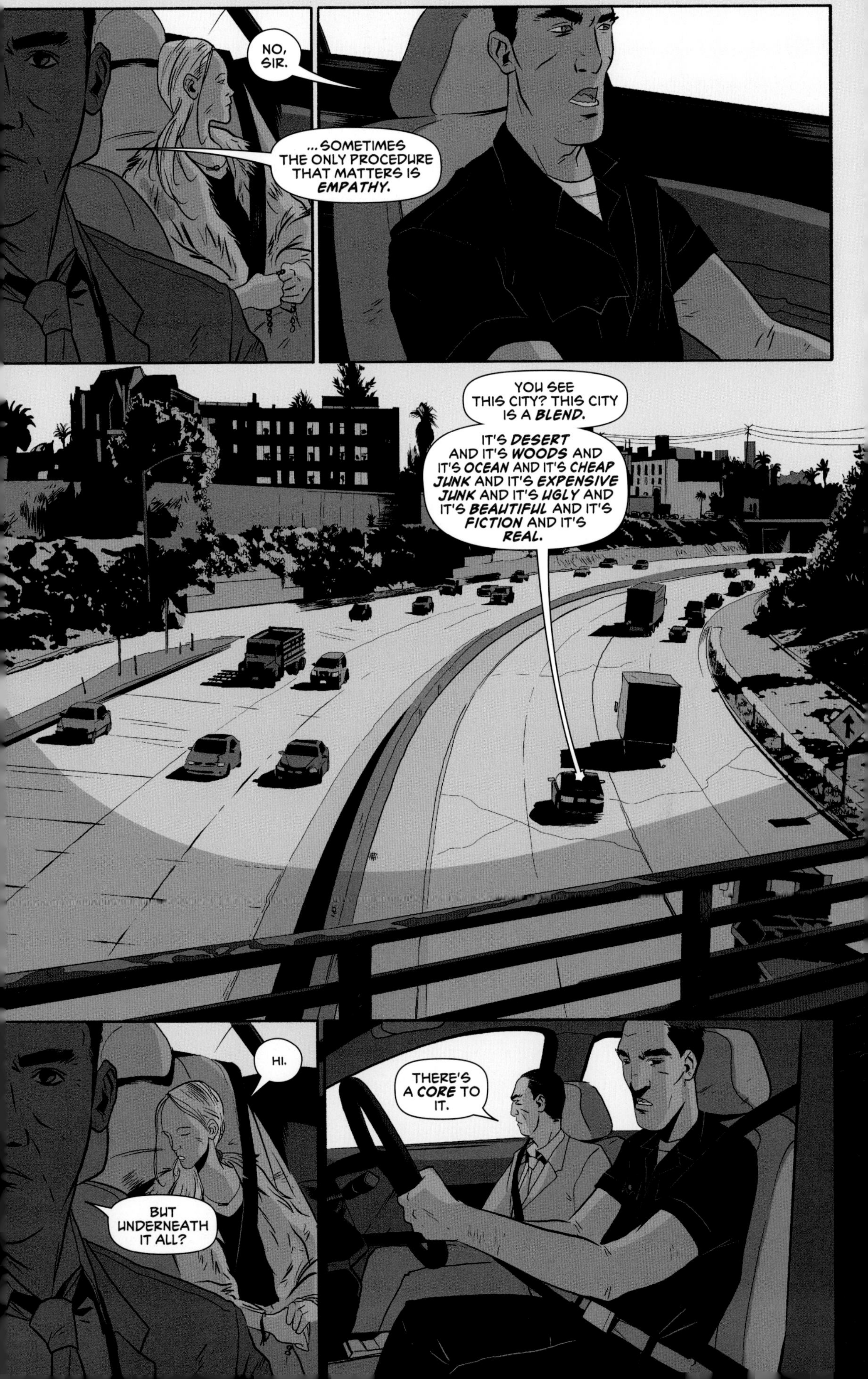
NO, SIR.
...SOMETIMES THE ONLY PROCEDURE THAT MATTERS IS EMPATHY.
YOU SEE THIS CITY? THIS CITY IS A BLEND.
IT'S DESERT AND IT'S WOODS AND IT'S OCEAN AND IT'S CHEAP JUNK AND IT'S EXPENSIVE JUNK AND IT'S UGLY AND IT'S BEAUTIFUL AND IT'S FICTION AND IT'S REAL.
HI.
BUT UNDERNEATH IT ALL?
THERE'S A CORE TO IT.

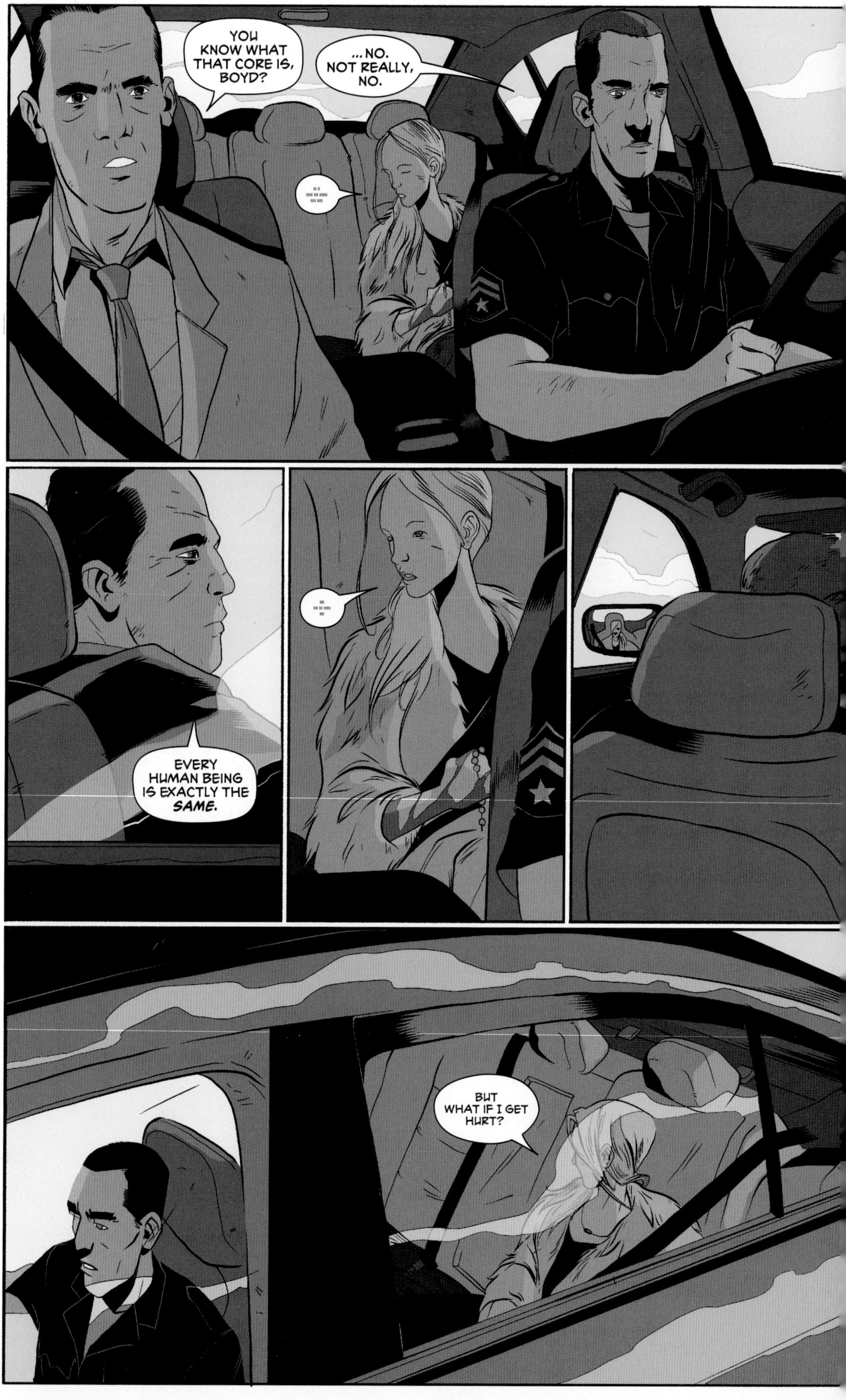
YOU KNOW WHAT THAT CORE IS, BOYD?
...NO. NOT REALLY, NO.
EVERY HUMAN BEING IS EXACTLY THE *SAME.*
BUT WHAT IF I GET HURT?

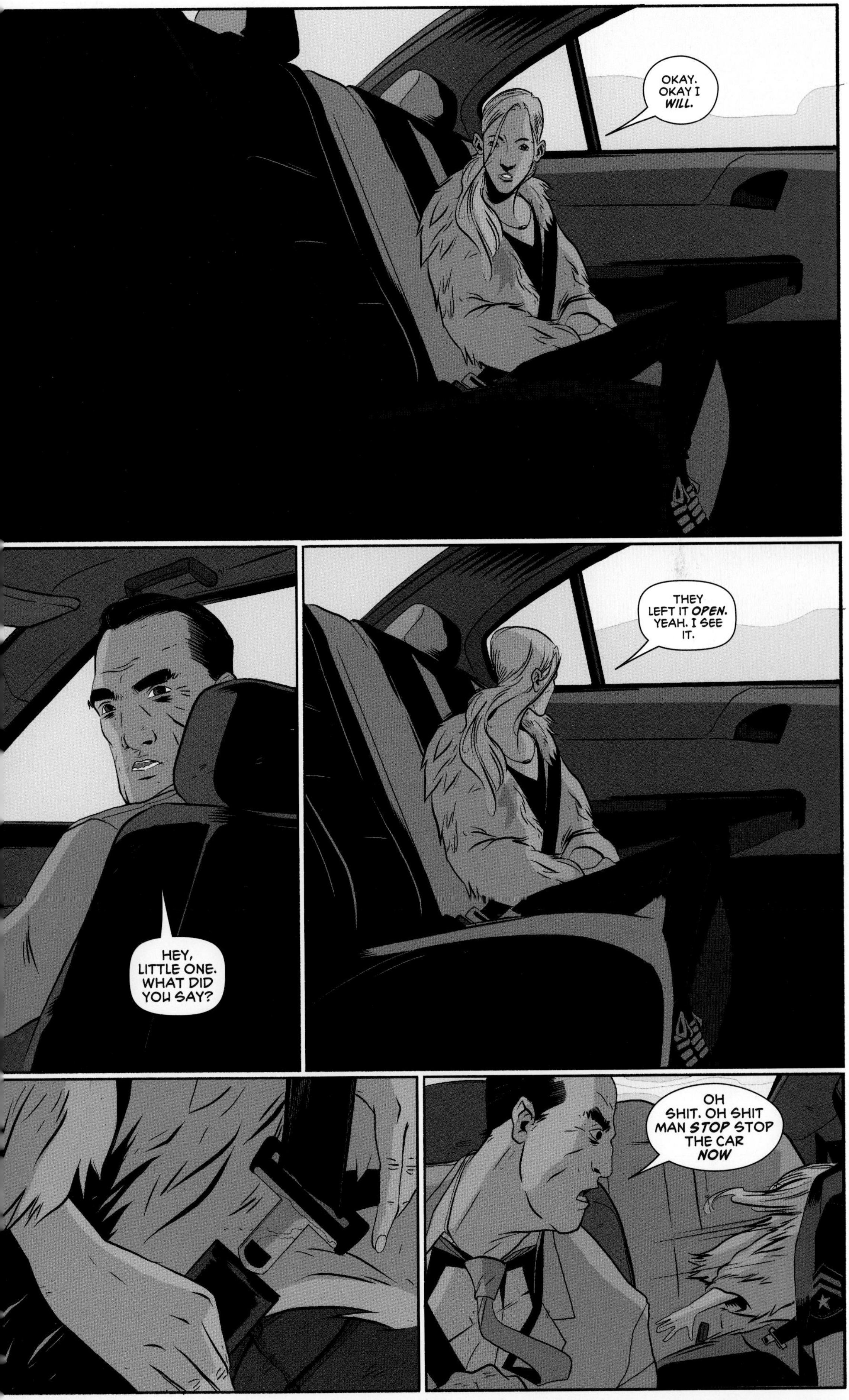
OKAY. OKAY I *WILL.*
HEY, LITTLE ONE. WHAT DID YOU SAY?
THEY LEFT IT *OPEN.* YEAH. I SEE IT.
OH SHIT. OH SHIT MAN *STOP* STOP THE CAR *NOW*

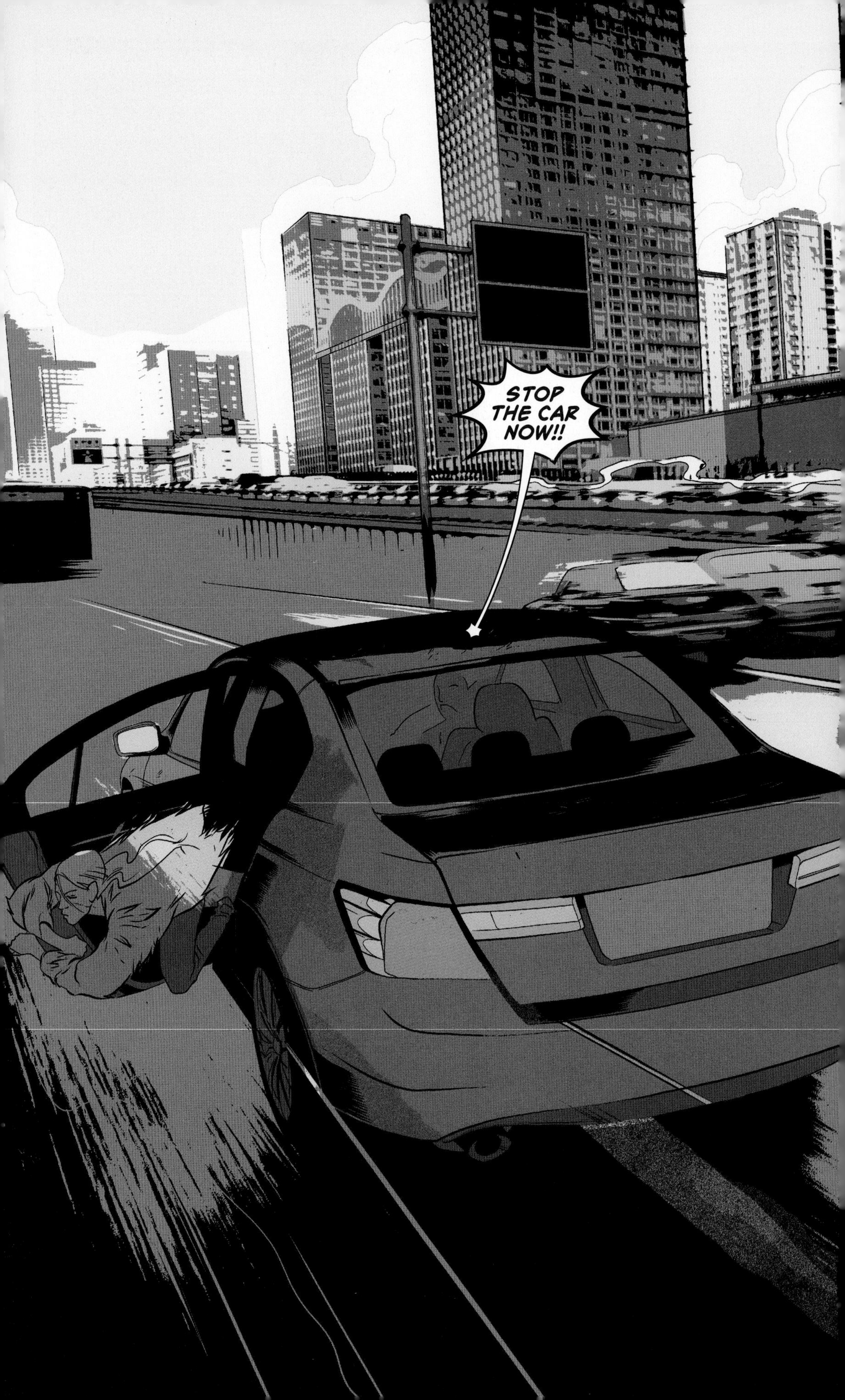
STOP THE CAR NOW!!

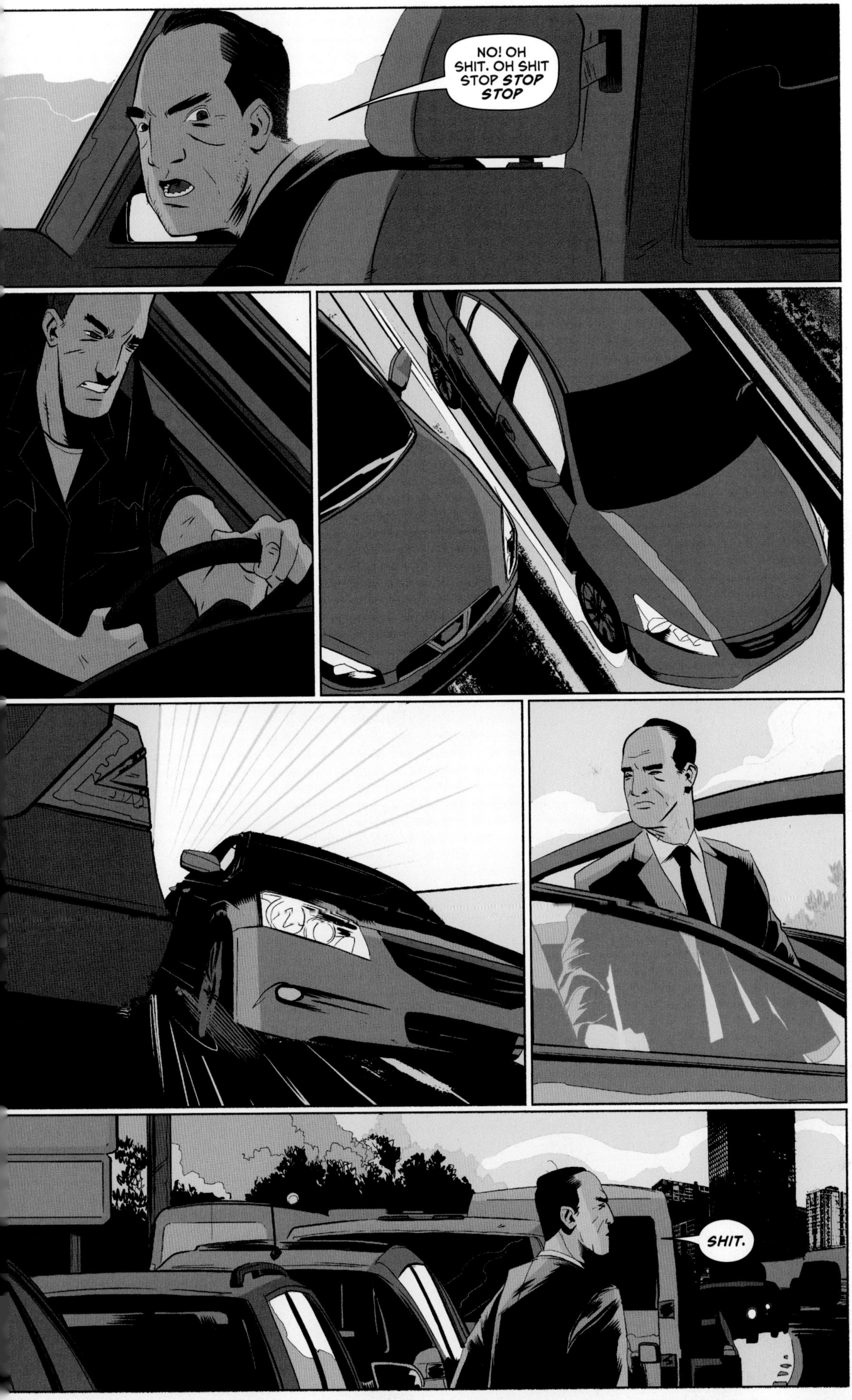
NO! OH SHIT. OH SHIT STOP STOP STOP
SHIT.

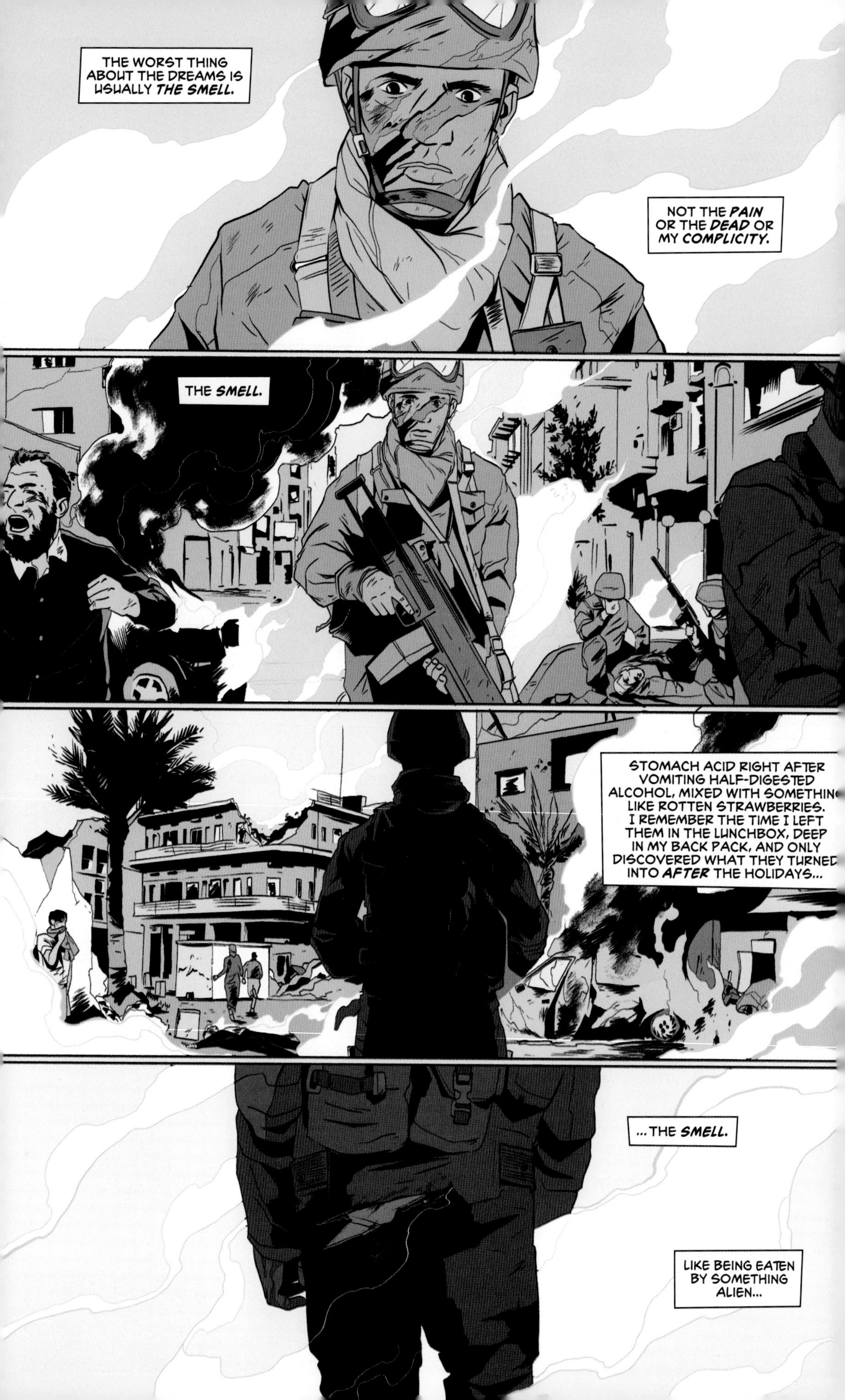
THE WORST THING ABOUT THE DREAMS IS USUALLY *THE SMELL.*
NOT THE *PAIN* OR THE *DEAD* OR MY *COMPLICITY.*
THE *SMELL.*
STOMACH ACID RIGHT AFTER VOMITING HALF-DIGESTED ALCOHOL, MIXED WITH SOMETHING LIKE ROTTEN STRAWBERRIES. I REMEMBER THE TIME I LEFT THEM IN THE LUNCHBOX, DEEP IN MY BACK PACK, AND ONLY DISCOVERED WHAT THEY TURNED INTO *AFTER* THE HOLIDAYS...
...THE *SMELL.*
LIKE BEING EATEN BY SOMETHING ALIEN...

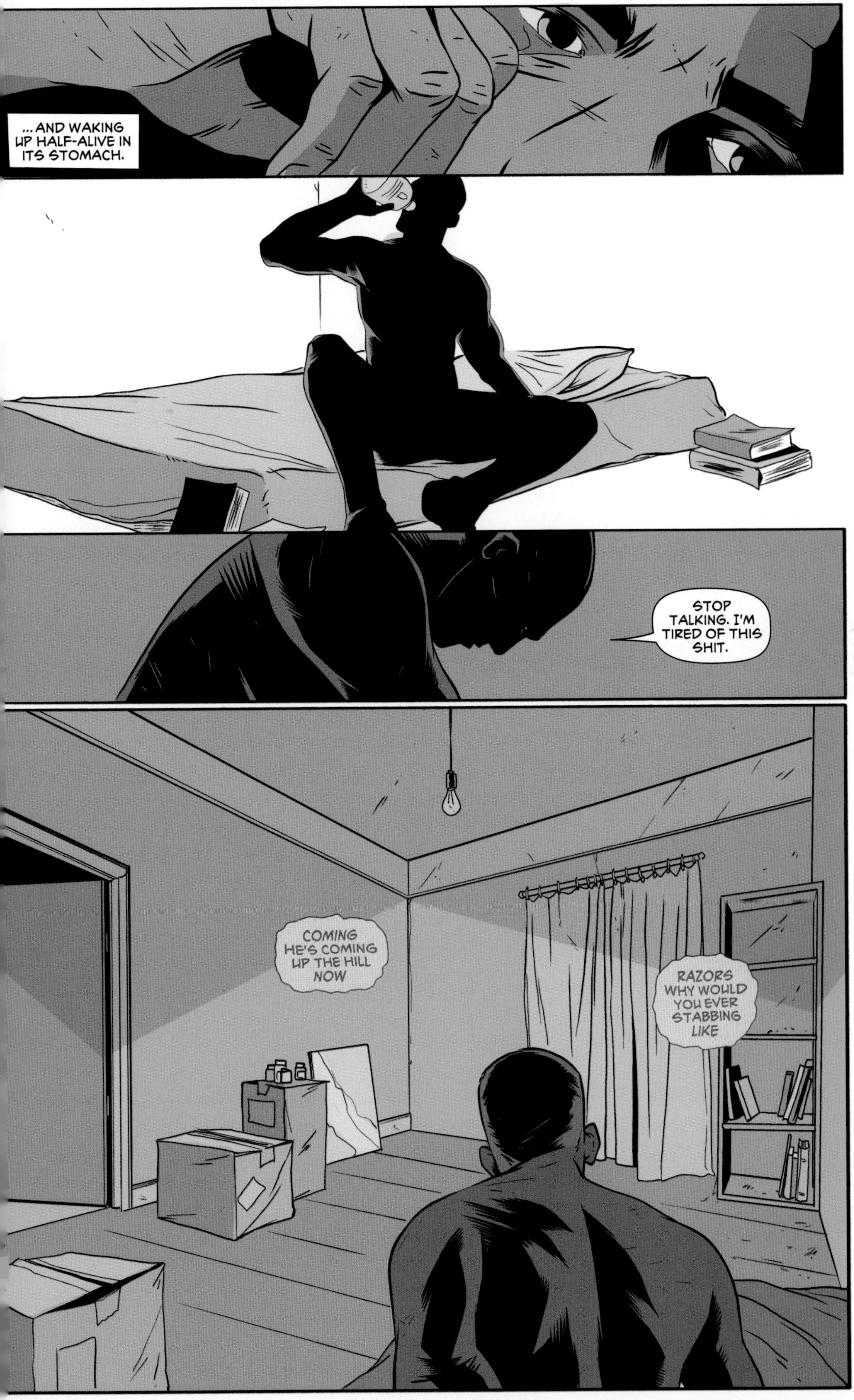
...AND WAKING UP HALF-ALIVE IN ITS STOMACH.
STOP TALKING. I'M TIRED OF THIS SHIT.
COMING HE'S COMING UP THE HILL NOW
RAZORS WHY WOULD YOU EVER STABBING LIKE

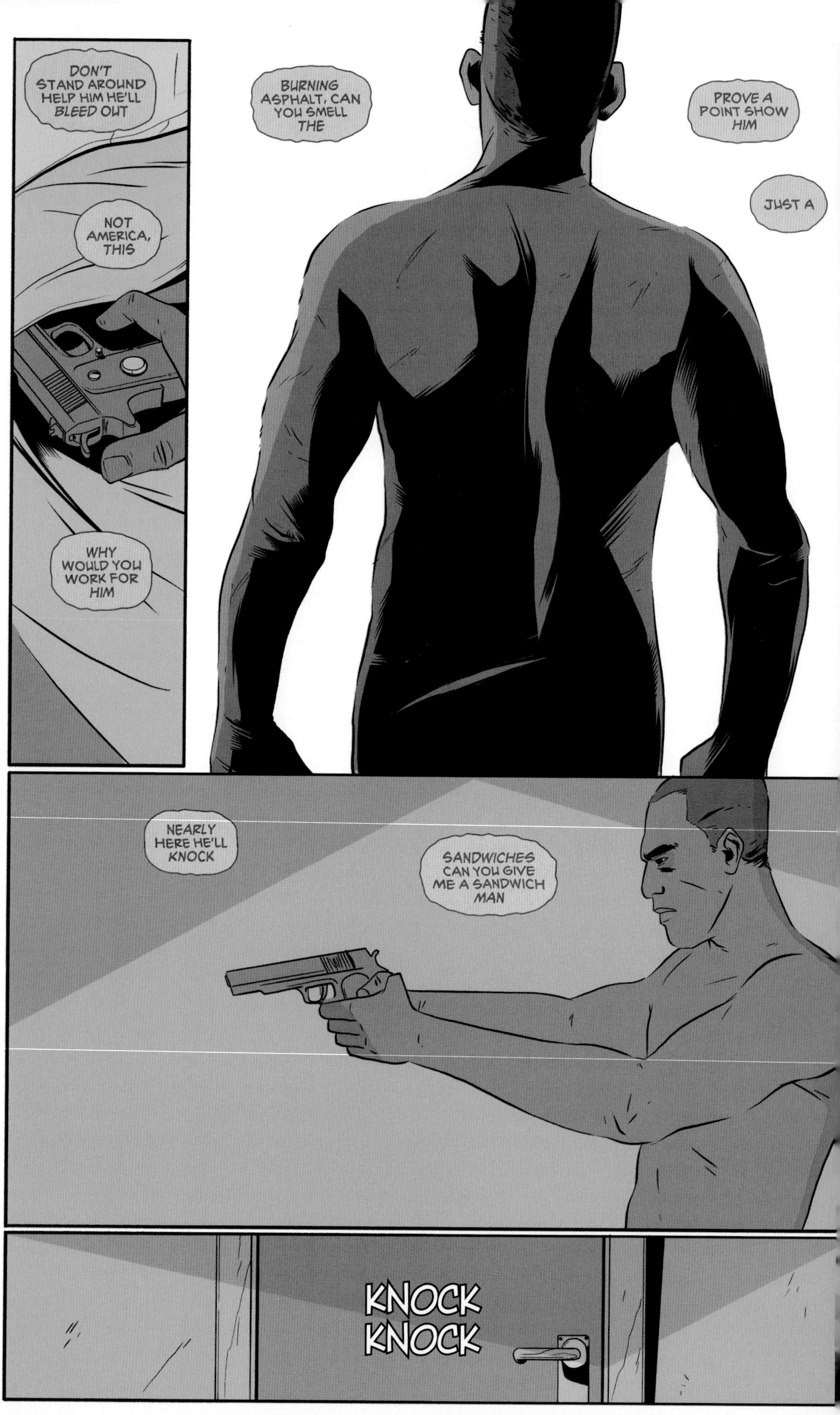
DON'T STAND AROUND HELP HIM HE'LL BLEED OUT
BURNING ASPHALT, CAN YOU SMELL THE
PROVE A POINT SHOW HIM
JUST A
NOT AMERICA, THIS
WHY WOULD YOU WORK FOR HIM
NEARLY HERE HE'LL KNOCK
SANDWICHES CAN YOU GIVE ME A SANDWICH MAN
KNOCK KNOCK

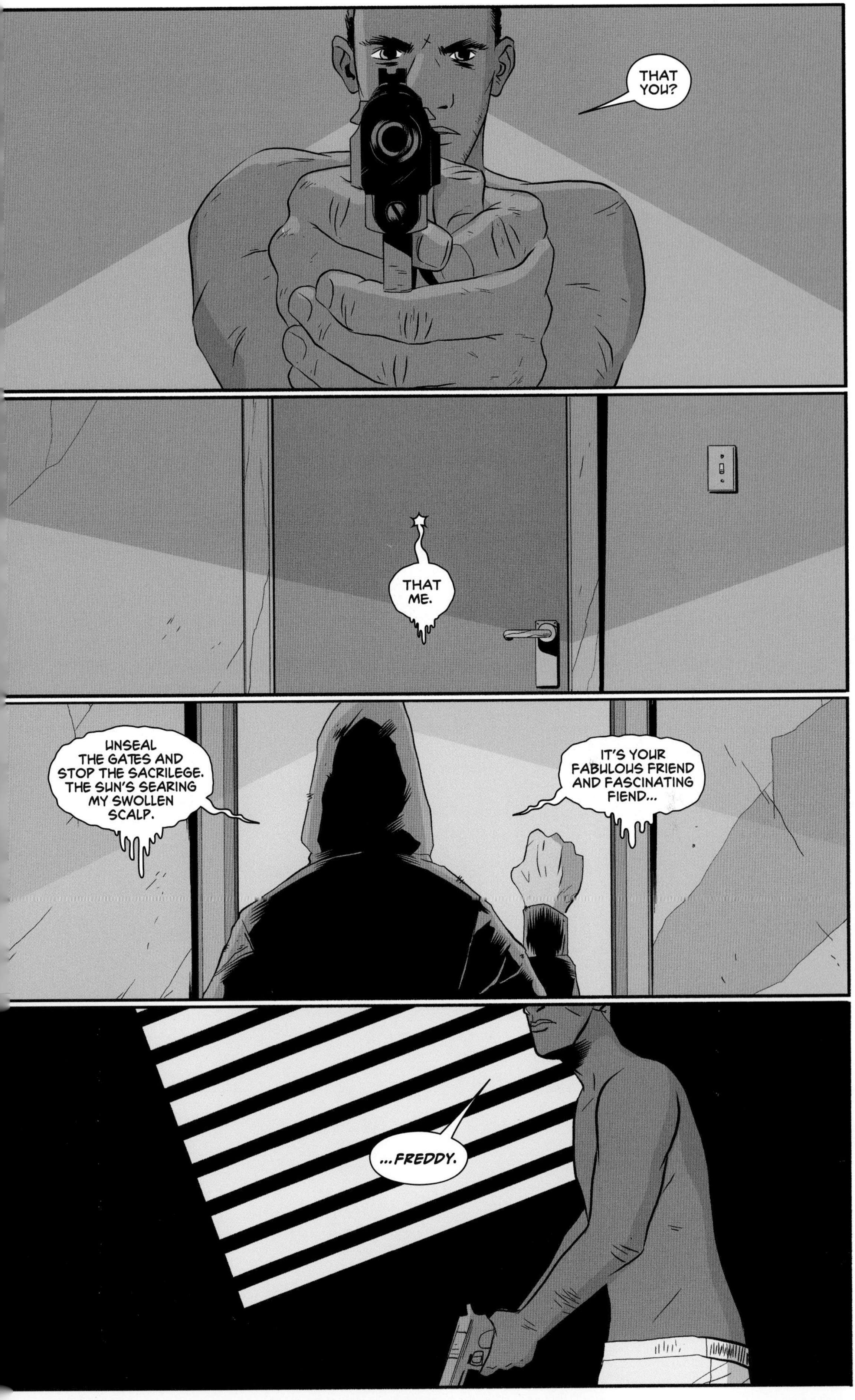
THAT YOU?
THAT ME.
UNSEAL THE GATES AND STOP THE SACRILEGE. THE SUN'S SEARING MY SWOLLEN SCALP.
IT'S YOUR FABULOUS FRIEND AND FASCINATING FIEND...
...FREDDY.

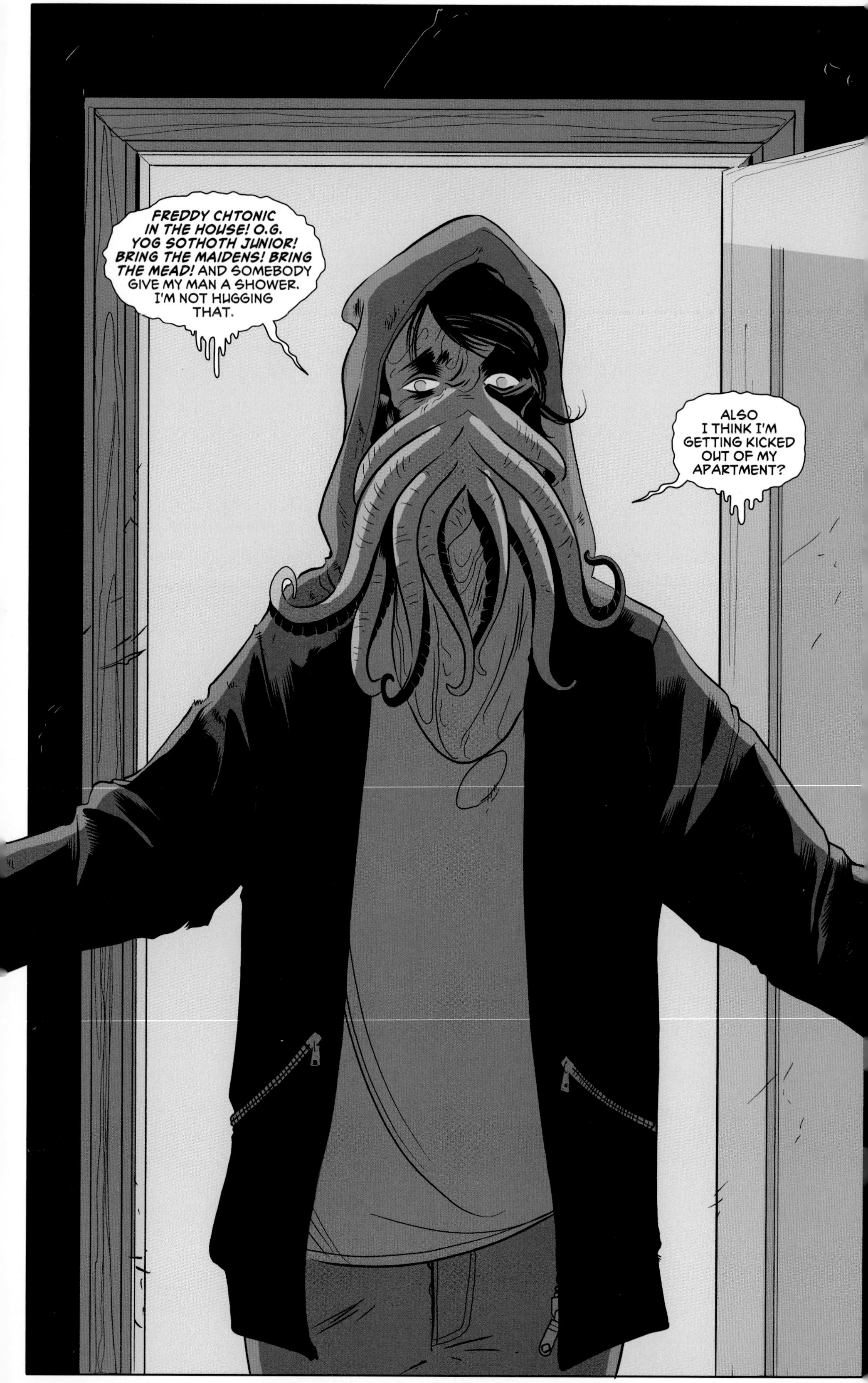
FREDDY CHTONIC IN THE HOUSE! O.G. YOG SOTHOTH JUNIOR! BRING THE MAIDENS! BRING THE MEAD! AND SOMEBODY GIVE MY MAN A SHOWER. I'M NOT HUGGING THAT.
ALSO I THINK I'M GETTING KICKED OUT OF MY APARTMENT?

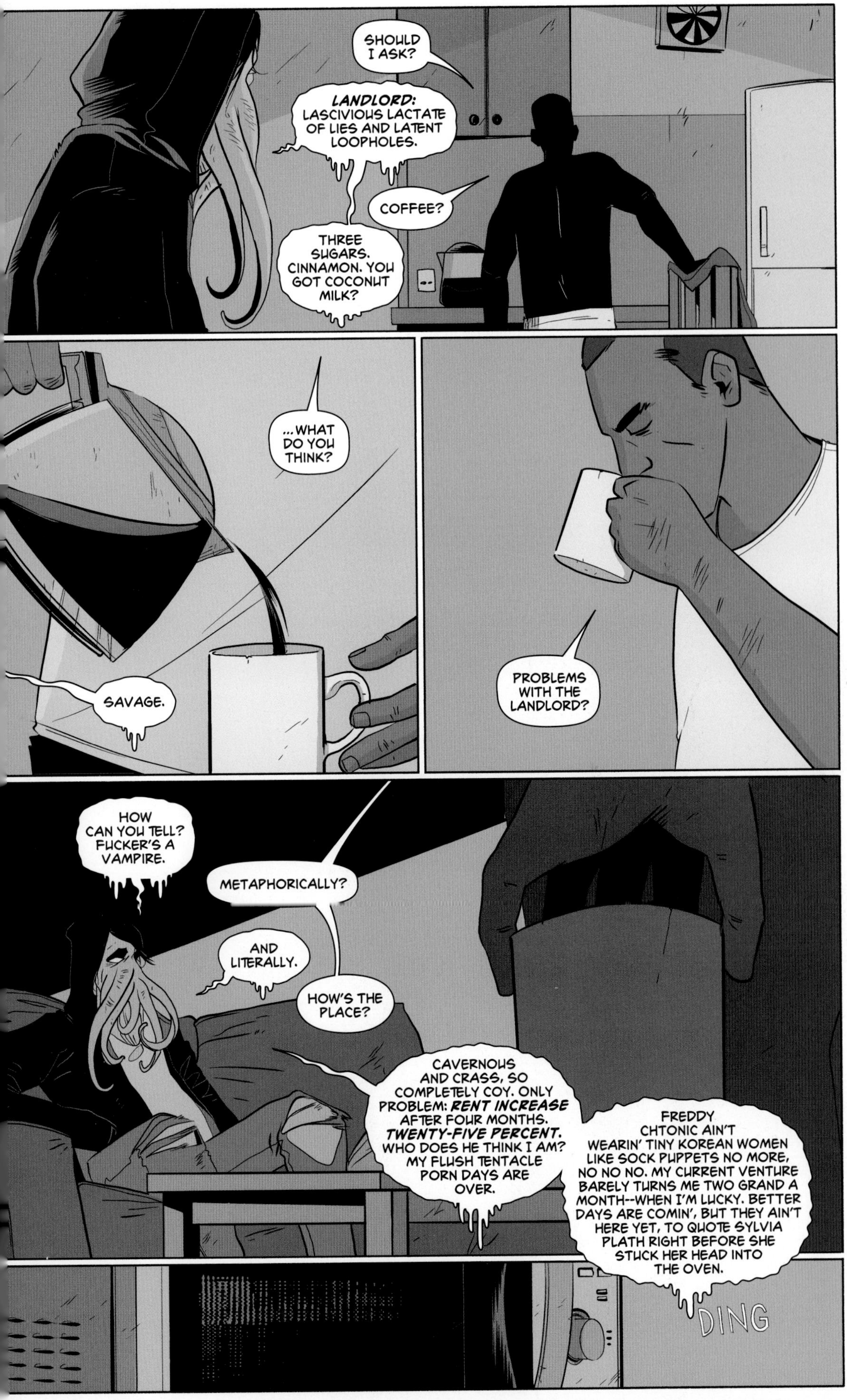
SHOULD I ASK?
LANDLORD: LASCIVIOUS LACTATE OF LIES AND LATENT LOOPHOLES.
COFFEE?
THREE SUGARS. CINNAMON. YOU GOT COCONUT MILK?
...WHAT DO YOU THINK?
SAVAGE.
PROBLEMS WITH THE LANDLORD?
HOW CAN YOU TELL? FUCKER'S A VAMPIRE.
METAPHORICALLY?
AND LITERALLY.
HOW'S THE PLACE?
CAVERNOUS AND CRASS, SO COMPLETELY COY. ONLY PROBLEM: RENT INCREASE AFTER FOUR MONTHS. TWENTY-FIVE PERCENT. WHO DOES HE THINK I AM? MY FLUSH TENTACLE PORN DAYS ARE OVER.
FREDDY CHTONIC AIN'T WEARIN' TINY KOREAN WOMEN LIKE SOCK PUPPETS NO MORE, NO NO NO. MY CURRENT VENTURE BARELY TURNS ME TWO GRAND A MONTH--WHEN I'M LUCKY. BETTER DAYS ARE COMIN', BUT THEY AIN'T HERE YET, TO QUOTE SYLVIA PLATH RIGHT BEFORE SHE STUCK HER HEAD INTO THE OVEN.
DING

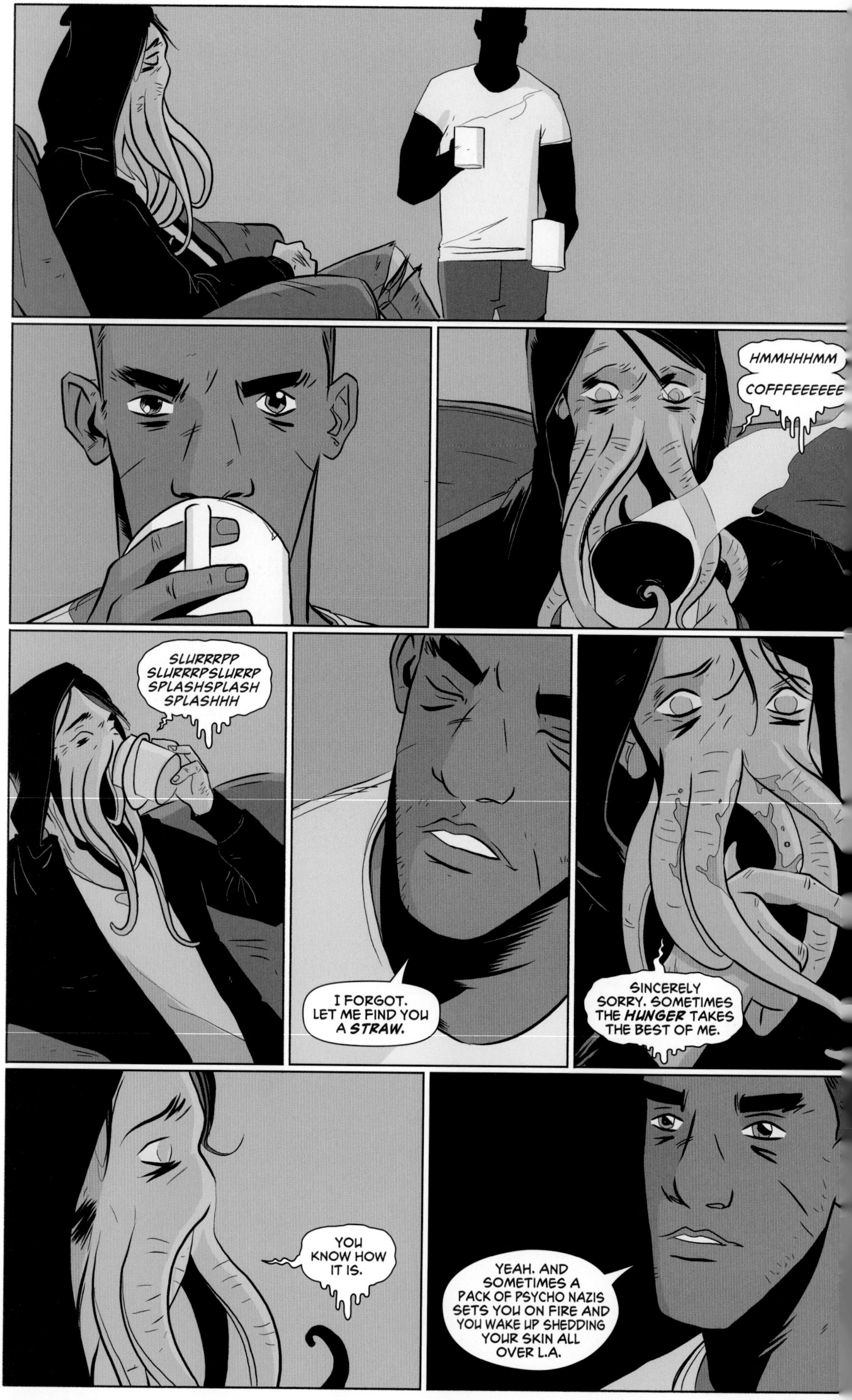
HMMHHHMM
COFFFEEEEEE
SLURRRPP SLURRRPSLURRP SPLASHSPLASH SPLASHHH
I FORGOT. LET ME FIND YOU A STRAW.
SINCERELY SORRY. SOMETIMES THE HUNGER TAKES THE BEST OF ME.
YOU KNOW HOW IT IS.
YEAH. AND SOMETIMES A PACK OF PSYCHO NAZIS SETS YOU ON FIRE AND YOU WAKE UP SHEDDING YOUR SKIN ALL OVER L.A.

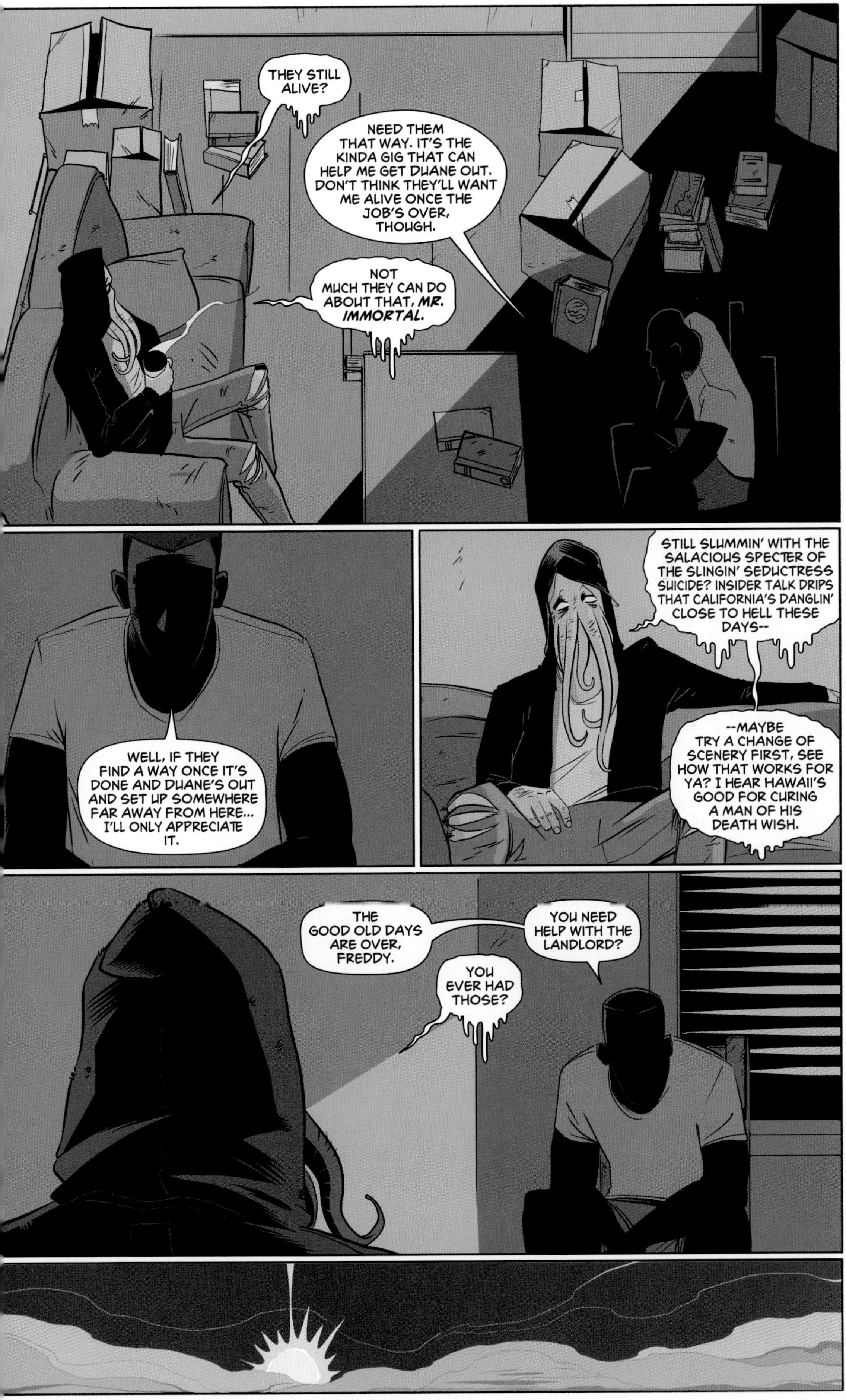
THEY STILL ALIVE?
NEED THEM THAT WAY. IT'S THE KINDA GIG THAT CAN HELP ME GET DUANE OUT. DON'T THINK THEY'LL WANT ME ALIVE ONCE THE JOB'S OVER, THOUGH.
NOT MUCH THEY CAN DO ABOUT THAT, MR. IMMORTAL.
WELL, IF THEY FIND A WAY ONCE IT'S DONE AND DUANE'S OUT AND SET UP SOMEWHERE FAR AWAY FROM HERE... I'LL ONLY APPRECIATE IT.
STILL SLUMMIN' WITH THE SALACIOUS SPECTER OF THE SLINGIN' SEDUCTRESS SUICIDE? INSIDER TALK DRIPS THAT CALIFORNIA'S DANGLIN' CLOSE TO HELL THESE DAYS--
--MAYBE TRY A CHANGE OF SCENERY FIRST, SEE HOW THAT WORKS FOR YA? I HEAR HAWAII'S GOOD FOR CURING A MAN OF HIS DEATH WISH.
YOU NEED HELP WITH THE LANDLORD?
THE GOOD OLD DAYS ARE OVER, FREDDY.
YOU EVER HAD THOSE?

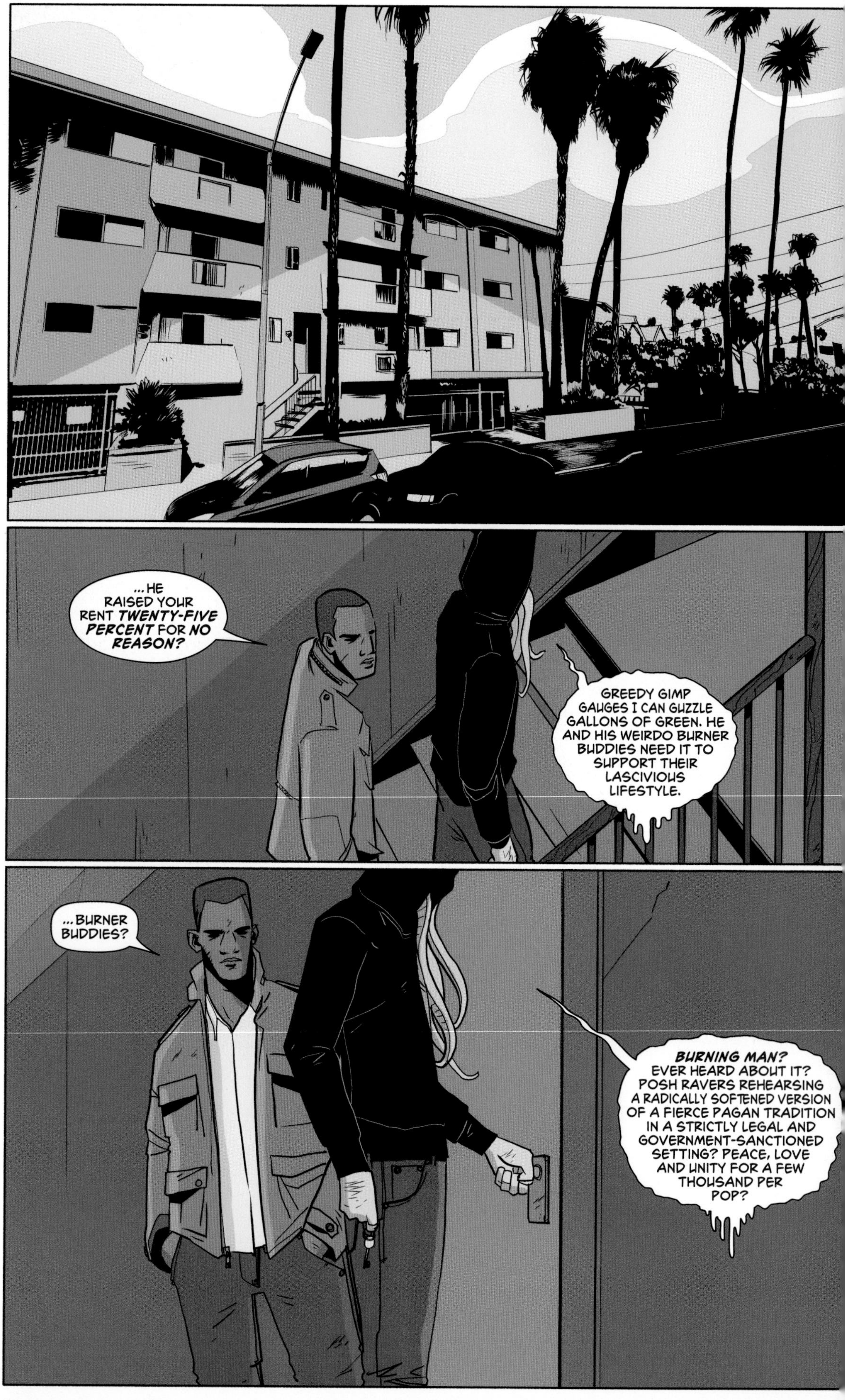
...HE RAISED YOUR RENT TWENTY-FIVE PERCENT FOR NO REASON?
GREEDY GIMP GAUGES I CAN GUZZLE GALLONS OF GREEN. HE AND HIS WEIRDO BURNER BUDDIES NEED IT TO SUPPORT THEIR LASCIVIOUS LIFESTYLE.
...BURNER BUDDIES?
BURNING MAN? EVER HEARD ABOUT IT? POSH RAVERS REHEARSING A RADICALLY SOFTENED VERSION OF A FIERCE PAGAN TRADITION IN A STRICTLY LEGAL AND GOVERNMENT-SANCTIONED SETTING? PEACE, LOVE AND UNITY FOR A FEW THOUSAND PER POP?

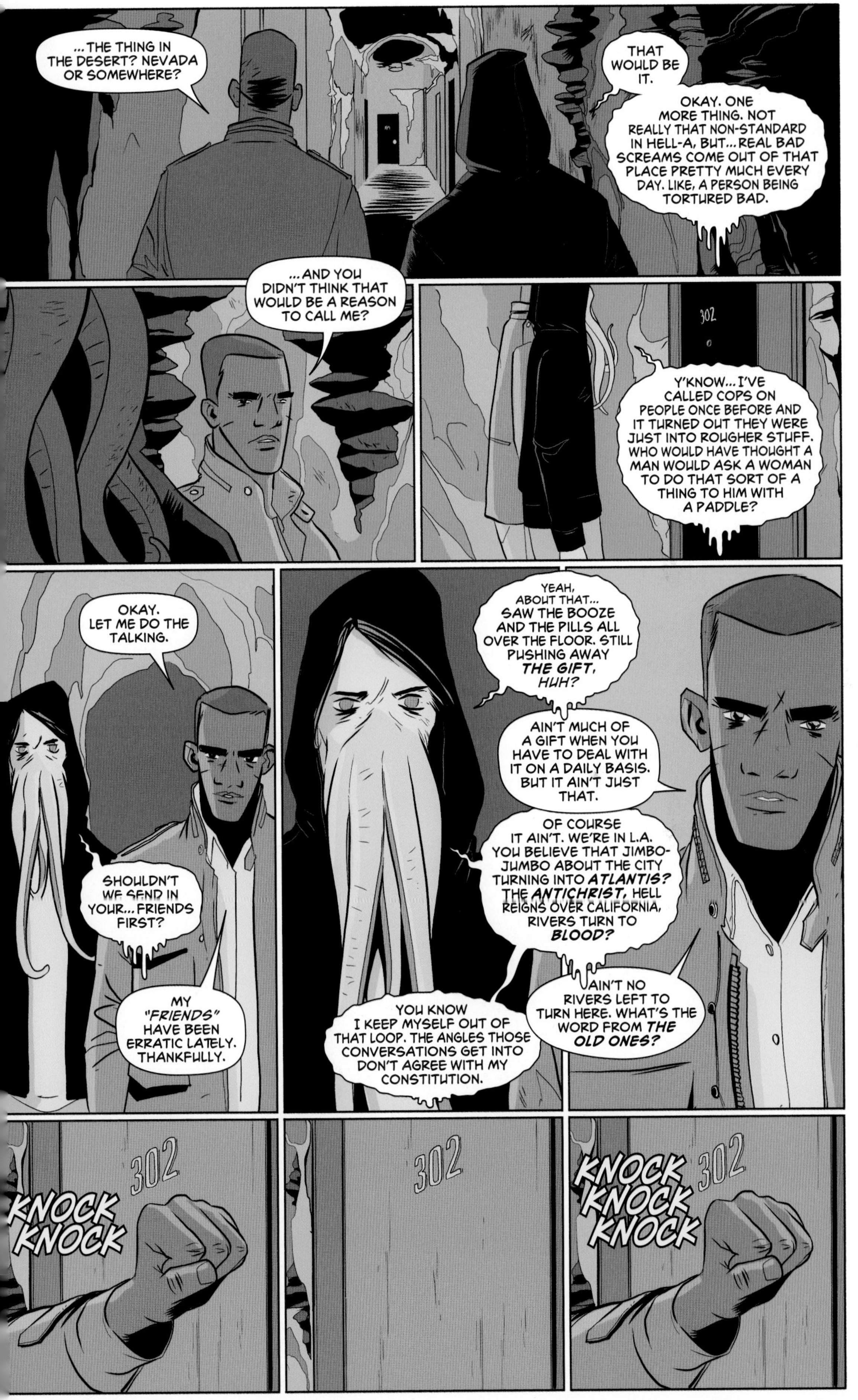
...THE THING IN THE DESERT? NEVADA OR SOMEWHERE?
THAT WOULD BE IT.
OKAY. ONE MORE THING. NOT REALLY THAT NON-STANDARD IN HELL-A, BUT...REAL BAD SCREAMS COME OUT OF THAT PLACE PRETTY MUCH EVERY DAY. LIKE, A PERSON BEING TORTURED BAD.
...AND YOU DIDN'T THINK THAT WOULD BE A REASON TO CALL ME?
302
Y'KNOW...I'VE CALLED COPS ON PEOPLE ONCE BEFORE AND IT TURNED OUT THEY WERE JUST INTO ROUGHER STUFF. WHO WOULD HAVE THOUGHT A MAN WOULD ASK A WOMAN TO DO THAT SORT OF A THING TO HIM WITH A PADDLE?
OKAY. LET ME DO THE TALKING.
SHOULDN'T WE SEND IN YOUR...FRIENDS FIRST?
MY "FRIENDS" HAVE BEEN ERRATIC LATELY. THANKFULLY.
YEAH, ABOUT THAT... SAW THE BOOZE AND THE PILLS ALL OVER THE FLOOR. STILL PUSHING AWAY THE GIFT, HUH?
AIN'T MUCH OF A GIFT WHEN YOU HAVE TO DEAL WITH IT ON A DAILY BASIS. BUT IT AIN'T JUST THAT.
OF COURSE IT AIN'T. WE'RE IN L.A. YOU BELIEVE THAT JIMBO-JUMBO ABOUT THE CITY TURNING INTO ATLANTIS? THE ANTICHRIST, HELL REIGNS OVER CALIFORNIA, RIVERS TURN TO BLOOD?
AIN'T NO RIVERS LEFT TO TURN HERE. WHAT'S THE WORD FROM THE OLD ONES?
YOU KNOW I KEEP MYSELF OUT OF THAT LOOP. THE ANGLES THOSE CONVERSATIONS GET INTO DON'T AGREE WITH MY CONSTITUTION.
302
KNOCK KNOCK
302
302
KNOCK KNOCK KNOCK

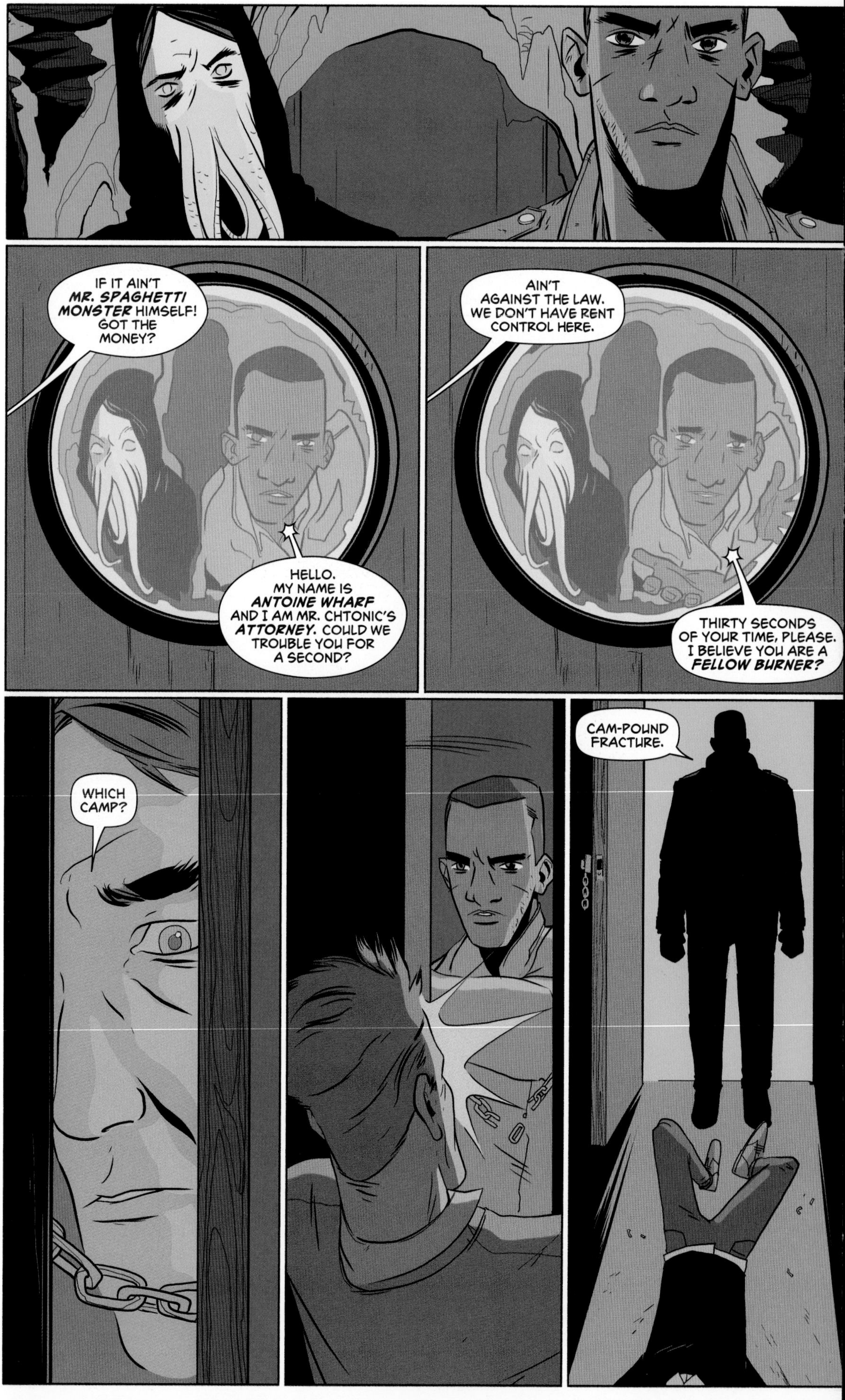

IF IT AIN'T MR. SPAGHETTI MONSTER HIMSELF! GOT THE MONEY?
HELLO. MY NAME IS ANTOINE WHARF AND I AM MR. CHTONIC'S ATTORNEY. COULD WE TROUBLE YOU FOR A SECOND?
AIN'T AGAINST THE LAW. WE DON'T HAVE RENT CONTROL HERE.
THIRTY SECONDS OF YOUR TIME, PLEASE. I BELIEVE YOU ARE A FELLOW BURNER?
WHICH CAMP?
CAM-POUND FRACTURE.

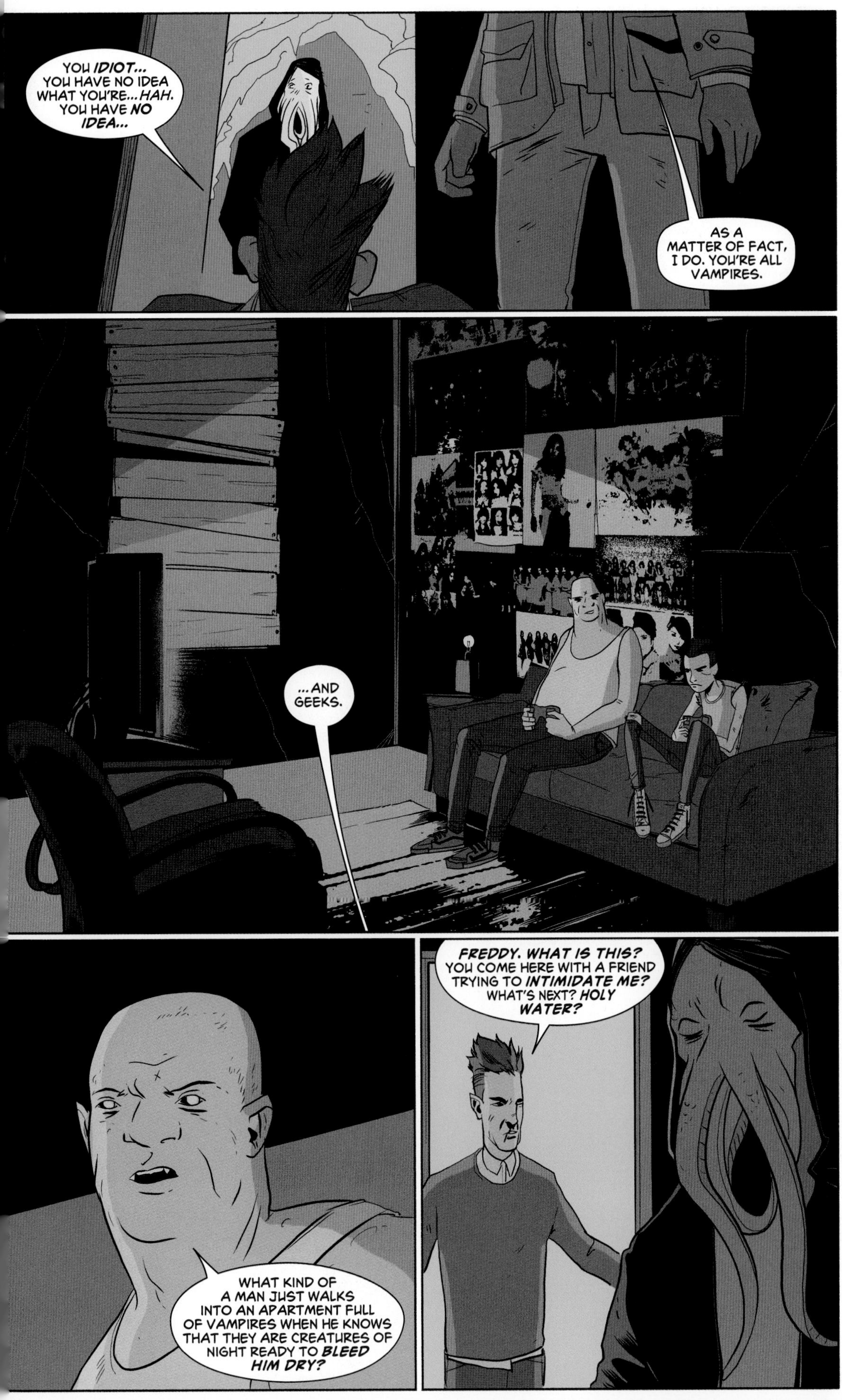
YOU IDIOT... YOU HAVE NO IDEA WHAT YOU'RE... HAH. YOU HAVE NO IDEA...
AS A MATTER OF FACT, I DO. YOU'RE ALL VAMPIRES.
...AND GEEKS.
WHAT KIND OF A MAN JUST WALKS INTO AN APARTMENT FULL OF VAMPIRES WHEN HE KNOWS THAT THEY ARE CREATURES OF NIGHT READY TO BLEED HIM DRY?
FREDDY. WHAT IS THIS? YOU COME HERE WITH A FRIEND TRYING TO INTIMIDATE ME? WHAT'S NEXT? HOLY WATER?

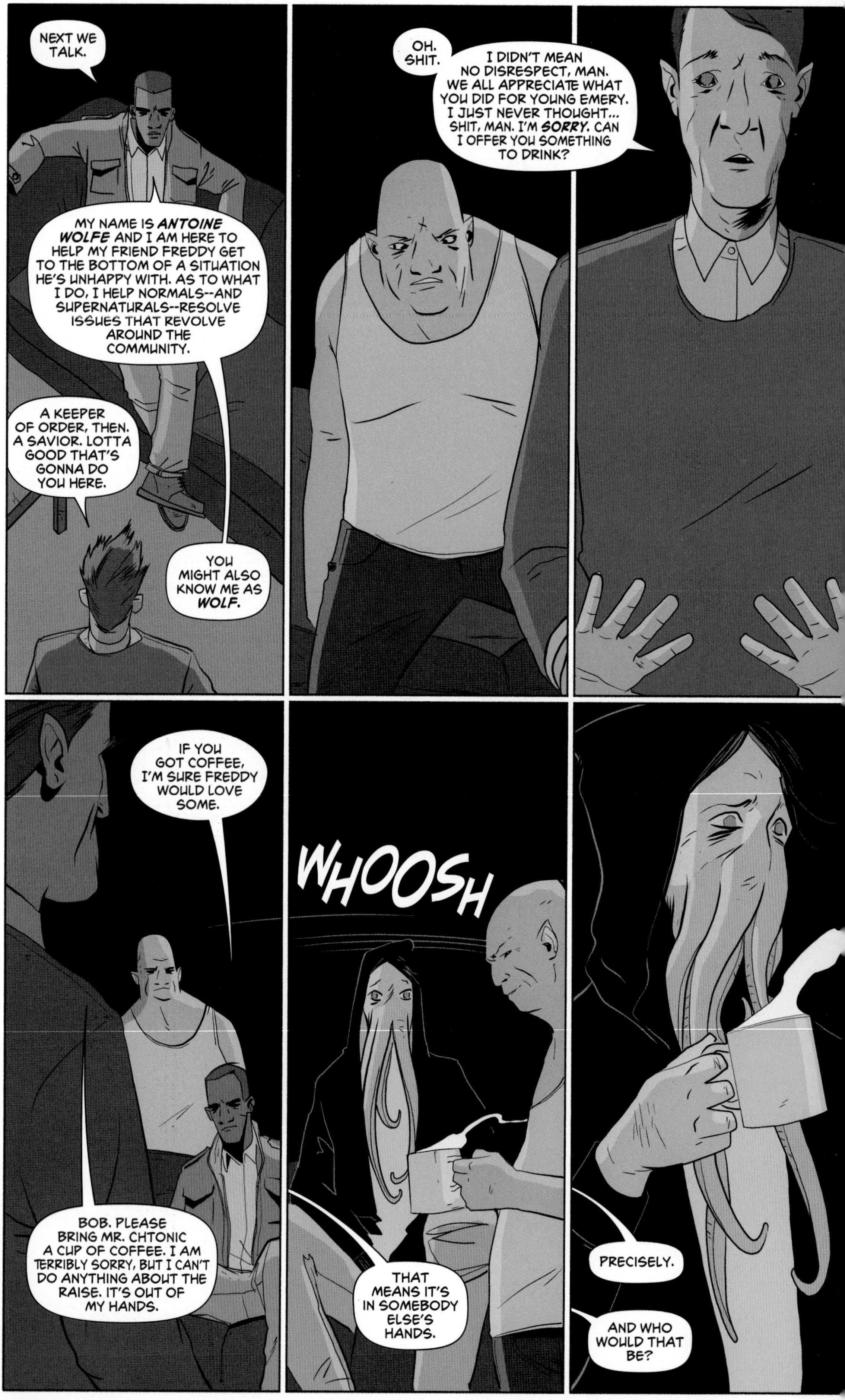
NEXT WE TALK.
MY NAME IS ANTOINE WOLFE AND I AM HERE TO HELP MY FRIEND FREDDY GET TO THE BOTTOM OF A SITUATION HE'S UNHAPPY WITH. AS TO WHAT I DO, I HELP NORMALS--AND SUPERNATURALS--RESOLVE ISSUES THAT REVOLVE AROUND THE COMMUNITY.
A KEEPER OF ORDER, THEN. A SAVIOR. LOTTA GOOD THAT'S GONNA DO YOU HERE.
YOU MIGHT ALSO KNOW ME AS WOLF.
OH. SHIT.
I DIDN'T MEAN NO DISRESPECT, MAN. WE ALL APPRECIATE WHAT YOU DID FOR YOUNG EMERY. I JUST NEVER THOUGHT... SHIT, MAN. I'M SORRY. CAN I OFFER YOU SOMETHING TO DRINK?
IF YOU GOT COFFEE, I'M SURE FREDDY WOULD LOVE SOME.
BOB. PLEASE BRING MR. CHTONIC A CUP OF COFFEE. I AM TERRIBLY SORRY, BUT I CAN'T DO ANYTHING ABOUT THE RAISE. IT'S OUT OF MY HANDS.
WHOOSH
THAT MEANS IT'S IN SOMEBODY ELSE'S HANDS.
PRECISELY.
AND WHO WOULD THAT BE?

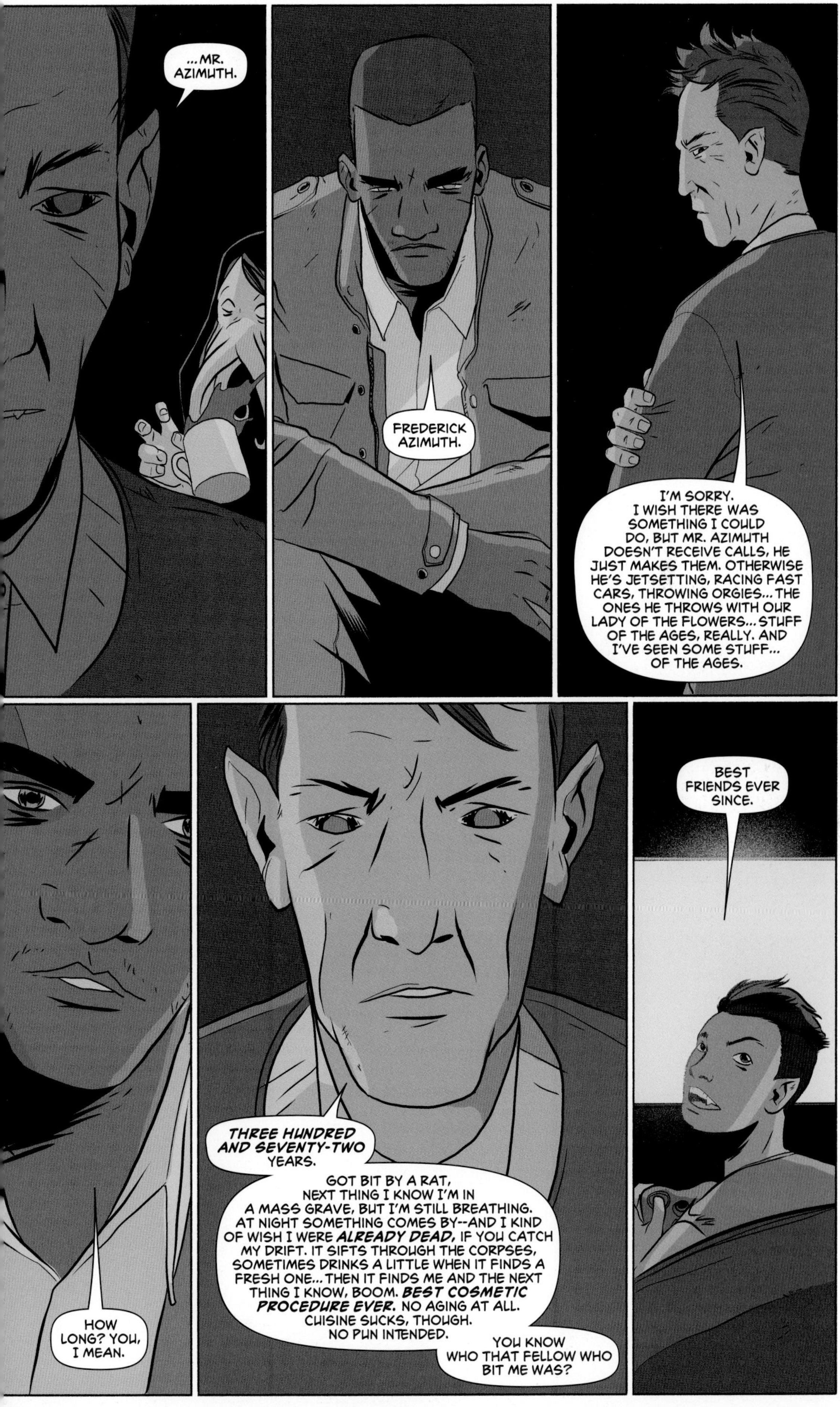
...MR. AZIMUTH.
FREDERICK AZIMUTH.
I'M SORRY. I WISH THERE WAS SOMETHING I COULD DO, BUT MR. AZIMUTH DOESN'T RECEIVE CALLS, HE JUST MAKES THEM. OTHERWISE HE'S JETSETTING, RACING FAST CARS, THROWING ORGIES... THE ONES HE THROWS WITH OUR LADY OF THE FLOWERS... STUFF OF THE AGES, REALLY. AND I'VE SEEN SOME STUFF... OF THE AGES.
HOW LONG? YOU, I MEAN.
THREE HUNDRED AND SEVENTY-TWO YEARS.
GOT BIT BY A RAT, NEXT THING I KNOW I'M IN A MASS GRAVE, BUT I'M STILL BREATHING. AT NIGHT SOMETHING COMES BY--AND I KIND OF WISH I WERE ALREADY DEAD, IF YOU CATCH MY DRIFT. IT SIFTS THROUGH THE CORPSES, SOMETIMES DRINKS A LITTLE WHEN IT FINDS A FRESH ONE... THEN IT FINDS ME AND THE NEXT THING I KNOW, BOOM. BEST COSMETIC PROCEDURE EVER. NO AGING AT ALL. CUISINE SUCKS, THOUGH. NO PUN INTENDED.
YOU KNOW WHO THAT FELLOW WHO BIT ME WAS?
BEST FRIENDS EVER SINCE.

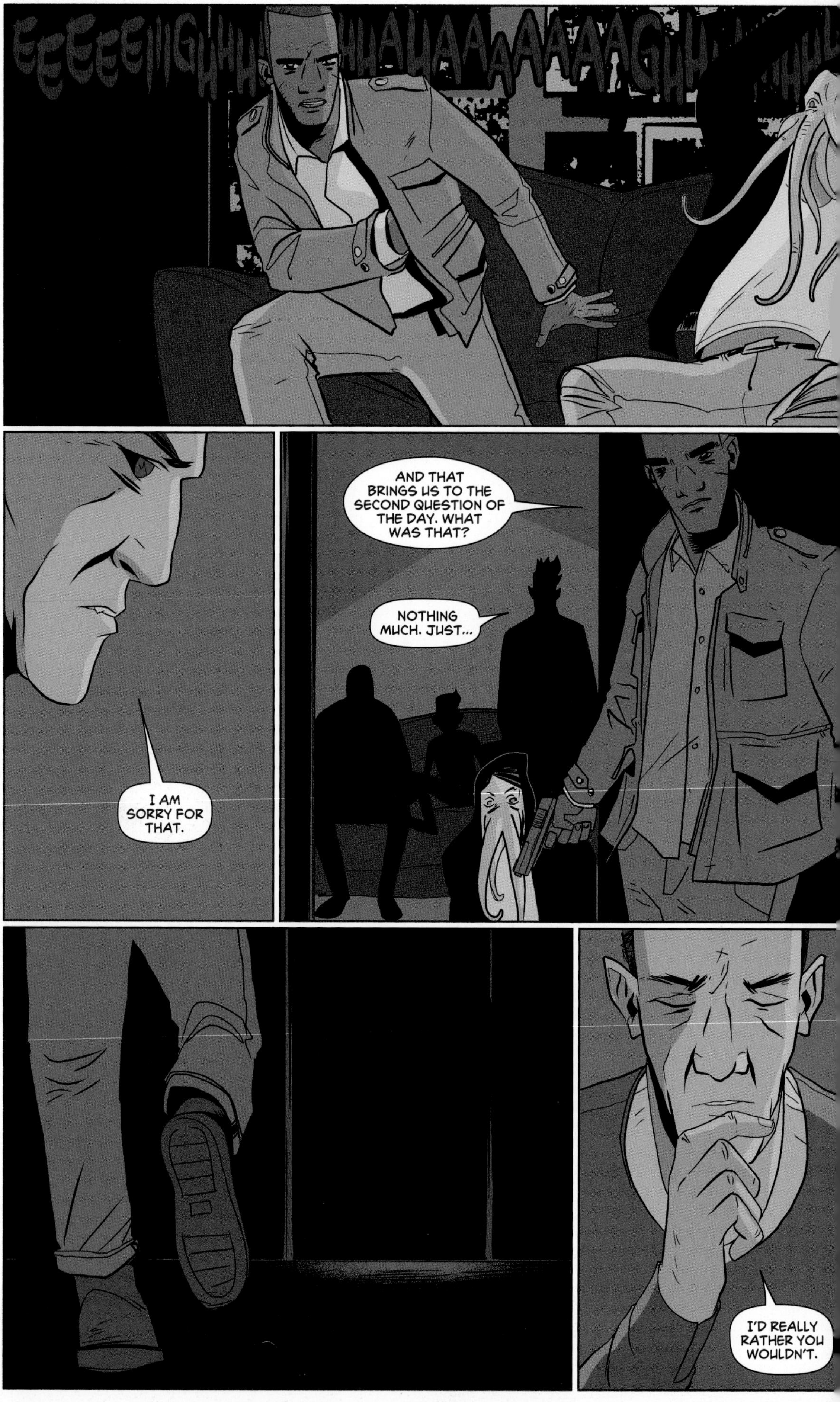
EEEEEEIIIGHHHHHUAUAAAAAAAAGHH
I AM SORRY FOR THAT.
AND THAT BRINGS US TO THE SECOND QUESTION OF THE DAY. WHAT WAS THAT?
NOTHING MUCH. JUST...
I'D REALLY RATHER YOU WOULDN'T.

DON'T WORRY.

WE'LL COME BACK TO THAT.

LATER THAT NIGHT.

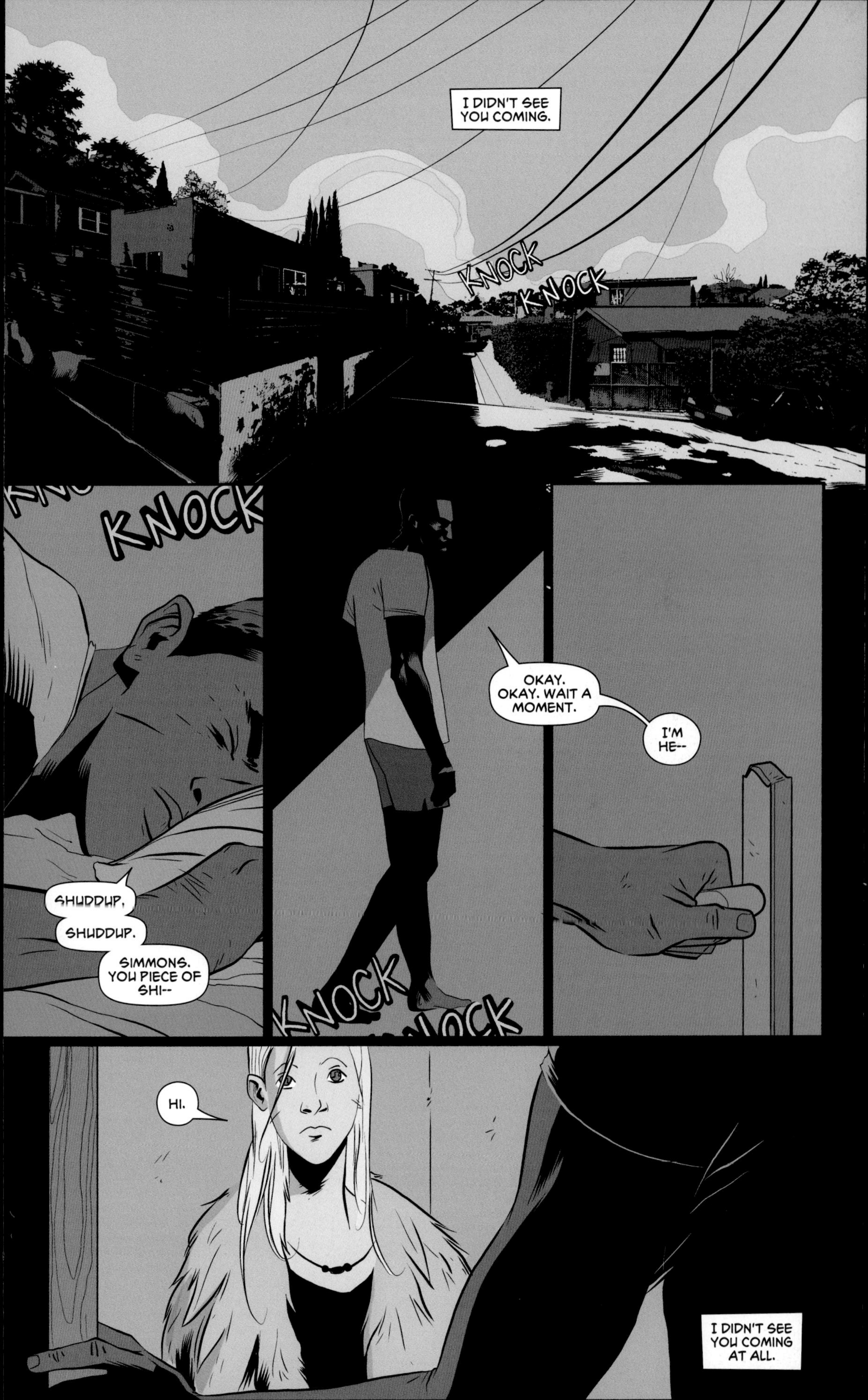
I DIDN'T SEE YOU COMING.
KNOCK
KNOCK
KNOCK
SHUDDUP,
SHUDDUP.
SIMMONS. YOU PIECE OF SHI--
OKAY. OKAY. WAIT A MOMENT.
I'M HE--
KNOCK
HI.
I DIDN'T SEE YOU COMING AT ALL.

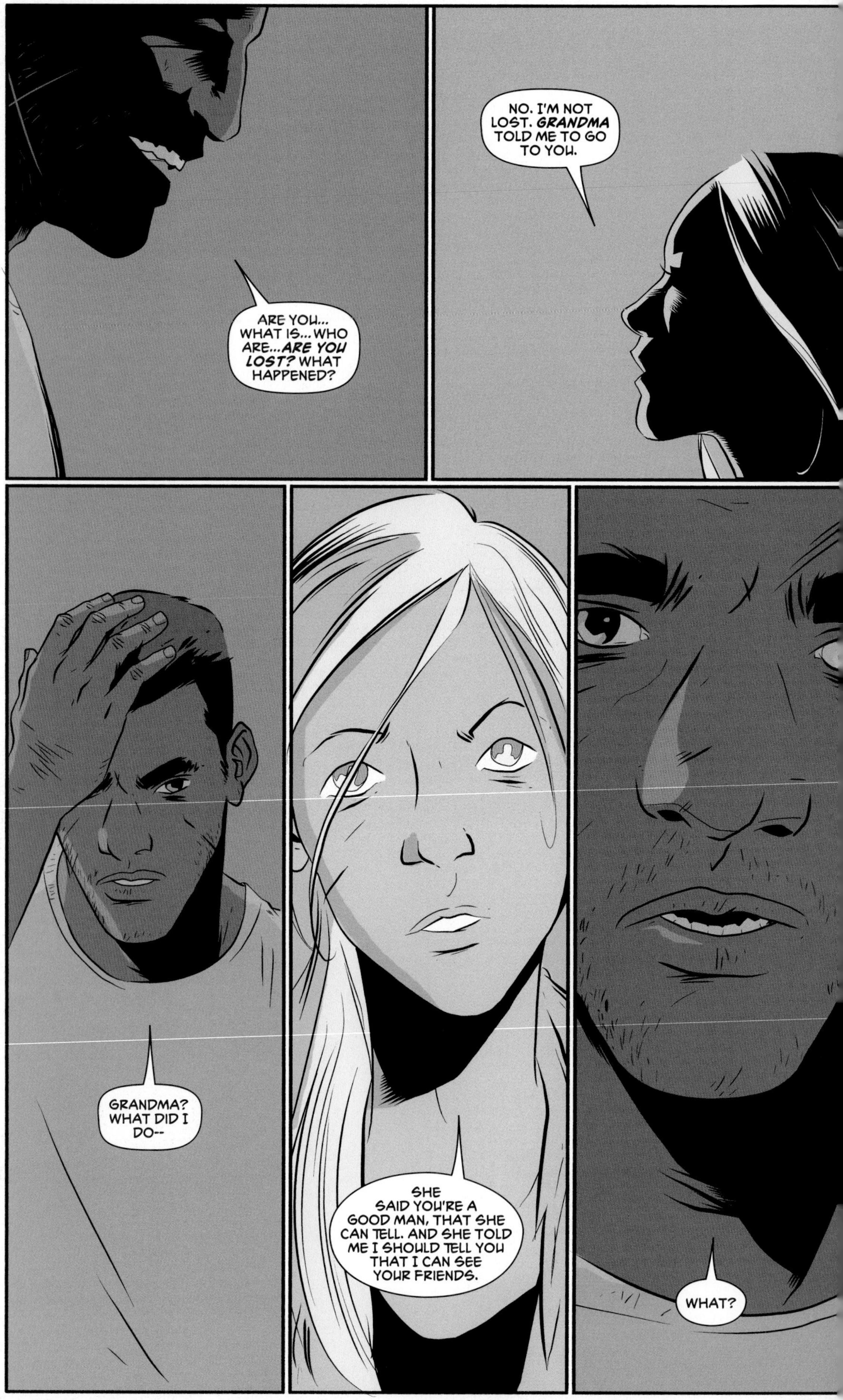
ARE YOU... WHAT IS...WHO ARE...ARE YOU LOST? WHAT HAPPENED?
NO. I'M NOT LOST. GRANDMA TOLD ME TO GO TO YOU.
GRANDMA? WHAT DID I DO--
SHE SAID YOU'RE A GOOD MAN, THAT SHE CAN TELL. AND SHE TOLD ME I SHOULD TELL YOU THAT I CAN SEE YOUR FRIENDS.
WHAT?

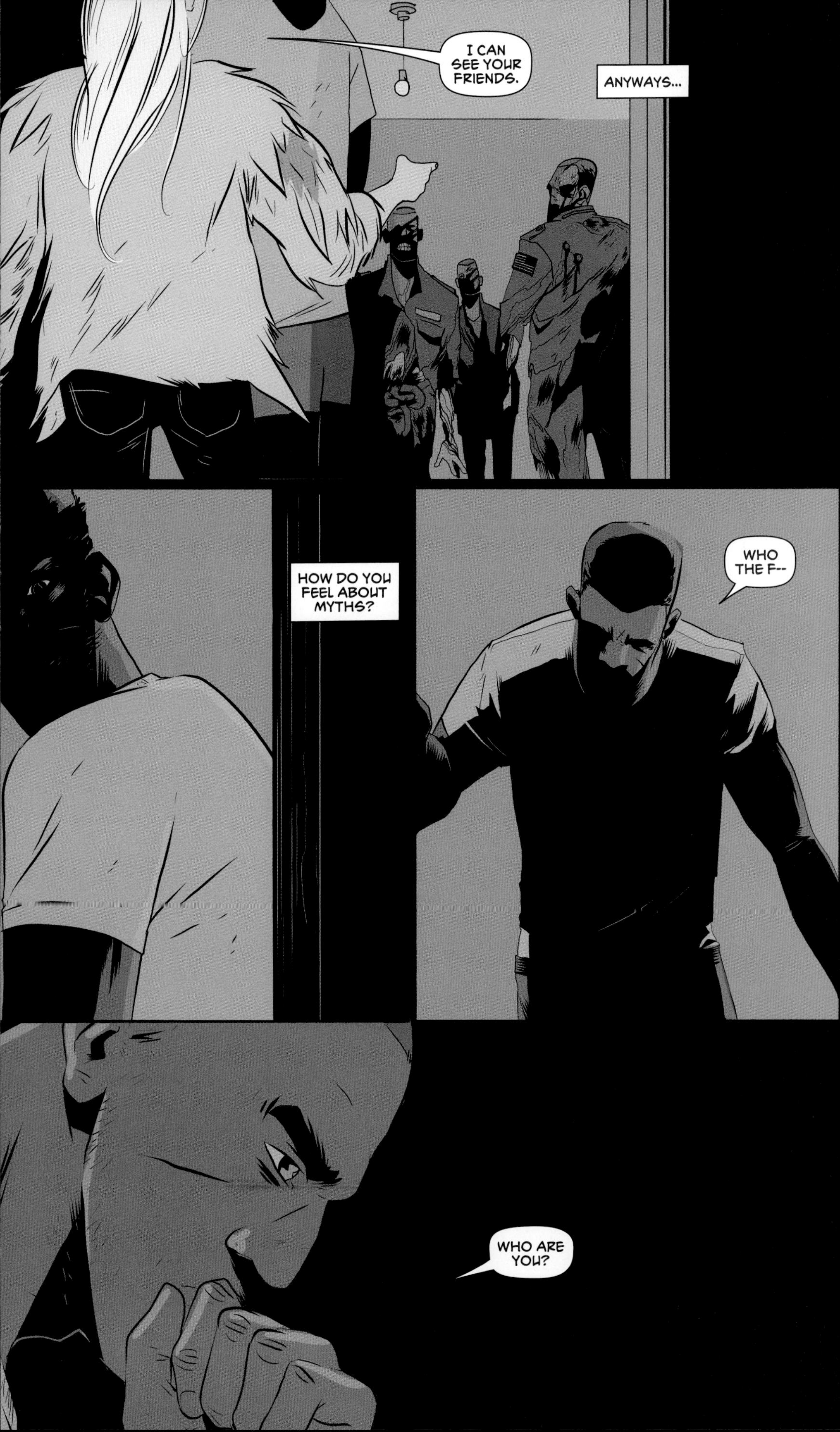
I CAN SEE YOUR FRIENDS.
ANYWAYS...
HOW DO YOU FEEL ABOUT MYTHS?
WHO THE F--
WHO ARE YOU?

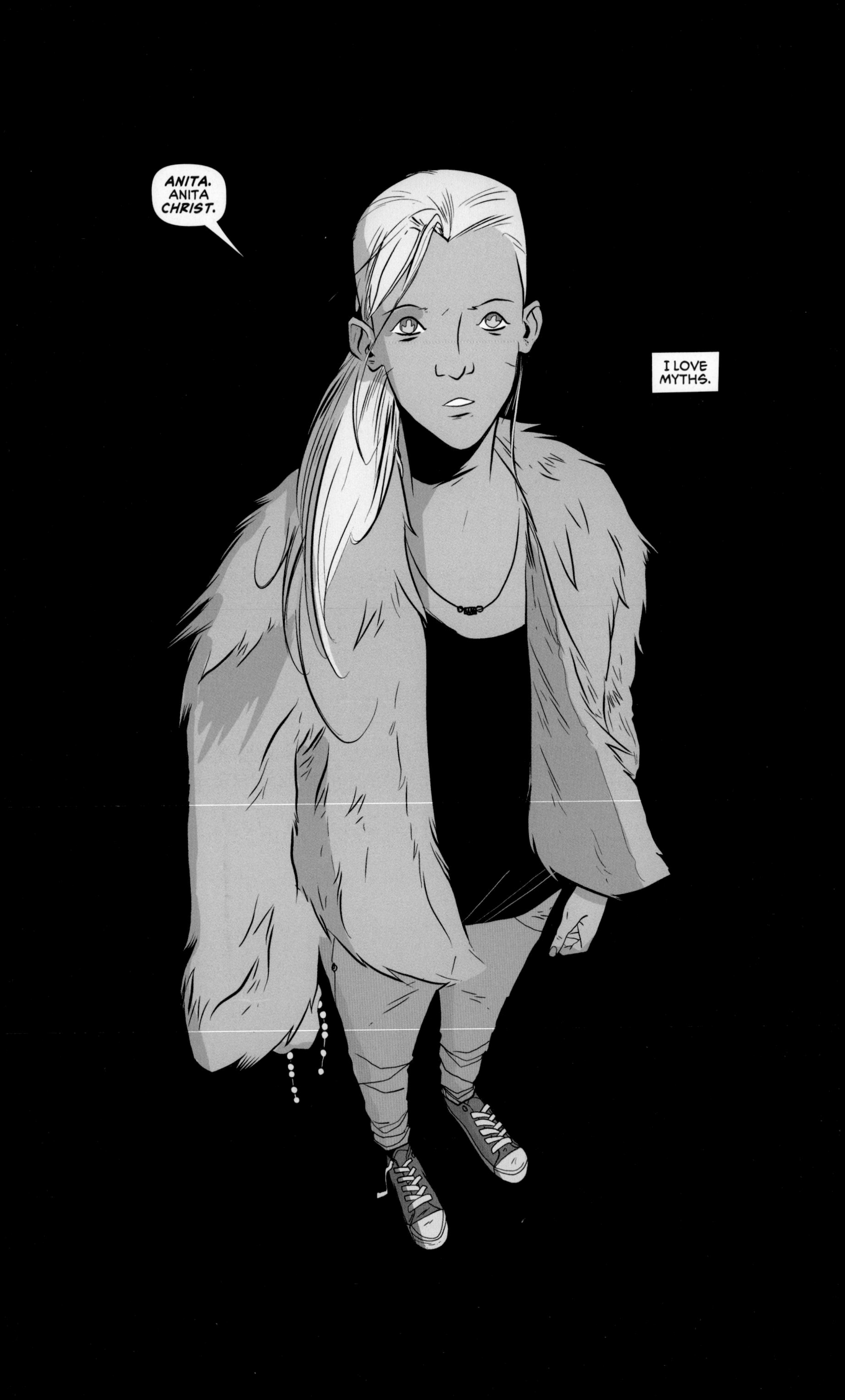
ANITA. ANITA CHRIST.
I LOVE MYTHS.

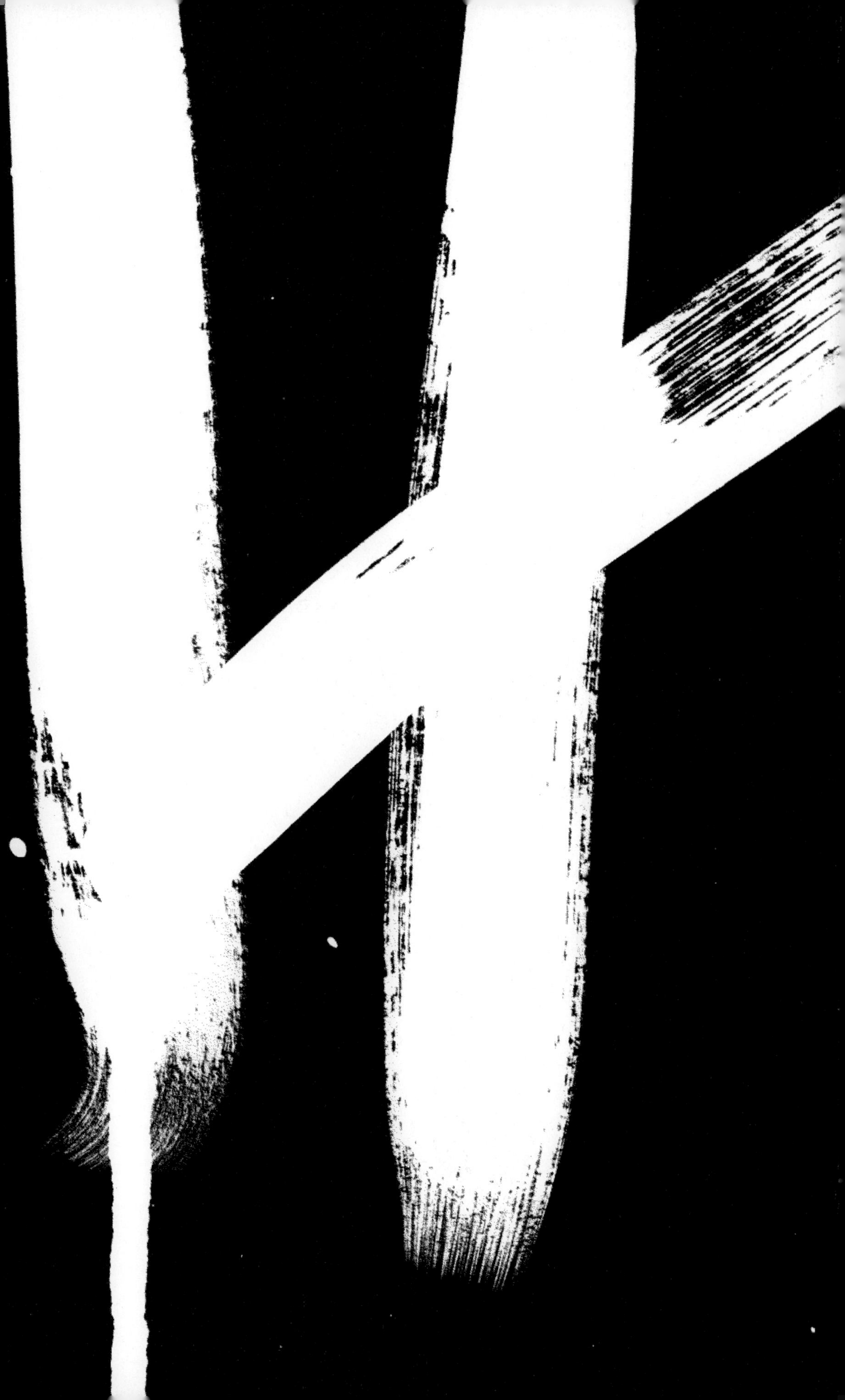

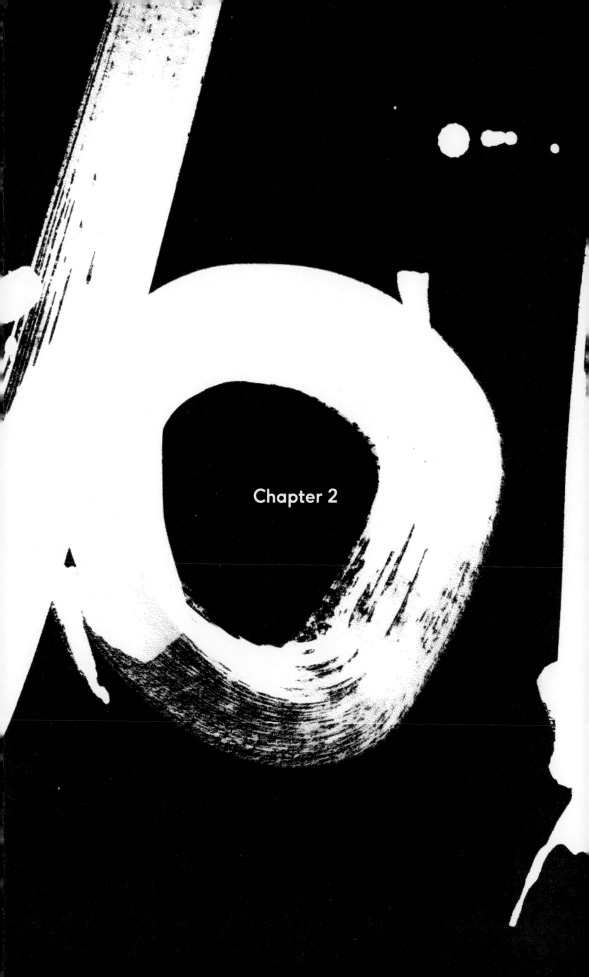

Chapter 2

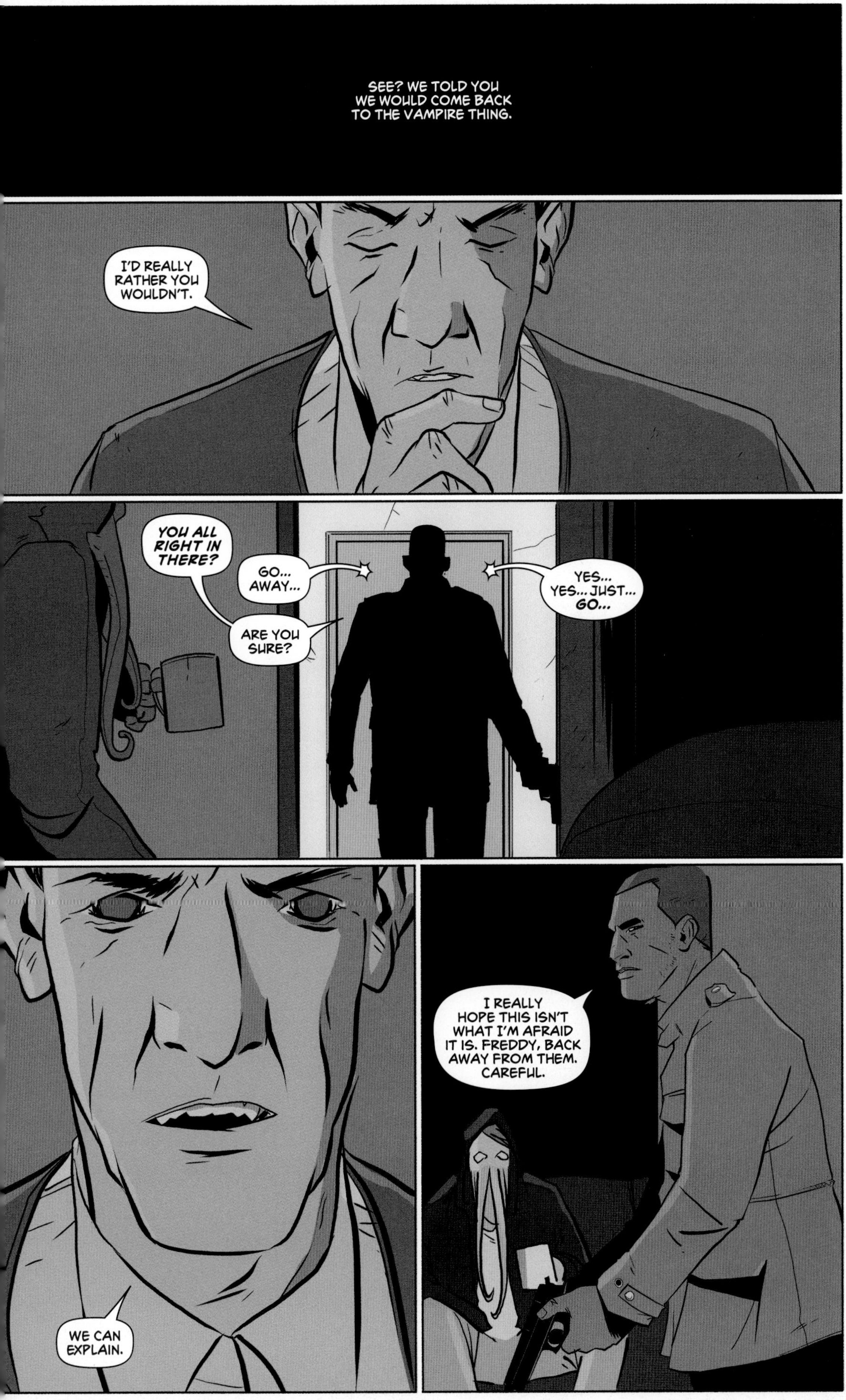
SEE? WE TOLD YOU WE WOULD COME BACK TO THE VAMPIRE THING.
I'D REALLY RATHER YOU WOULDN'T.
YOU ALL RIGHT IN THERE?
GO... AWAY...
ARE YOU SURE?
YES... YES... JUST... GO...
WE CAN EXPLAIN.
I REALLY HOPE THIS ISN'T WHAT I'M AFRAID IT IS. FREDDY, BACK AWAY FROM THEM. CAREFUL.

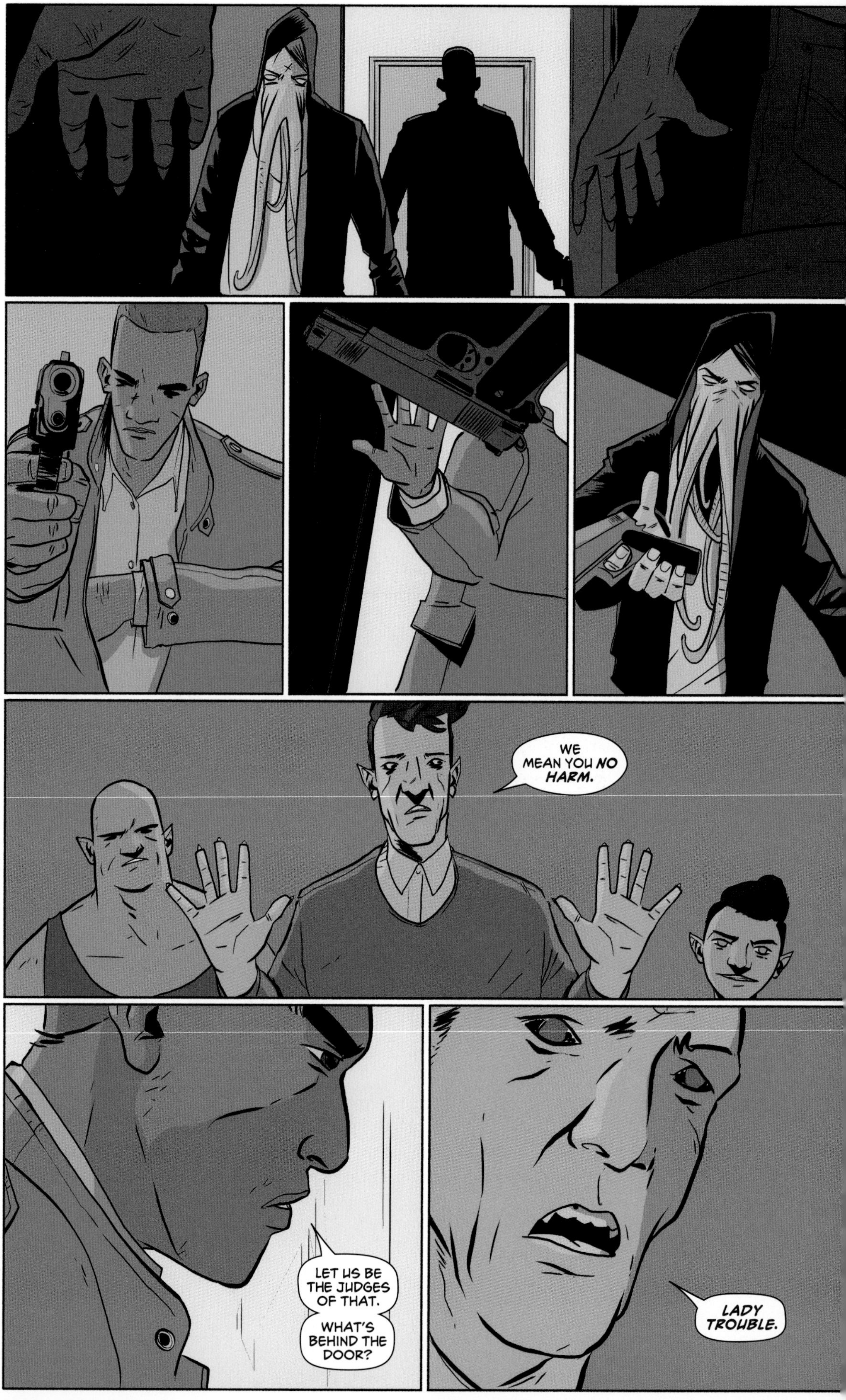

WE MEAN YOU *NO HARM.*
LET US BE THE JUDGES OF THAT.
WHAT'S BEHIND THE DOOR?
LADY TROUBLE.

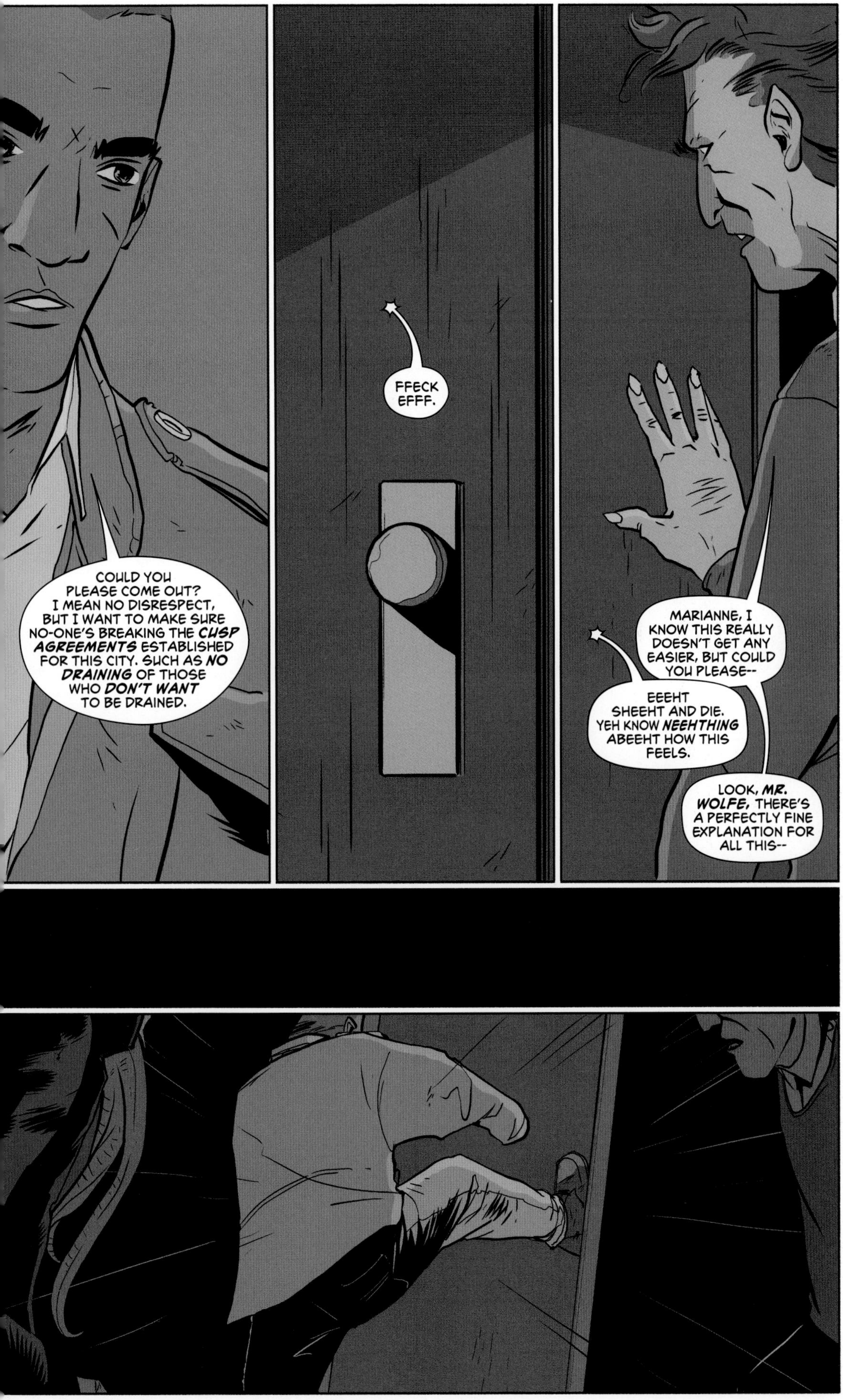

COULD YOU PLEASE COME OUT? I MEAN NO DISRESPECT, BUT I WANT TO MAKE SURE NO-ONE'S BREAKING THE *CUSP AGREEMENTS* ESTABLISHED FOR THIS CITY. SUCH AS *NO DRAINING* OF THOSE WHO *DON'T WANT* TO BE DRAINED.
FFECK EFFF.
MARIANNE, I KNOW THIS REALLY DOESN'T GET ANY EASIER, BUT COULD YOU PLEASE--
EEEHT SHEEHT AND DIE. YEH KNOW *NEEHTHING* ABEEHT HOW THIS FEELS.
LOOK, *MR. WOLFE,* THERE'S A PERFECTLY FINE EXPLANATION FOR ALL THIS--

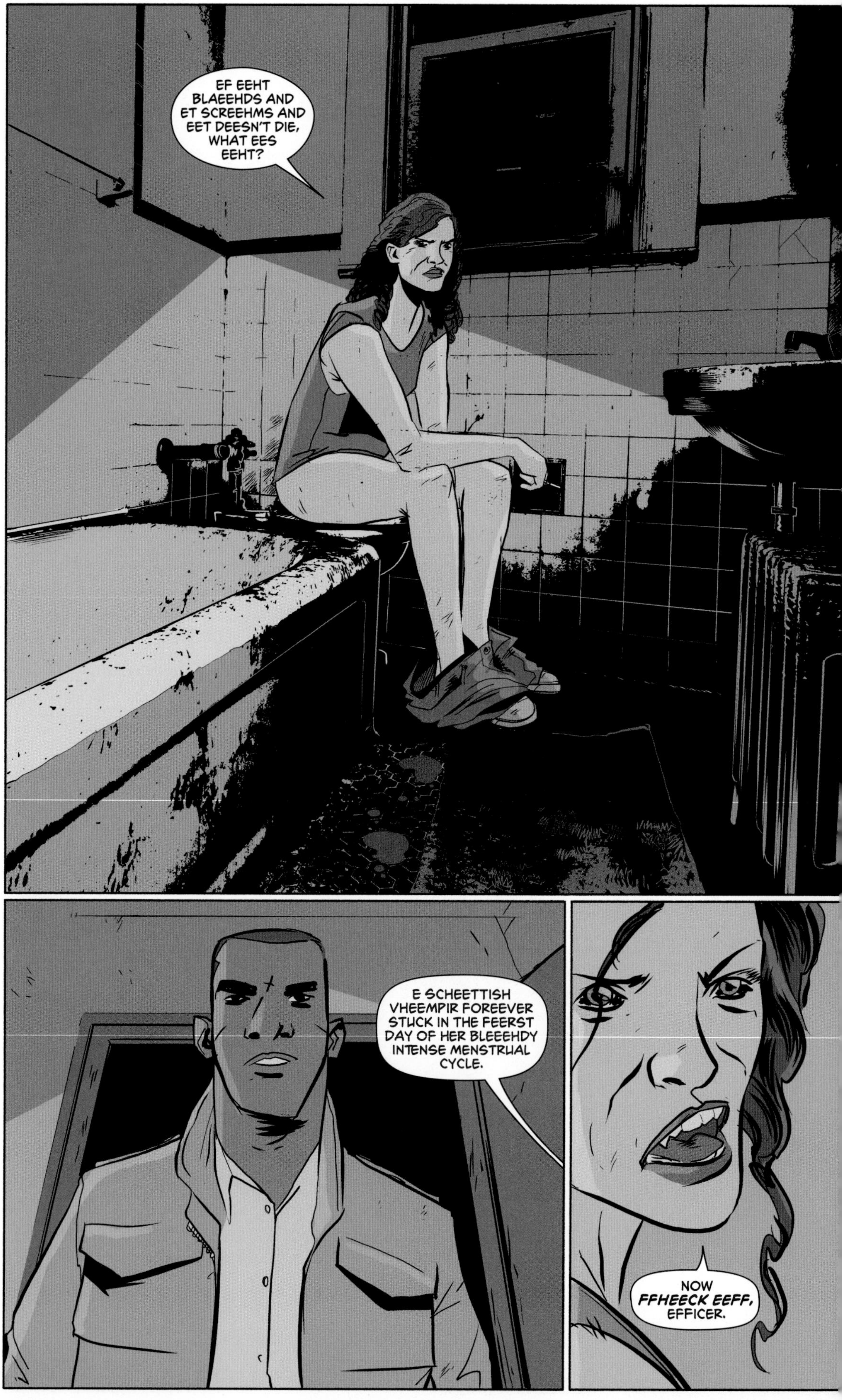
EF EEHT BLAEEHDS AND ET SCREEHMS AND EET DEESN'T DIE, WHAT EES EEHT?
E SCHEETTISH VHEEMPIR FOREEVER STUCK IN THE FEERST DAY OF HER BLEEEHDY INTENSE MENSTRUAL CYCLE.
NOW *FFHEECK EEFF,* EFFICER.

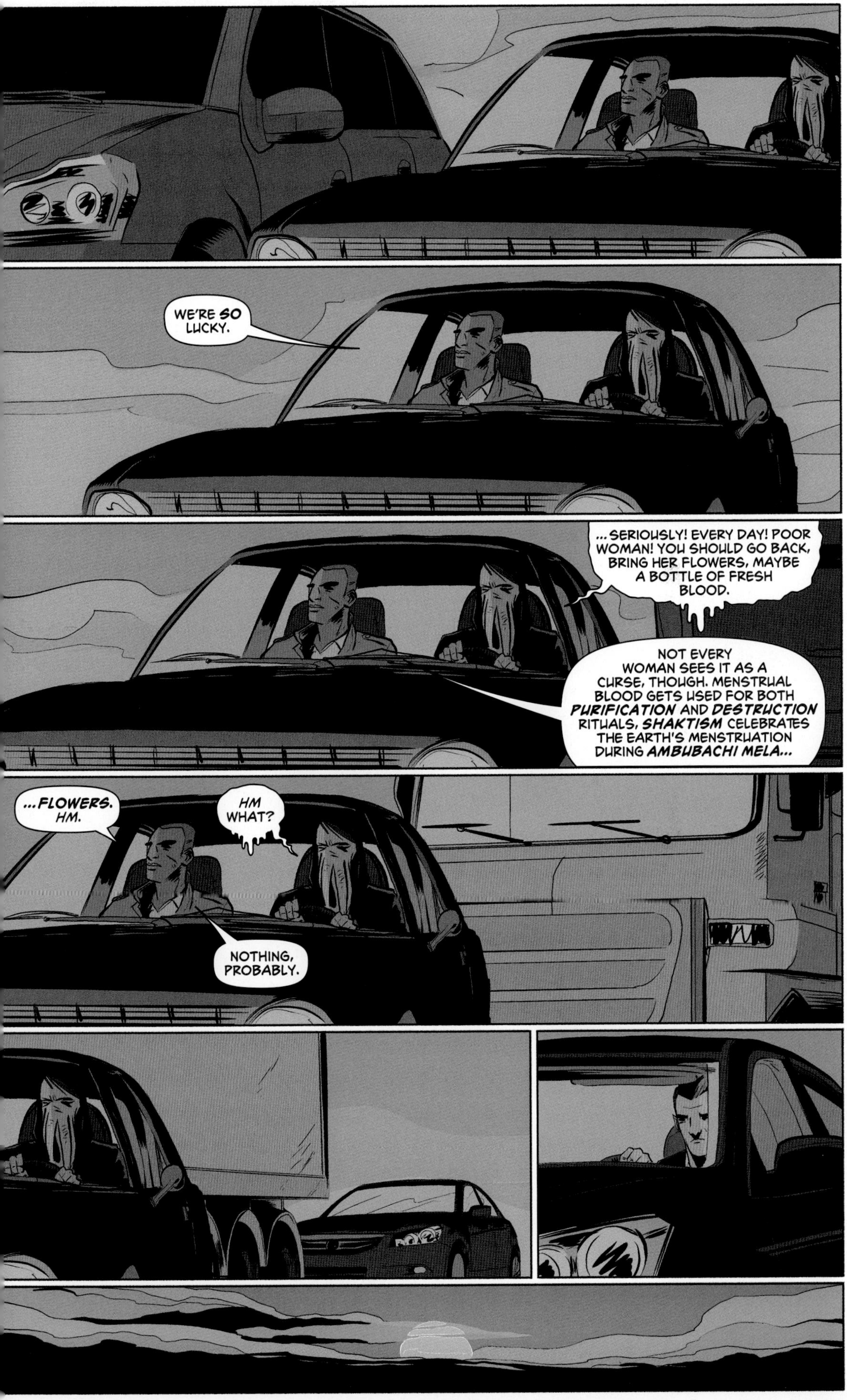
WE'RE SO LUCKY.
...SERIOUSLY! EVERY DAY! POOR WOMAN! YOU SHOULD GO BACK, BRING HER FLOWERS, MAYBE A BOTTLE OF FRESH BLOOD.
NOT EVERY WOMAN SEES IT AS A CURSE, THOUGH. MENSTRUAL BLOOD GETS USED FOR BOTH PURIFICATION AND DESTRUCTION RITUALS, SHAKTISM CELEBRATES THE EARTH'S MENSTRUATION DURING AMBUBACHI MELA...
...FLOWERS. HM.
HM WHAT?
NOTHING, PROBABLY.

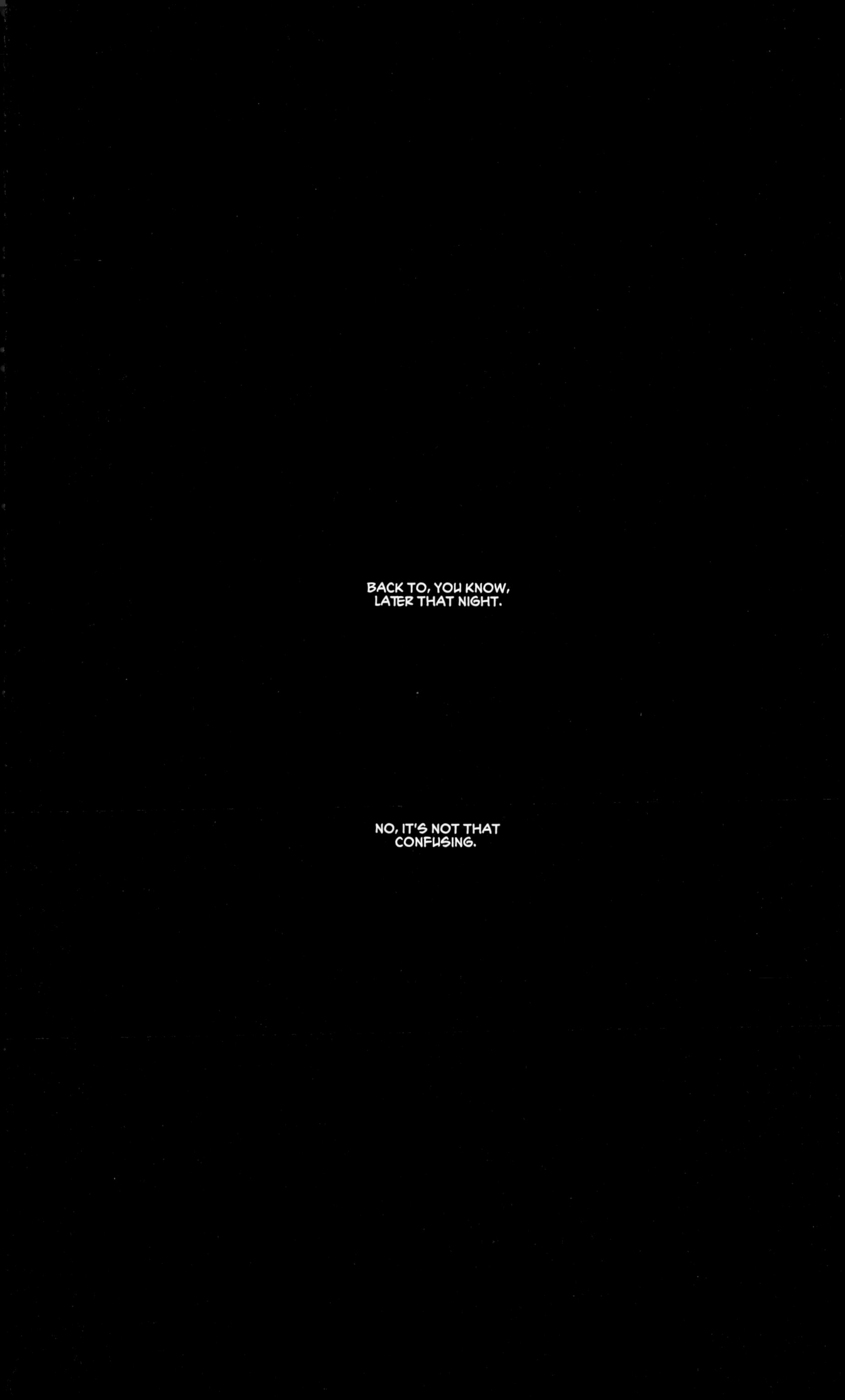
BACK TO, YOU KNOW, LATER THAT NIGHT.
NO, IT'S NOT THAT CONFUSING.

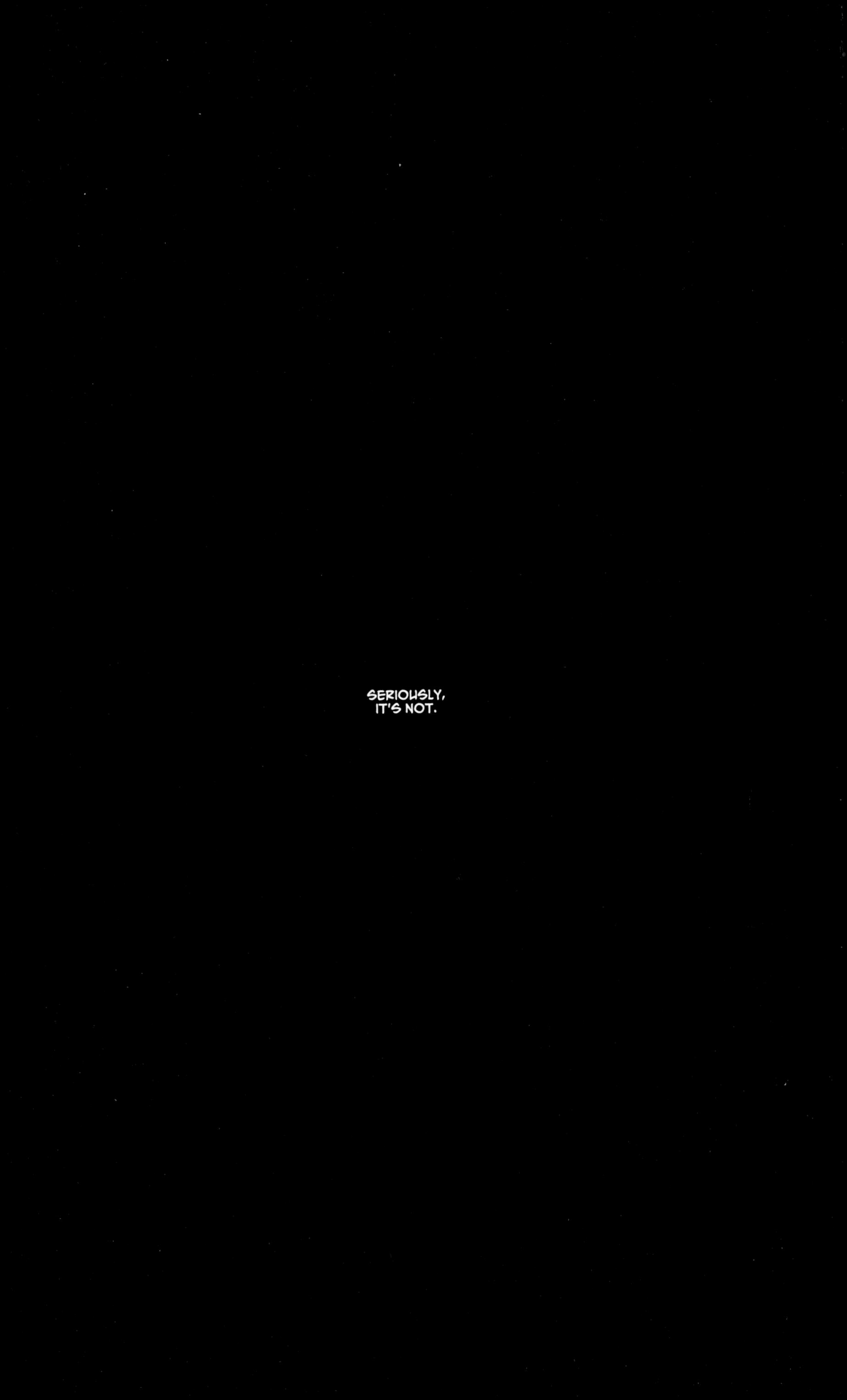
SERIOUSLY, IT'S NOT.

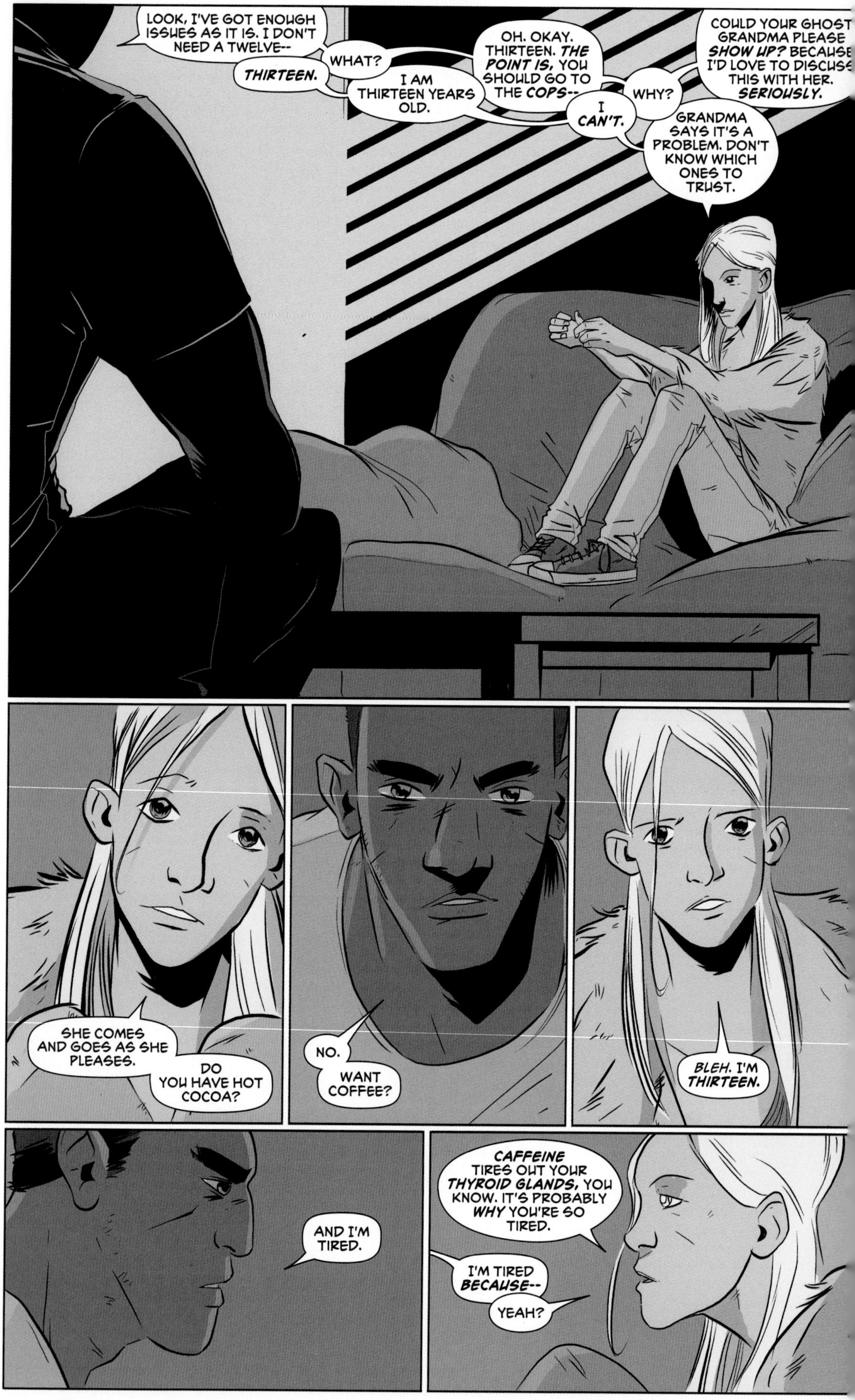

LOOK, I'VE GOT ENOUGH ISSUES AS IT IS. I DON'T NEED A TWELVE--
THIRTEEN.
WHAT?
I AM THIRTEEN YEARS OLD.
OH. OKAY. THIRTEEN. THE POINT IS, YOU SHOULD GO TO THE COPS--
I CAN'T.
WHY?
GRANDMA SAYS IT'S A PROBLEM. DON'T KNOW WHICH ONES TO TRUST.
COULD YOUR GHOST GRANDMA PLEASE SHOW UP? BECAUSE I'D LOVE TO DISCUSS THIS WITH HER. SERIOUSLY.
SHE COMES AND GOES AS SHE PLEASES.
DO YOU HAVE HOT COCOA?
NO.
WANT COFFEE?
BLEH. I'M THIRTEEN.
AND I'M TIRED.
CAFFEINE TIRES OUT YOUR THYROID GLANDS, YOU KNOW. IT'S PROBABLY WHY YOU'RE SO TIRED.
I'M TIRED BECAUSE--
YEAH?

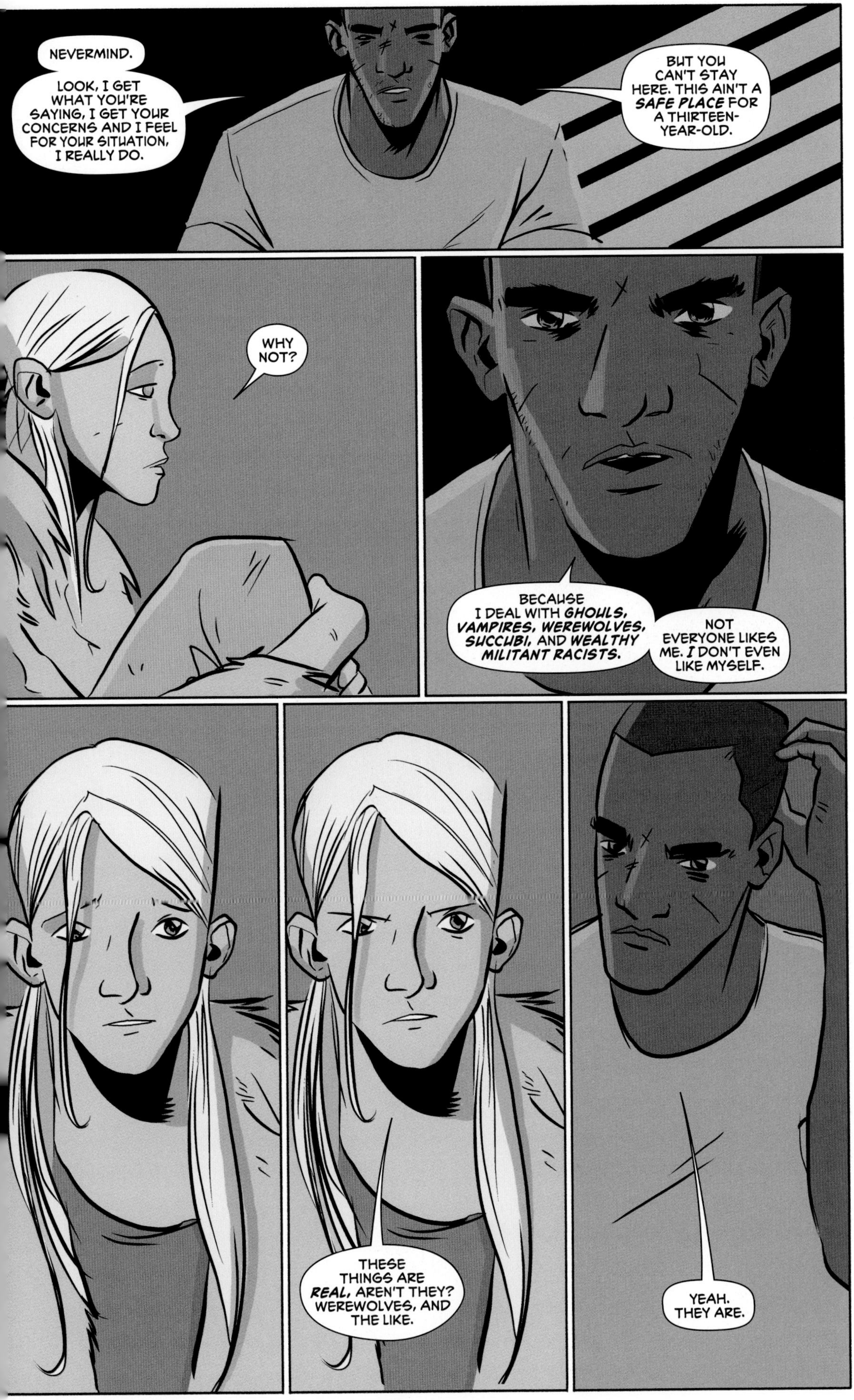
NEVERMIND.
LOOK, I GET WHAT YOU'RE SAYING, I GET YOUR CONCERNS AND I FEEL FOR YOUR SITUATION, I REALLY DO.
BUT YOU CAN'T STAY HERE. THIS AIN'T A SAFE PLACE FOR A THIRTEEN-YEAR-OLD.
WHY NOT?
BECAUSE I DEAL WITH GHOULS, VAMPIRES, WEREWOLVES, SUCCUBI, AND WEALTHY MILITANT RACISTS.
NOT EVERYONE LIKES ME. I DON'T EVEN LIKE MYSELF.
THESE THINGS ARE REAL, AREN'T THEY? WEREWOLVES, AND THE LIKE.
YEAH. THEY ARE.

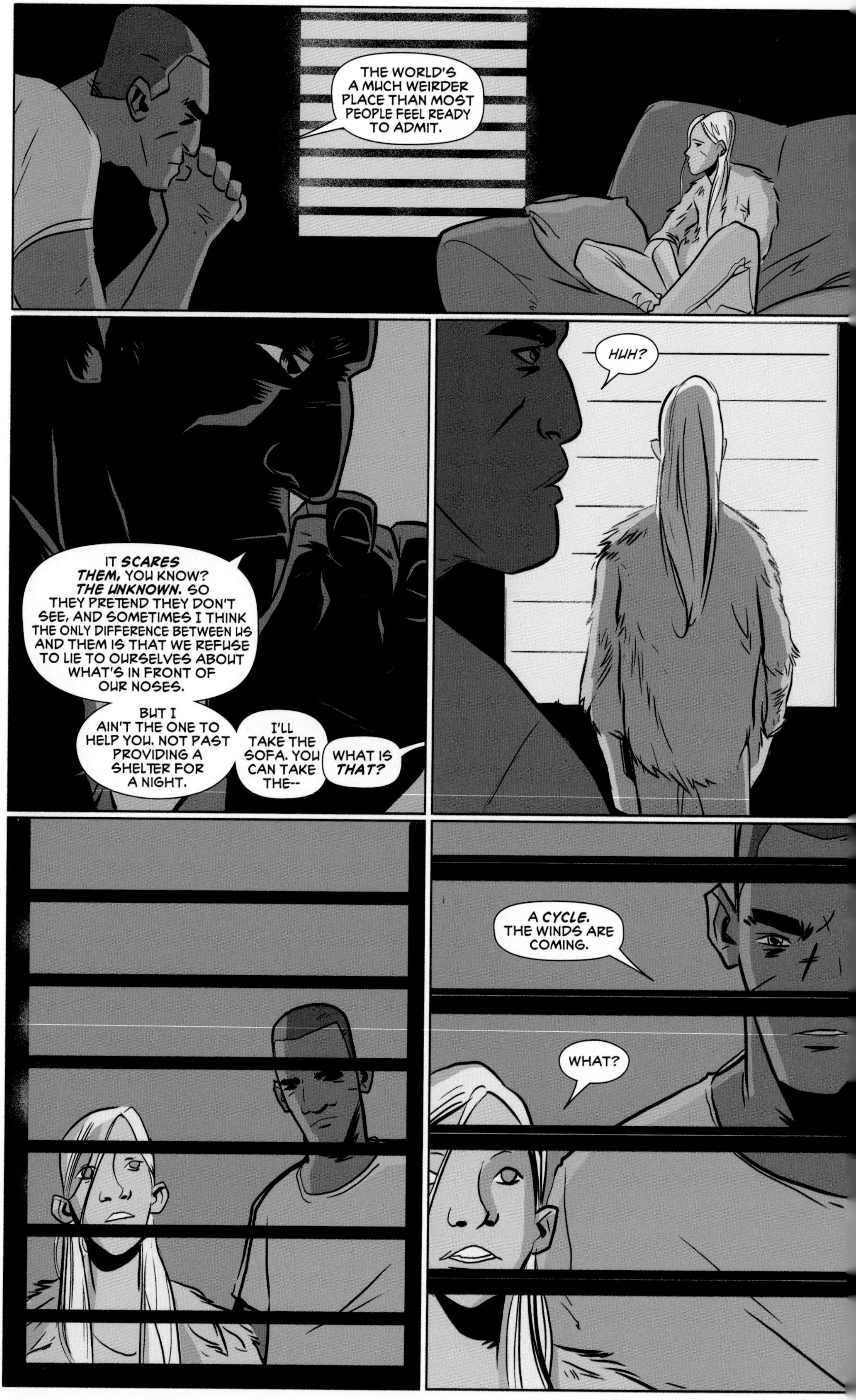
THE WORLD'S A MUCH WEIRDER PLACE THAN MOST PEOPLE FEEL READY TO ADMIT.
IT SCARES THEM, YOU KNOW? THE UNKNOWN. SO THEY PRETEND THEY DON'T SEE, AND SOMETIMES I THINK THE ONLY DIFFERENCE BETWEEN US AND THEM IS THAT WE REFUSE TO LIE TO OURSELVES ABOUT WHAT'S IN FRONT OF OUR NOSES.
BUT I AIN'T THE ONE TO HELP YOU. NOT PAST PROVIDING A SHELTER FOR A NIGHT.
I'LL TAKE THE SOFA. YOU CAN TAKE THE--
WHAT IS THAT?
HUH?
A CYCLE. THE WINDS ARE COMING.
WHAT?

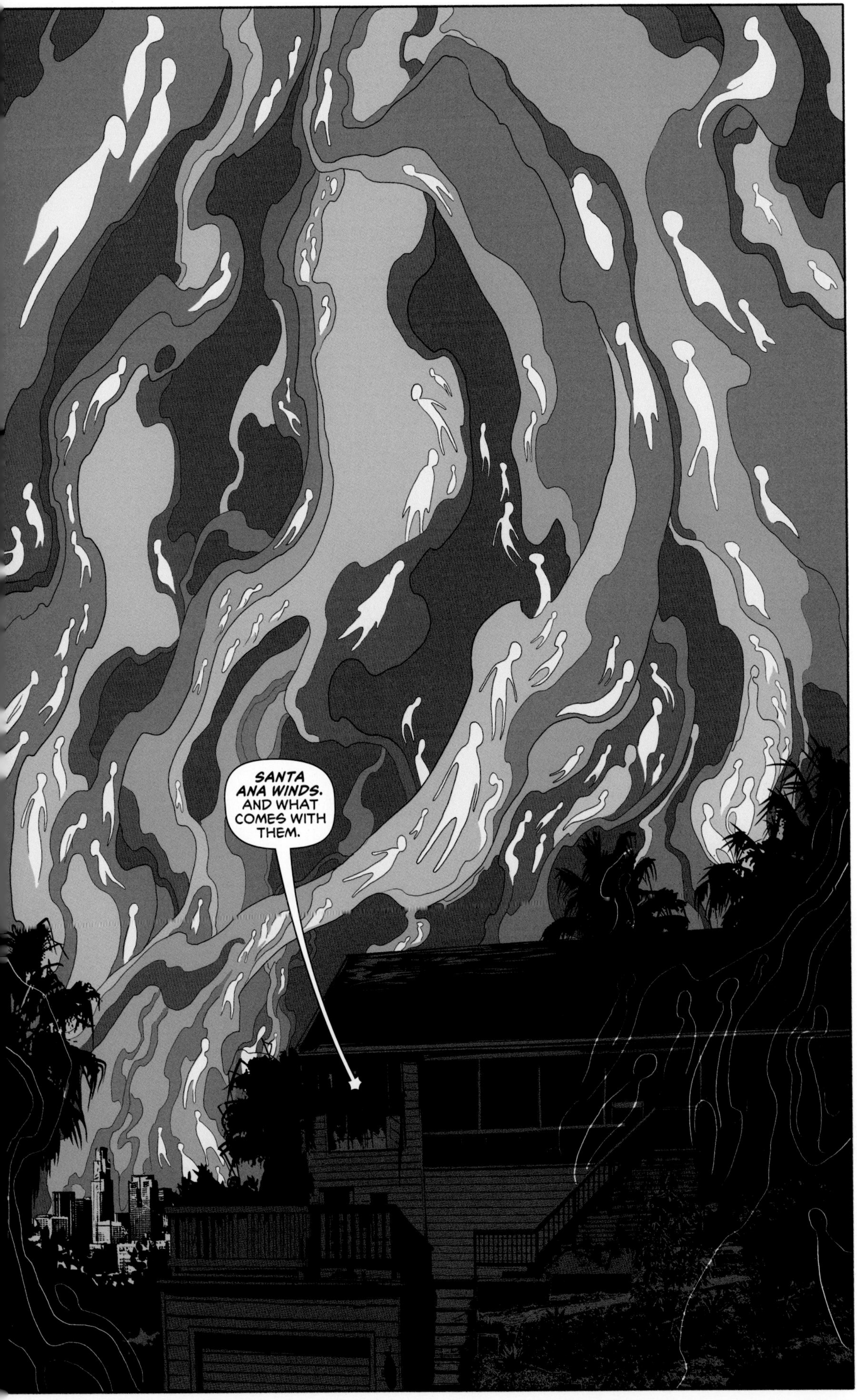
SANTA ANA WINDS. AND WHAT COMES WITH THEM.

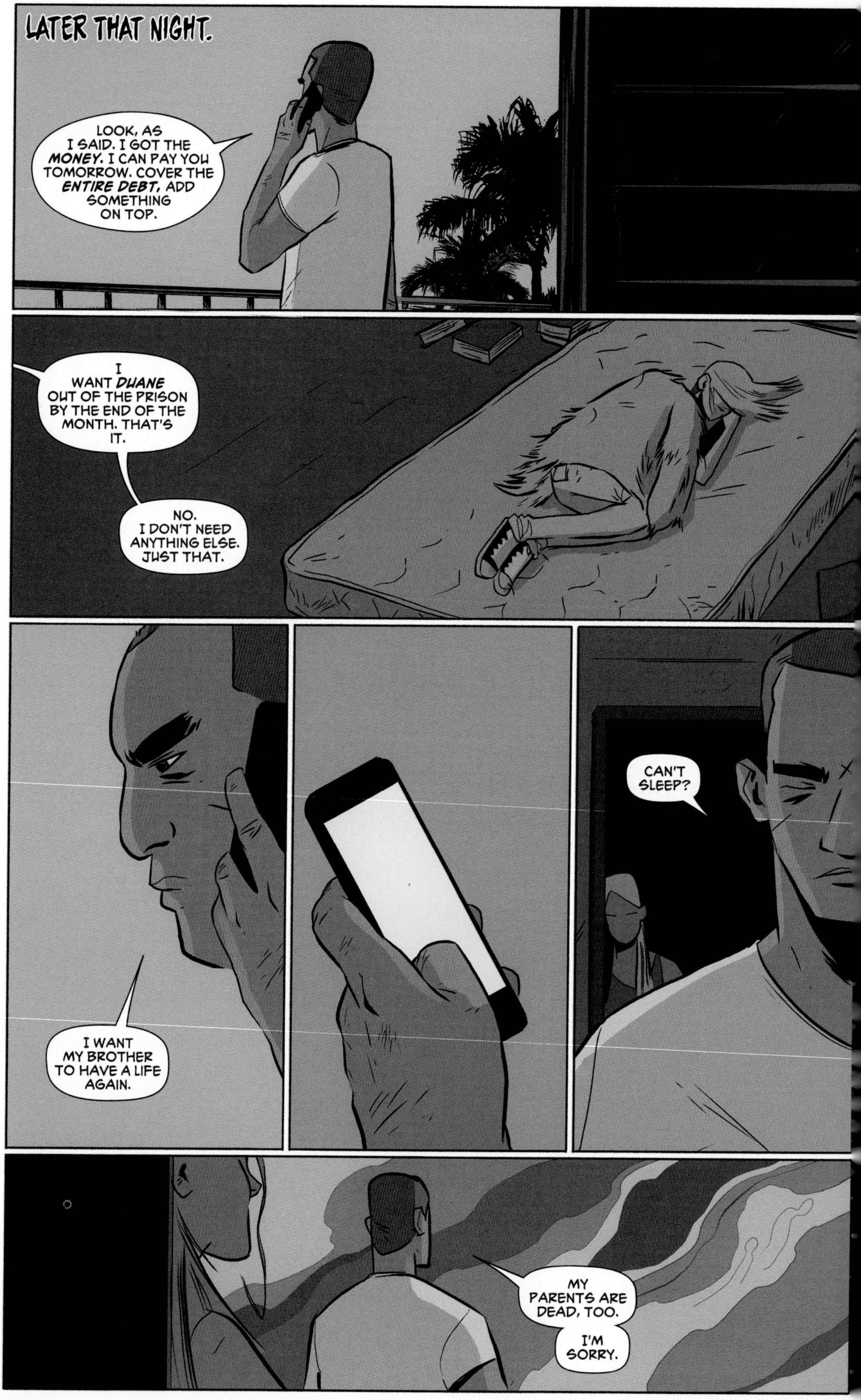
LATER THAT NIGHT.
LOOK, AS I SAID. I GOT THE MONEY. I CAN PAY YOU TOMORROW. COVER THE ENTIRE DEBT, ADD SOMETHING ON TOP.
I WANT DUANE OUT OF THE PRISON BY THE END OF THE MONTH. THAT'S IT.
NO. I DON'T NEED ANYTHING ELSE. JUST THAT.
I WANT MY BROTHER TO HAVE A LIFE AGAIN.
CAN'T SLEEP?
MY PARENTS ARE DEAD, TOO.
I'M SORRY.

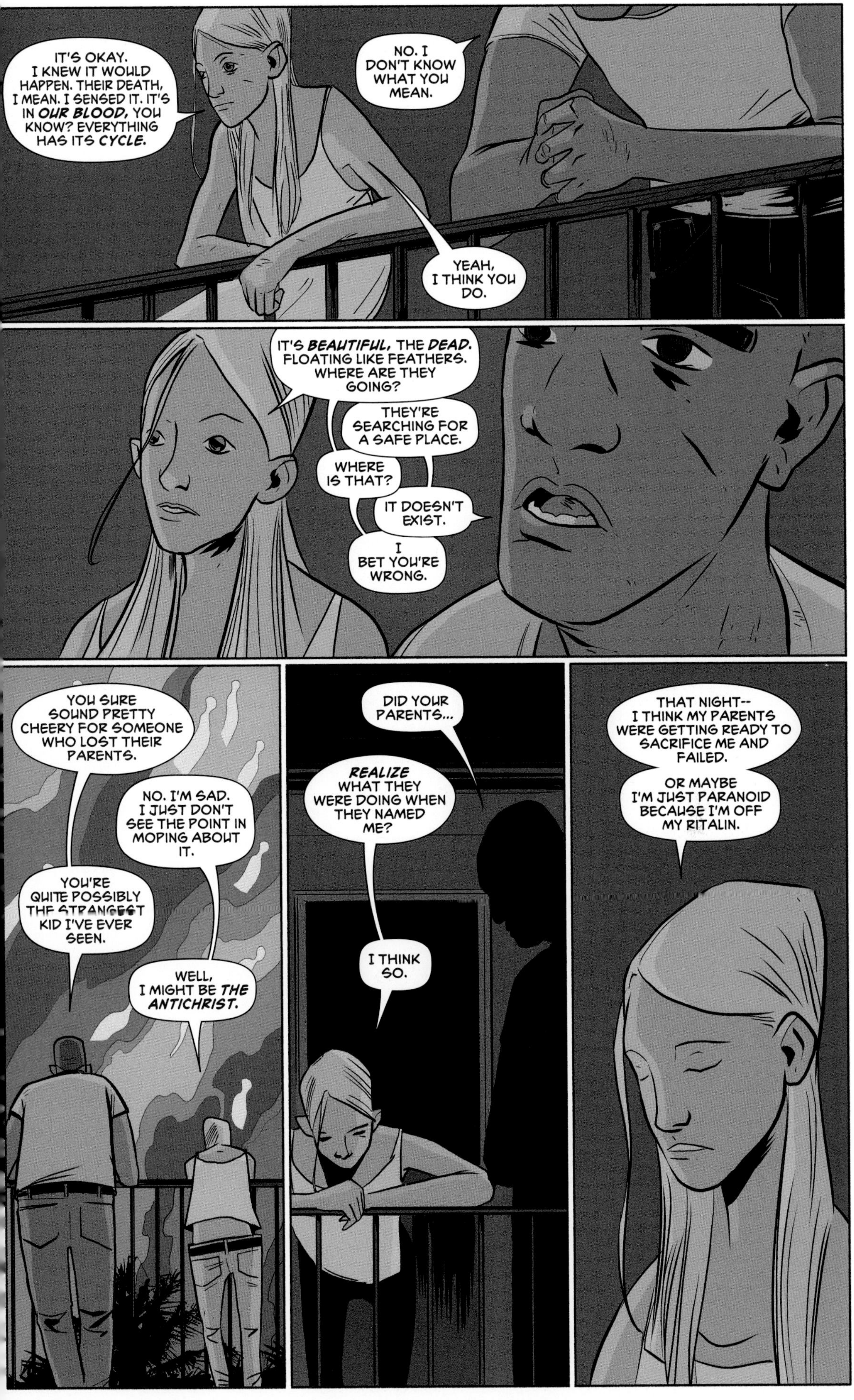
IT'S OKAY. I KNEW IT WOULD HAPPEN. THEIR DEATH, I MEAN. I SENSED IT. IT'S IN OUR BLOOD, YOU KNOW? EVERYTHING HAS ITS CYCLE.
NO. I DON'T KNOW WHAT YOU MEAN.
YEAH, I THINK YOU DO.
IT'S BEAUTIFUL, THE DEAD. FLOATING LIKE FEATHERS. WHERE ARE THEY GOING?
THEY'RE SEARCHING FOR A SAFE PLACE.
WHERE IS THAT?
IT DOESN'T EXIST.
I BET YOU'RE WRONG.
YOU SURE SOUND PRETTY CHEERY FOR SOMEONE WHO LOST THEIR PARENTS.
NO. I'M SAD. I JUST DON'T SEE THE POINT IN MOPING ABOUT IT.
YOU'RE QUITE POSSIBLY THE STRANGEST KID I'VE EVER SEEN.
WELL, I MIGHT BE THE ANTICHRIST.
DID YOUR PARENTS...
REALIZE WHAT THEY WERE DOING WHEN THEY NAMED ME?
I THINK SO.
THAT NIGHT-- I THINK MY PARENTS WERE GETTING READY TO SACRIFICE ME AND FAILED.
OR MAYBE I'M JUST PARANOID BECAUSE I'M OFF MY RITALIN.

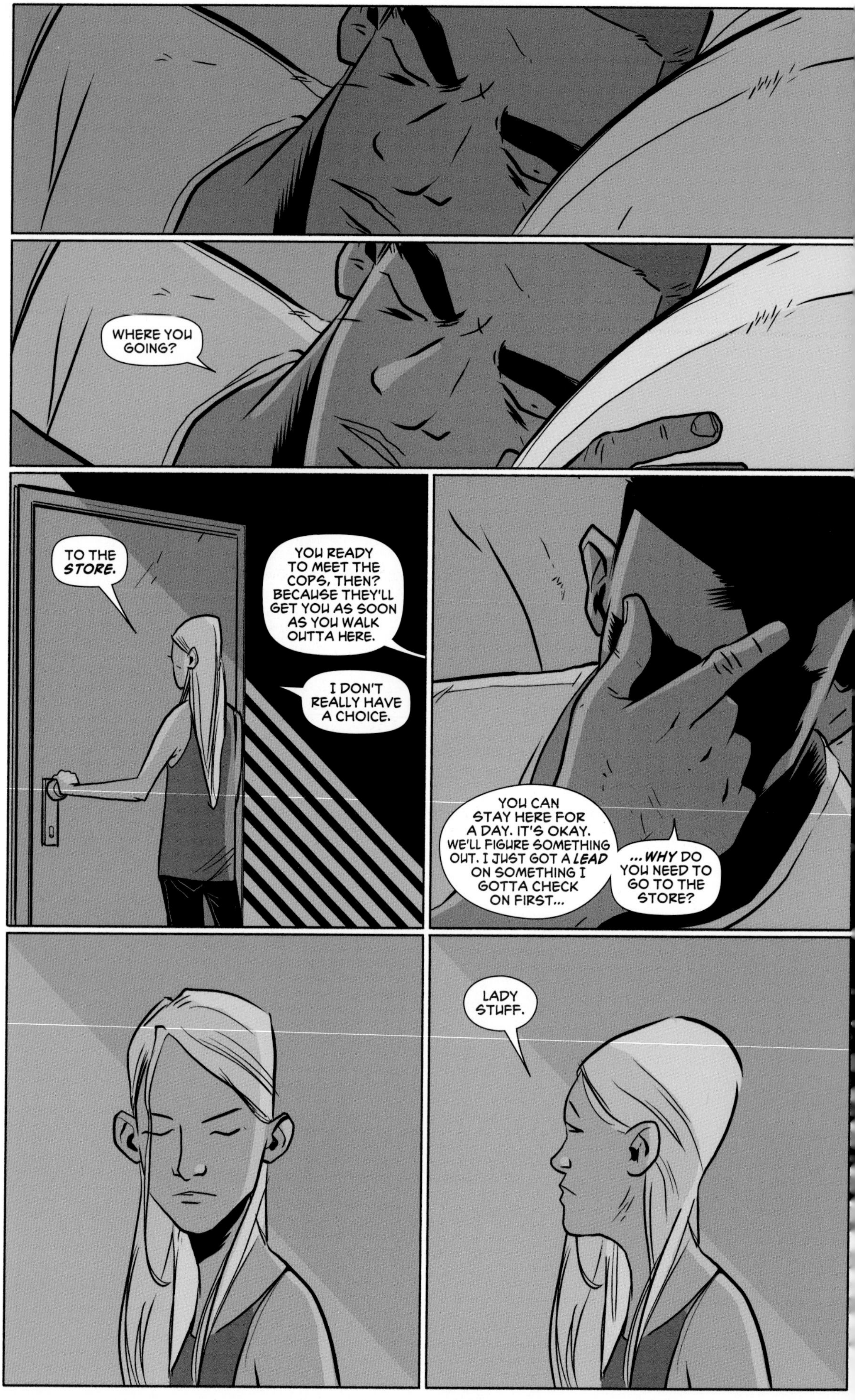
WHERE YOU GOING?
TO THE *STORE*.
YOU READY TO MEET THE COPS, THEN? BECAUSE THEY'LL GET YOU AS SOON AS YOU WALK OUTTA HERE.
I DON'T REALLY HAVE A CHOICE.
YOU CAN STAY HERE FOR A DAY. IT'S OKAY. WE'LL FIGURE SOMETHING OUT. I JUST GOT A *LEAD* ON SOMETHING I GOTTA CHECK ON FIRST...
...*WHY* DO YOU NEED TO GO TO THE STORE?
LADY STUFF.

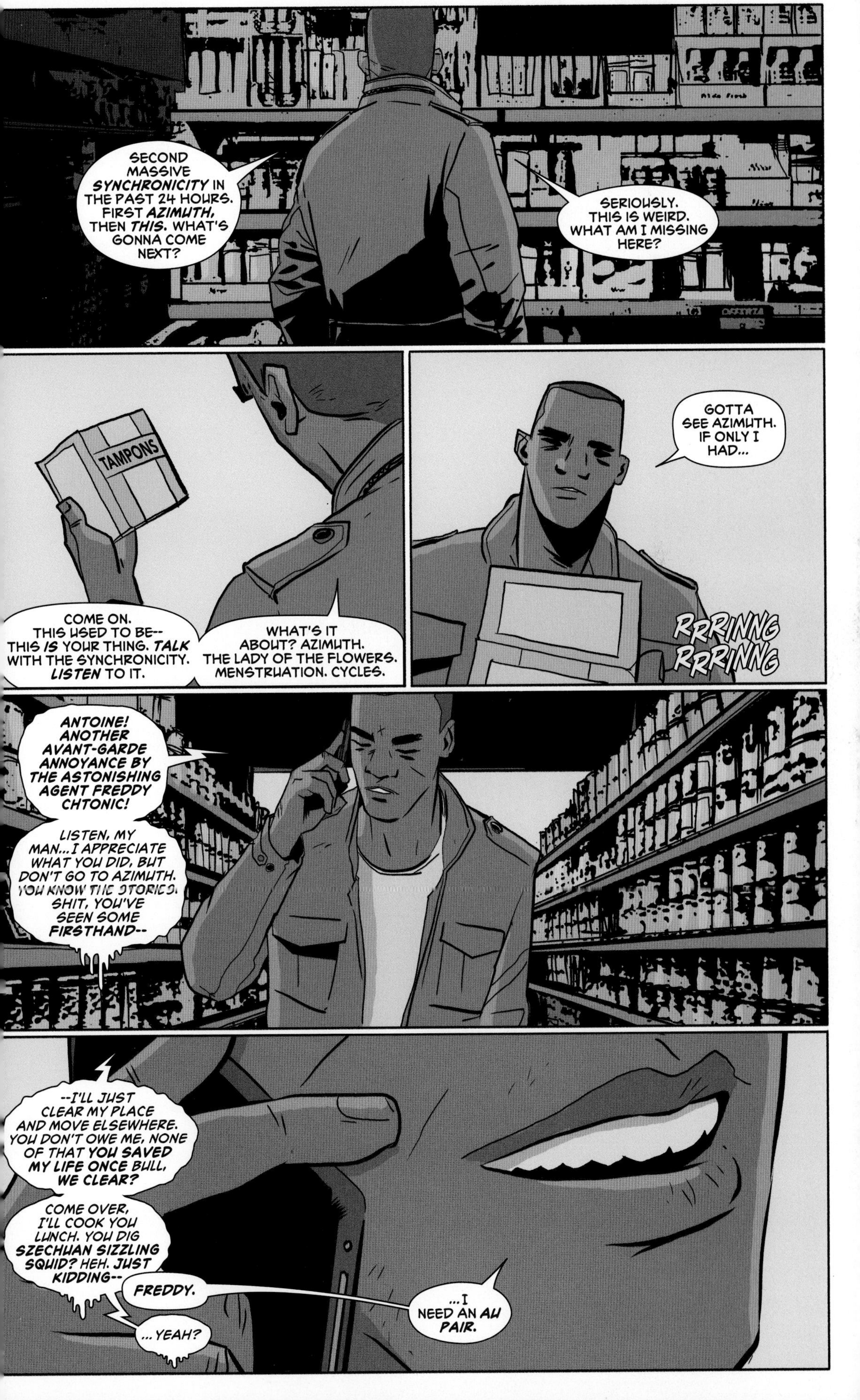
SECOND MASSIVE SYNCHRONICITY IN THE PAST 24 HOURS. FIRST AZIMUTH, THEN THIS. WHAT'S GONNA COME NEXT?
SERIOUSLY. THIS IS WEIRD. WHAT AM I MISSING HERE?
TAMPONS
COME ON. THIS USED TO BE-- THIS IS YOUR THING. TALK WITH THE SYNCHRONICITY. LISTEN TO IT.
WHAT'S IT ABOUT? AZIMUTH. THE LADY OF THE FLOWERS. MENSTRUATION. CYCLES.
GOTTA SEE AZIMUTH. IF ONLY I HAD...
RRRINNG RRRINNG
ANTOINE! ANOTHER AVANT-GARDE ANNOYANCE BY THE ASTONISHING AGENT FREDDY CHTONIC!
LISTEN, MY MAN...I APPRECIATE WHAT YOU DID, BUT DON'T GO TO AZIMUTH. YOU KNOW THE STORIES. SHIT, YOU'VE SEEN SOME FIRSTHAND--
--I'LL JUST CLEAR MY PLACE AND MOVE ELSEWHERE. YOU DON'T OWE ME, NONE OF THAT YOU SAVED MY LIFE ONCE BULL, WE CLEAR?
COME OVER, I'LL COOK YOU LUNCH. YOU DIG SZECHUAN SIZZLING SQUID? HEH. JUST KIDDING--
FREDDY.
...YEAH?
...I NEED AN AU PAIR.

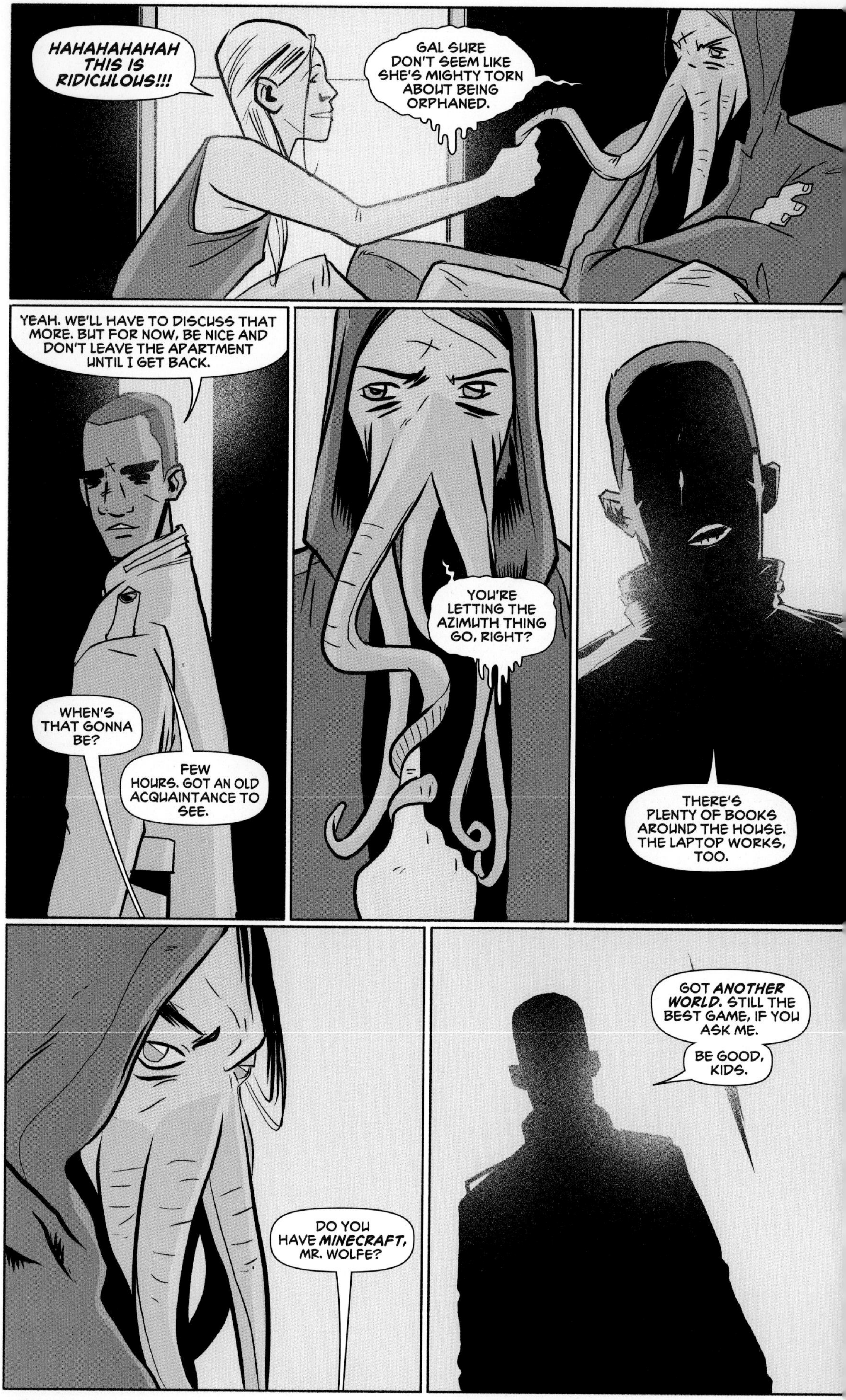
HAHAHAHAHAH THIS IS RIDICULOUS!!!
GAL SURE DON'T SEEM LIKE SHE'S MIGHTY TORN ABOUT BEING ORPHANED.
YEAH. WE'LL HAVE TO DISCUSS THAT MORE. BUT FOR NOW, BE NICE AND DON'T LEAVE THE APARTMENT UNTIL I GET BACK.
WHEN'S THAT GONNA BE?
FEW HOURS. GOT AN OLD ACQUAINTANCE TO SEE.
YOU'RE LETTING THE AZIMUTH THING GO, RIGHT?
THERE'S PLENTY OF BOOKS AROUND THE HOUSE. THE LAPTOP WORKS, TOO.
DO YOU HAVE MINECRAFT, MR. WOLFE?
GOT ANOTHER WORLD. STILL THE BEST GAME, IF YOU ASK ME.
BE GOOD, KIDS.

WHAT AM I MISSING? A GIRL APPEARS AT MY DOORSTEP, MIGHT BE THE *ANTICHRIST.* THE CITY BURNS A HOLE INTO MY HEAD AS I GET CLOSER TO GETTING DUANE OUT OF A *PRISON* HE SHOULD HAVE NEVER BEEN SENT TO IN THE FIRST PLACE.

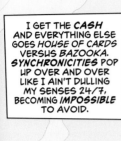

I GET THE *CASH* AND EVERYTHING ELSE GOES *HOUSE OF CARDS* VERSUS *BAZOOKA.* *SYNCHRONICITIES* POP UP OVER AND OVER LIKE I AIN'T DULLING MY SENSES 24/7, BECOMING *IMPOSSIBLE* TO AVOID.

BLOOD. MOON. APOCALYPSE TALK. LADY OF THE FLOWERS. AND NOW AZIMUTH. THE TIMES IN IRAQ STRETCH THEIR ELONGATED, SCALY NECK AND EXTEND THEIR JAW, THE TEETH INSIDE WAY TOO SHARP FOR ANY ORDINARY ANIMAL.

THE JAW CRACKS, ALL UNNATURAL, BONES SNAPPING LIKE TWIGS.

SOUNDS OF THE PAST AND THE FUTURE CONVERGING.

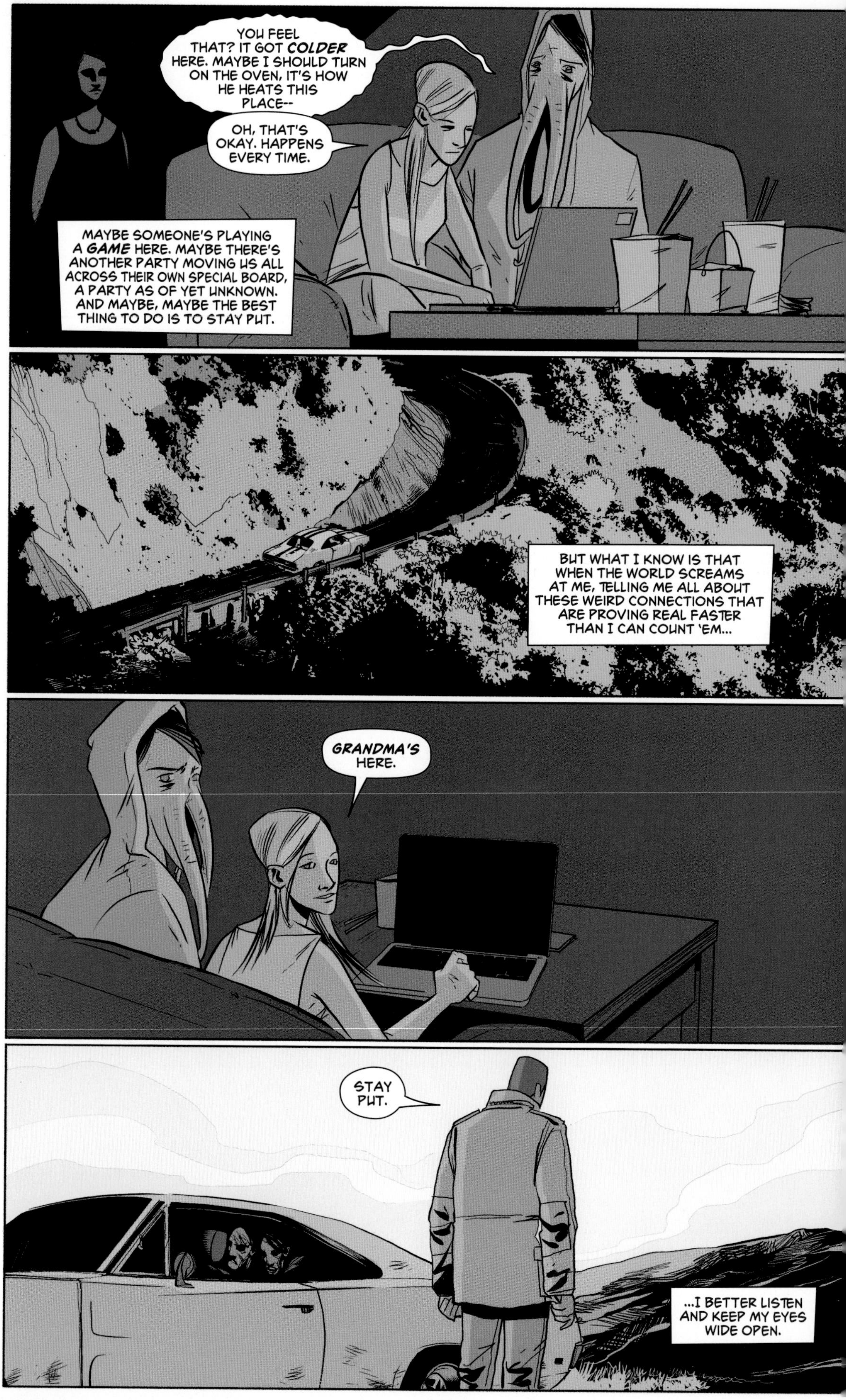
YOU FEEL THAT? IT GOT COLDER HERE. MAYBE I SHOULD TURN ON THE OVEN, IT'S HOW HE HEATS THIS PLACE--
OH, THAT'S OKAY. HAPPENS EVERY TIME.
MAYBE SOMEONE'S PLAYING A GAME HERE. MAYBE THERE'S ANOTHER PARTY MOVING US ALL ACROSS THEIR OWN SPECIAL BOARD, A PARTY AS OF YET UNKNOWN. AND MAYBE, MAYBE THE BEST THING TO DO IS TO STAY PUT.
BUT WHAT I KNOW IS THAT WHEN THE WORLD SCREAMS AT ME, TELLING ME ALL ABOUT THESE WEIRD CONNECTIONS THAT ARE PROVING REAL FASTER THAN I CAN COUNT 'EM...
GRANDMA'S HERE.
STAY PUT.
...I BETTER LISTEN AND KEEP MY EYES WIDE OPEN.

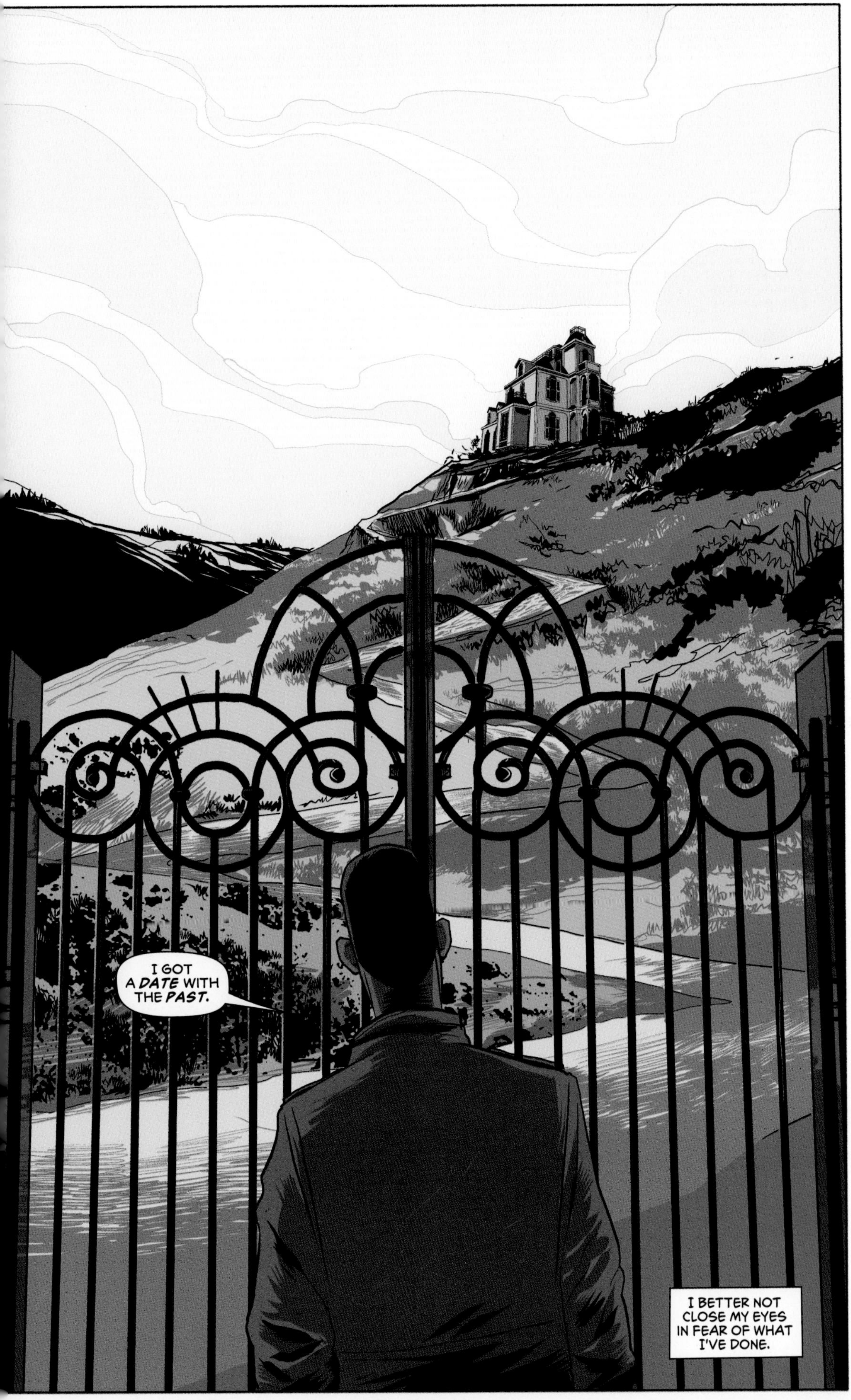
I GOT A *DATE* WITH THE *PAST*.
I BETTER NOT CLOSE MY EYES IN FEAR OF WHAT I'VE DONE.

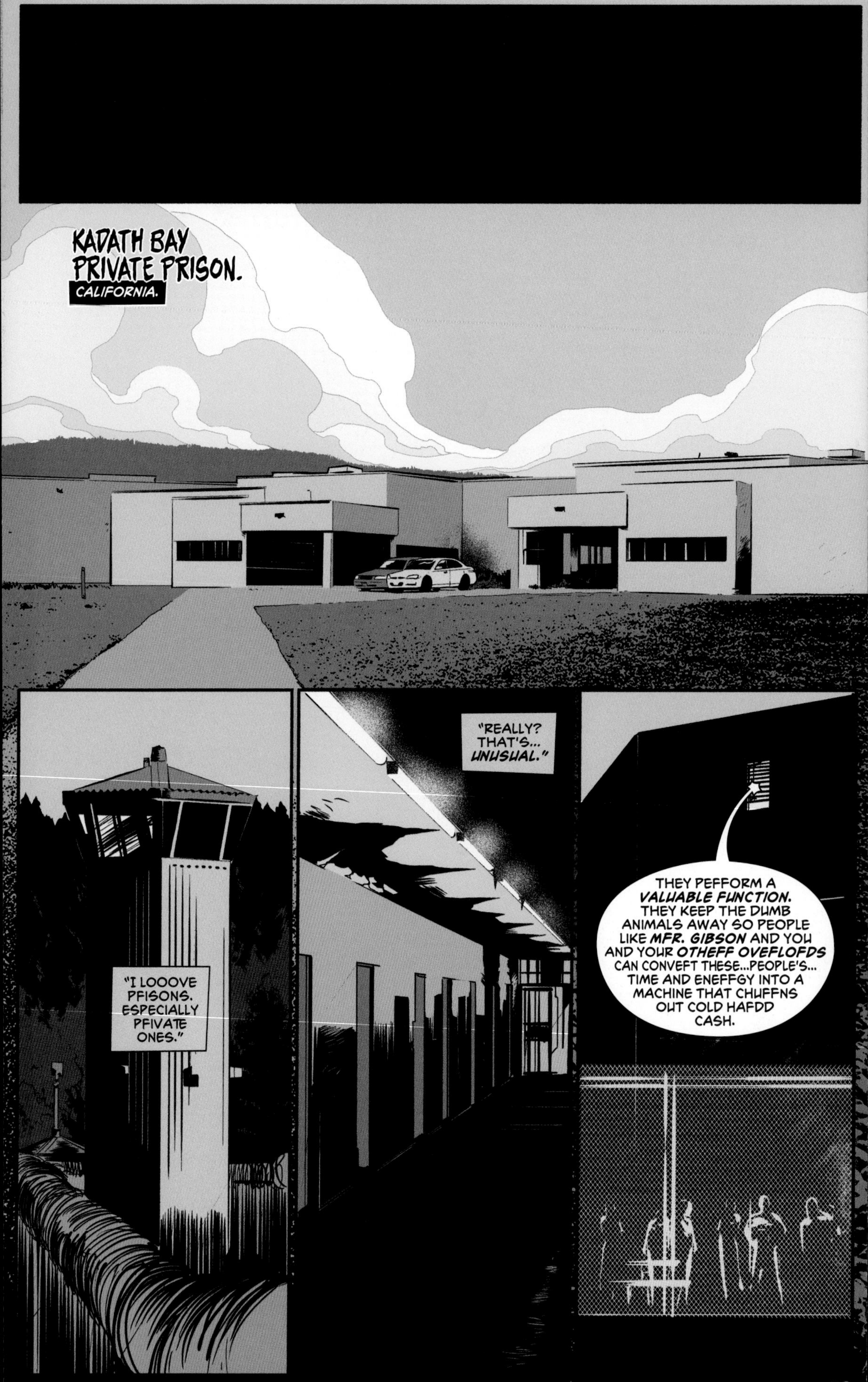
KADATH BAY PRIVATE PRISON.
CALIFORNIA.
"I LOOOVE PFISONS. ESPECIALLY PFIVATE ONES."
"REALLY? THAT'S... UNUSUAL."
THEY PEFFORM A VALUABLE FUNCTION. THEY KEEP THE DUMB ANIMALS AWAY SO PEOPLE LIKE MFR. GIBSON AND YOU AND YOUR OTHEFF OVEFLOFDS CAN CONVEFT THESE...PEOPLE'S... TIME AND ENEFFGY INTO A MACHINE THAT CHUFFNS OUT COLD HAFDD CASH.

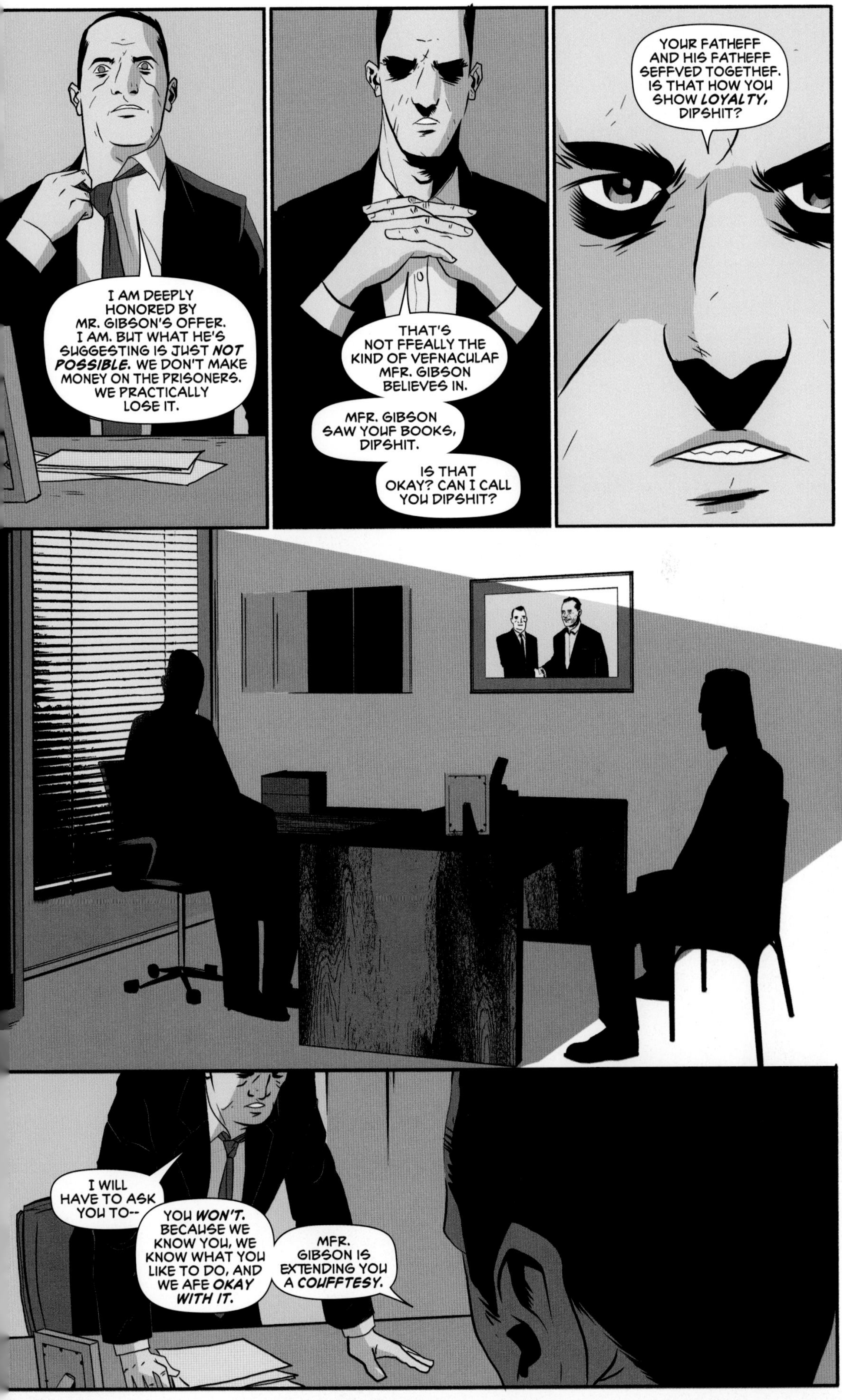

I AM DEEPLY HONORED BY MR. GIBSON'S OFFER. I AM. BUT WHAT HE'S SUGGESTING IS JUST *NOT POSSIBLE.* WE DON'T MAKE MONEY ON THE PRISONERS. WE PRACTICALLY LOSE IT.
THAT'S NOT FFEALLY THE KIND OF VEFNACULAF MFR. GIBSON BELIEVES IN.
MFR. GIBSON SAW YOUF BOOKS, DIPSHIT.
IS THAT OKAY? CAN I CALL YOU DIPSHIT?
YOUR FATHEFF AND HIS FATHEFF SEFFVED TOGETHEF. IS THAT HOW YOU SHOW *LOYALTY,* DIPSHIT?
I WILL HAVE TO ASK YOU TO--
YOU *WON'T.* BECAUSE WE KNOW YOU, WE KNOW WHAT YOU LIKE TO DO, AND WE AFE *OKAY WITH IT.*
MFR. GIBSON IS EXTENDING YOU A *COUFFTESY.*

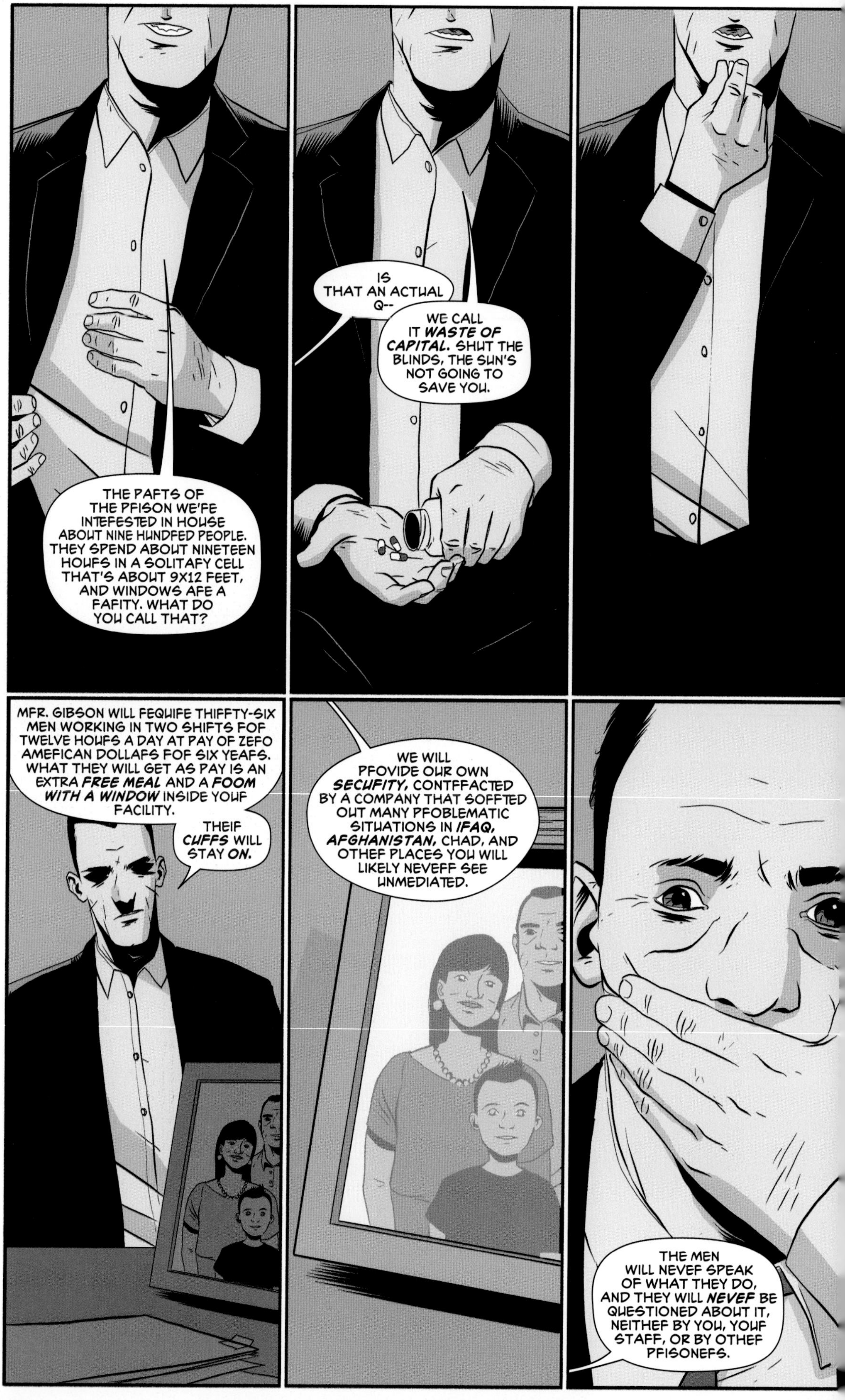
THE PAFTS OF THE PFISON WE'FE INTEFESTED IN HOUSE ABOUT NINE HUNDFED PEOPLE. THEY SPEND ABOUT NINETEEN HOUFS IN A SOLITAFY CELL THAT'S ABOUT 9X12 FEET, AND WINDOWS AFE A FAFITY. WHAT DO YOU CALL THAT?
IS THAT AN ACTUAL Q--
WE CALL IT WASTE OF CAPITAL. SHUT THE BLINDS, THE SUN'S NOT GOING TO SAVE YOU.
MFR. GIBSON WILL FEQUIFE THIFTY-SIX MEN WORKING IN TWO SHIFTS FOF TWELVE HOUFS A DAY AT PAY OF ZEFO AMEFICAN DOLLAFS FOF SIX YEAFS. WHAT THEY WILL GET AS PAY IS AN EXTRA FREE MEAL AND A FOOM WITH A WINDOW INSIDE YOUF FACILITY.
THEIF CUFFS WILL STAY ON.
WE WILL PFOVIDE OUR OWN SECUFITY, CONTFFACTED BY A COMPANY THAT SOFTED OUT MANY PFOBLEMATIC SITUATIONS IN IFAQ, AFGHANISTAN, CHAD, AND OTHEF PLACES YOU WILL LIKELY NEVEFF SEE UNMEDIATED.
THE MEN WILL NEVEF SPEAK OF WHAT THEY DO, AND THEY WILL NEVEF BE QUESTIONED ABOUT IT, NEITHEF BY YOU, YOUF STAFF, OR BY OTHEF PFISONEFS.

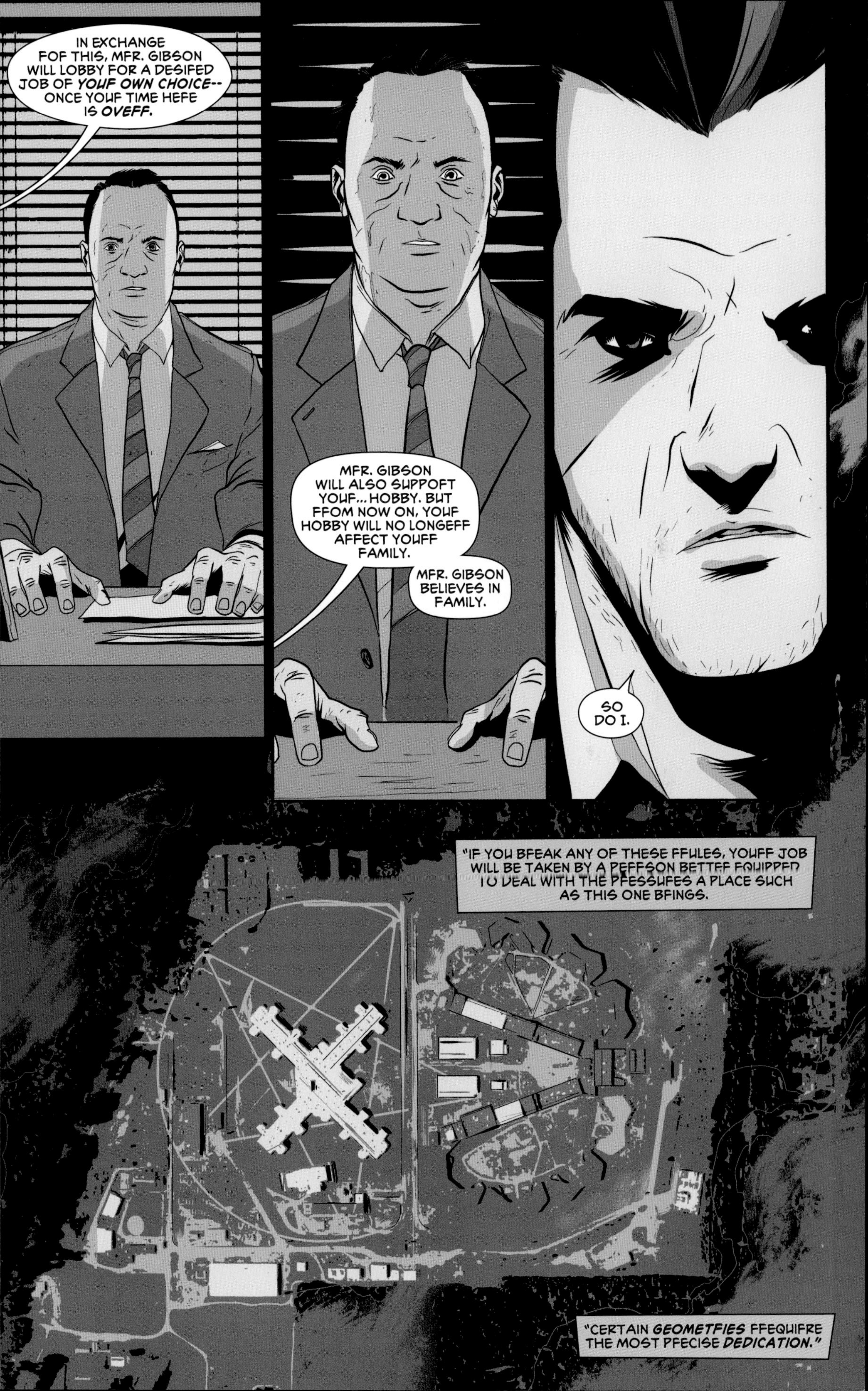
IN EXCHANGE FOR THIS, MFR. GIBSON WILL LOBBY FOR A DESIFED JOB OF *YOUF OWN CHOICE*-- ONCE YOUF TIME HEFE IS *OVEFF.*
MFR. GIBSON WILL ALSO SUPPOFT YOUF... HOBBY. BUT FFOM NOW ON, YOUF HOBBY WILL NO LONGEFF AFFECT YOUFF FAMILY.
MFR. GIBSON BELIEVES IN FAMILY.
SO DO I.
"IF YOU BFEAK ANY OF THESE FFULES, YOUFF JOB WILL BE TAKEN BY A PEFFSON BETTEFF EQUIPPED TO DEAL WITH THE PFESSUFES A PLACE SUCH AS THIS ONE BFINGS.
"CERTAIN *GEOMETFIES* FFEQUIFRE THE MOST PFECISE *DEDICATION.*"

Chapter 3

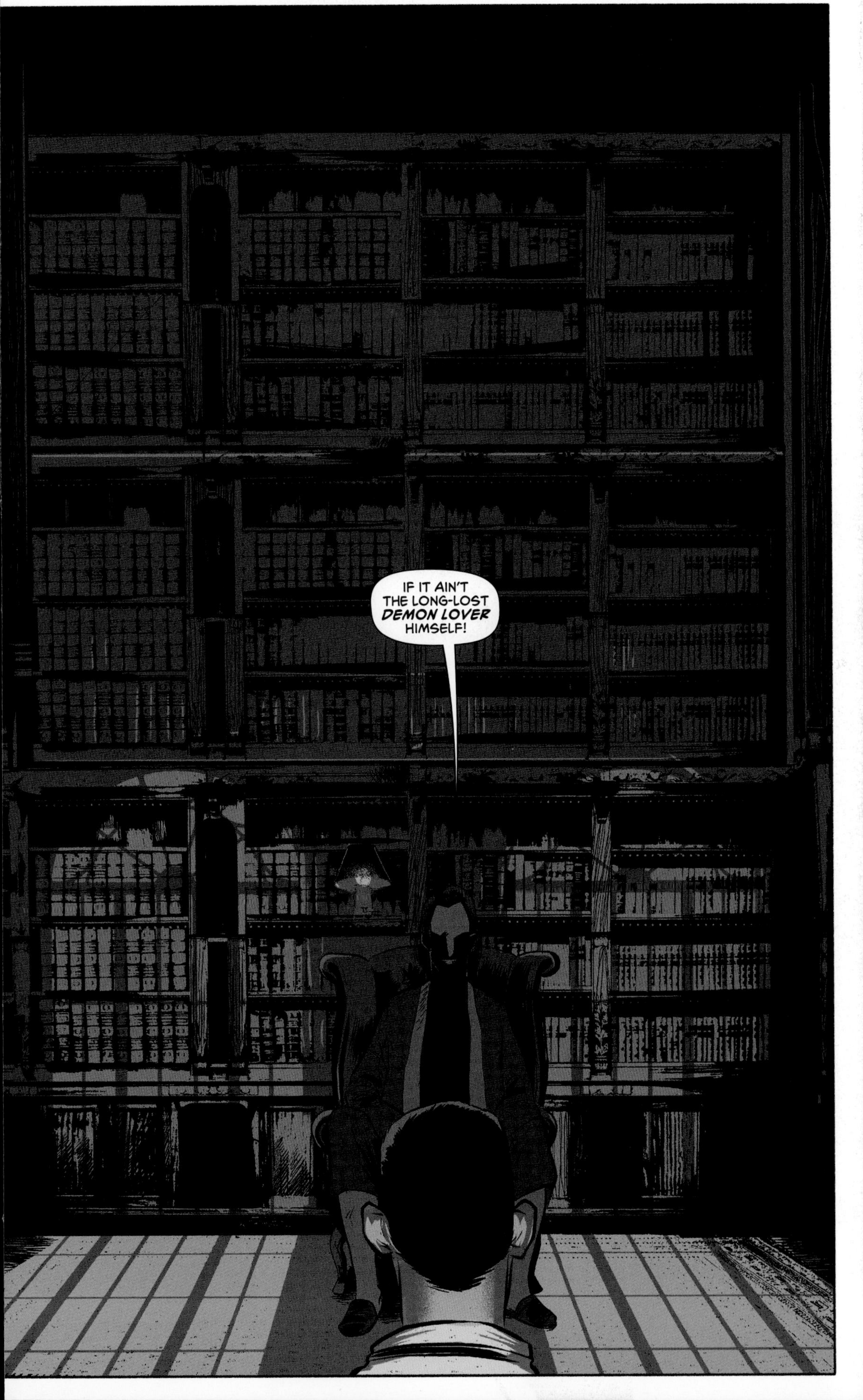
IF IT AIN'T THE LONG-LOST *DEMON LOVER* HIMSELF!

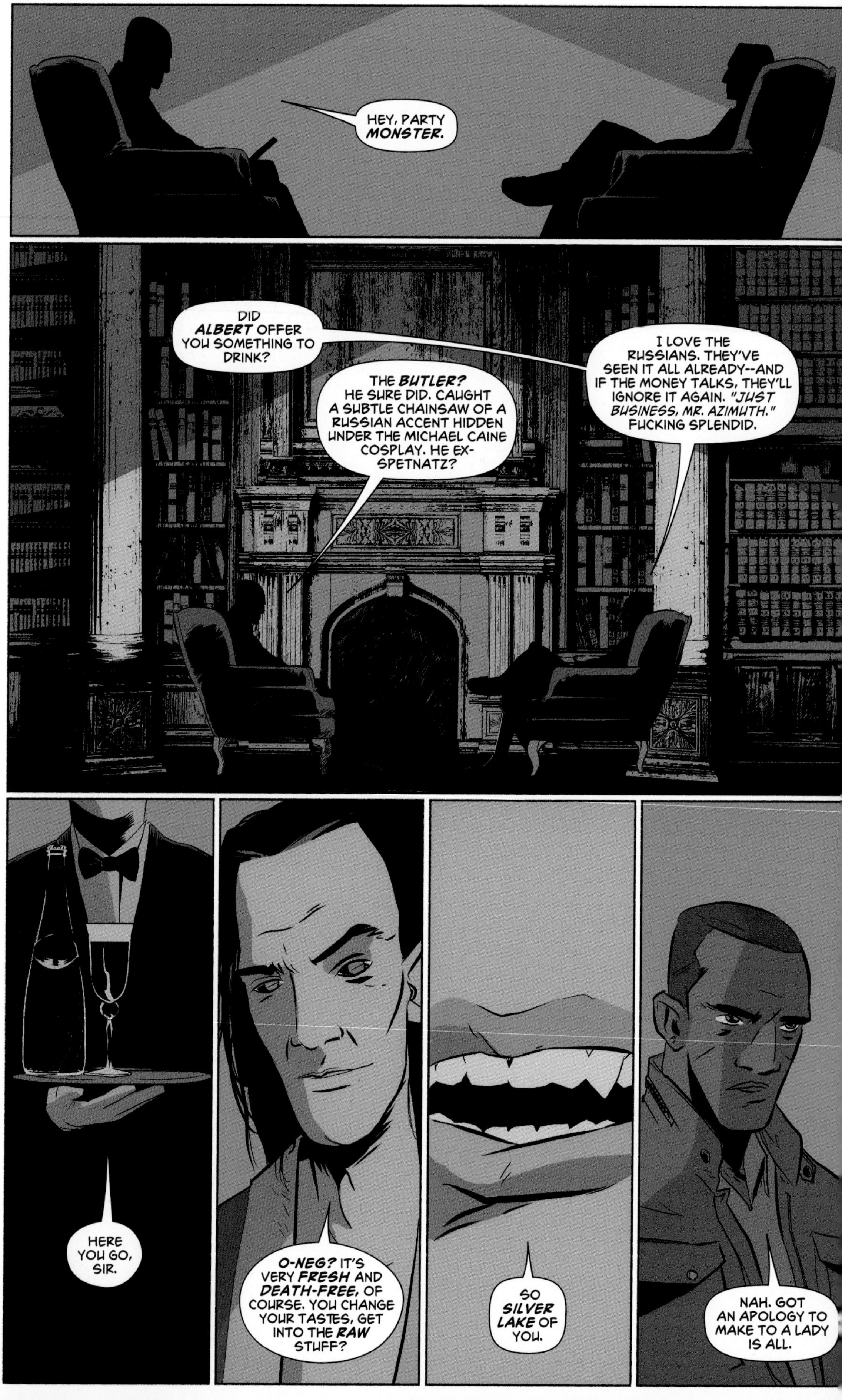
HEY, PARTY MONSTER.
DID ALBERT OFFER YOU SOMETHING TO DRINK?
THE BUTLER? HE SURE DID. CAUGHT A SUBTLE CHAINSAW OF A RUSSIAN ACCENT HIDDEN UNDER THE MICHAEL CAINE COSPLAY. HE EX-SPETNATZ?
I LOVE THE RUSSIANS. THEY'VE SEEN IT ALL ALREADY--AND IF THE MONEY TALKS, THEY'LL IGNORE IT AGAIN. "JUST BUSINESS, MR. AZIMUTH." FUCKING SPLENDID.
HERE YOU GO, SIR.
O-NEG? IT'S VERY FRESH AND DEATH-FREE, OF COURSE. YOU CHANGE YOUR TASTES, GET INTO THE RAW STUFF?
SO SILVER LAKE OF YOU.
NAH. GOT AN APOLOGY TO MAKE TO A LADY IS ALL.

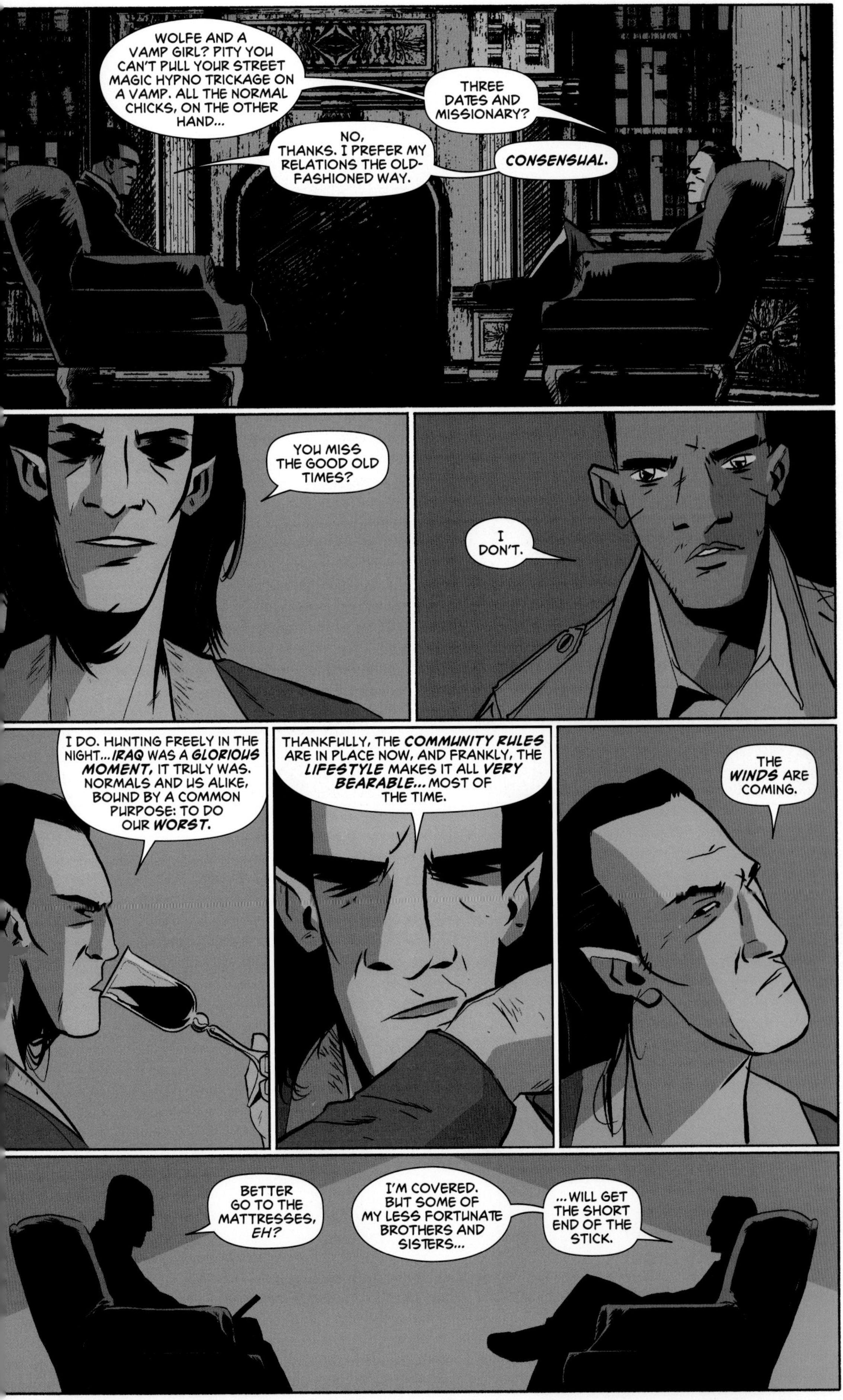
WOLFE AND A VAMP GIRL? PITY YOU CAN'T PULL YOUR STREET MAGIC HYPNO TRICKAGE ON A VAMP. ALL THE NORMAL CHICKS, ON THE OTHER HAND...
THREE DATES AND MISSIONARY?
NO, THANKS. I PREFER MY RELATIONS THE OLD-FASHIONED WAY.
CONSENSUAL.
YOU MISS THE GOOD OLD TIMES?
I DON'T.
I DO. HUNTING FREELY IN THE NIGHT... IRAQ WAS A GLORIOUS MOMENT, IT TRULY WAS. NORMALS AND US ALIKE, BOUND BY A COMMON PURPOSE: TO DO OUR WORST.
THANKFULLY, THE COMMUNITY RULES ARE IN PLACE NOW, AND FRANKLY, THE LIFESTYLE MAKES IT ALL VERY BEARABLE... MOST OF THE TIME.
THE WINDS ARE COMING.
BETTER GO TO THE MATTRESSES, EH?
I'M COVERED. BUT SOME OF MY LESS FORTUNATE BROTHERS AND SISTERS...
...WILL GET THE SHORT END OF THE STICK.

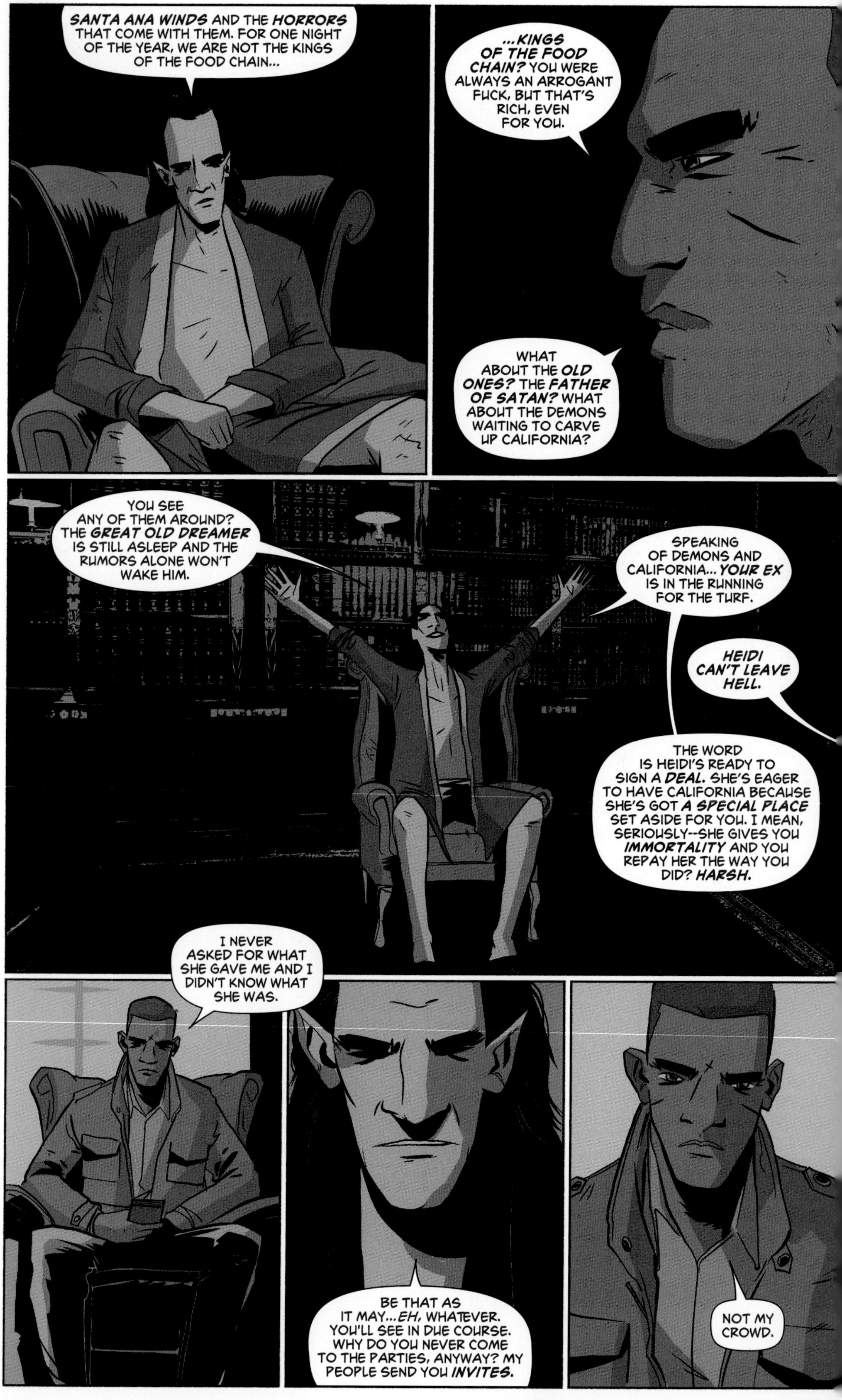
SANTA ANA WINDS AND THE HORRORS THAT COME WITH THEM. FOR ONE NIGHT OF THE YEAR, WE ARE NOT THE KINGS OF THE FOOD CHAIN...
...KINGS OF THE FOOD CHAIN? YOU WERE ALWAYS AN ARROGANT FUCK, BUT THAT'S RICH, EVEN FOR YOU.
WHAT ABOUT THE OLD ONES? THE FATHER OF SATAN? WHAT ABOUT THE DEMONS WAITING TO CARVE UP CALIFORNIA?
YOU SEE ANY OF THEM AROUND? THE GREAT OLD DREAMER IS STILL ASLEEP AND THE RUMORS ALONE WON'T WAKE HIM.
SPEAKING OF DEMONS AND CALIFORNIA... YOUR EX IS IN THE RUNNING FOR THE TURF.
HEIDI CAN'T LEAVE HELL.
THE WORD IS HEIDI'S READY TO SIGN A DEAL. SHE'S EAGER TO HAVE CALIFORNIA BECAUSE SHE'S GOT A SPECIAL PLACE SET ASIDE FOR YOU. I MEAN, SERIOUSLY--SHE GIVES YOU IMMORTALITY AND YOU REPAY HER THE WAY YOU DID? HARSH.
I NEVER ASKED FOR WHAT SHE GAVE ME AND I DIDN'T KNOW WHAT SHE WAS.
BE THAT AS IT MAY... EH, WHATEVER. YOU'LL SEE IN DUE COURSE. WHY DO YOU NEVER COME TO THE PARTIES, ANYWAY? MY PEOPLE SEND YOU INVITES.
NOT MY CROWD.

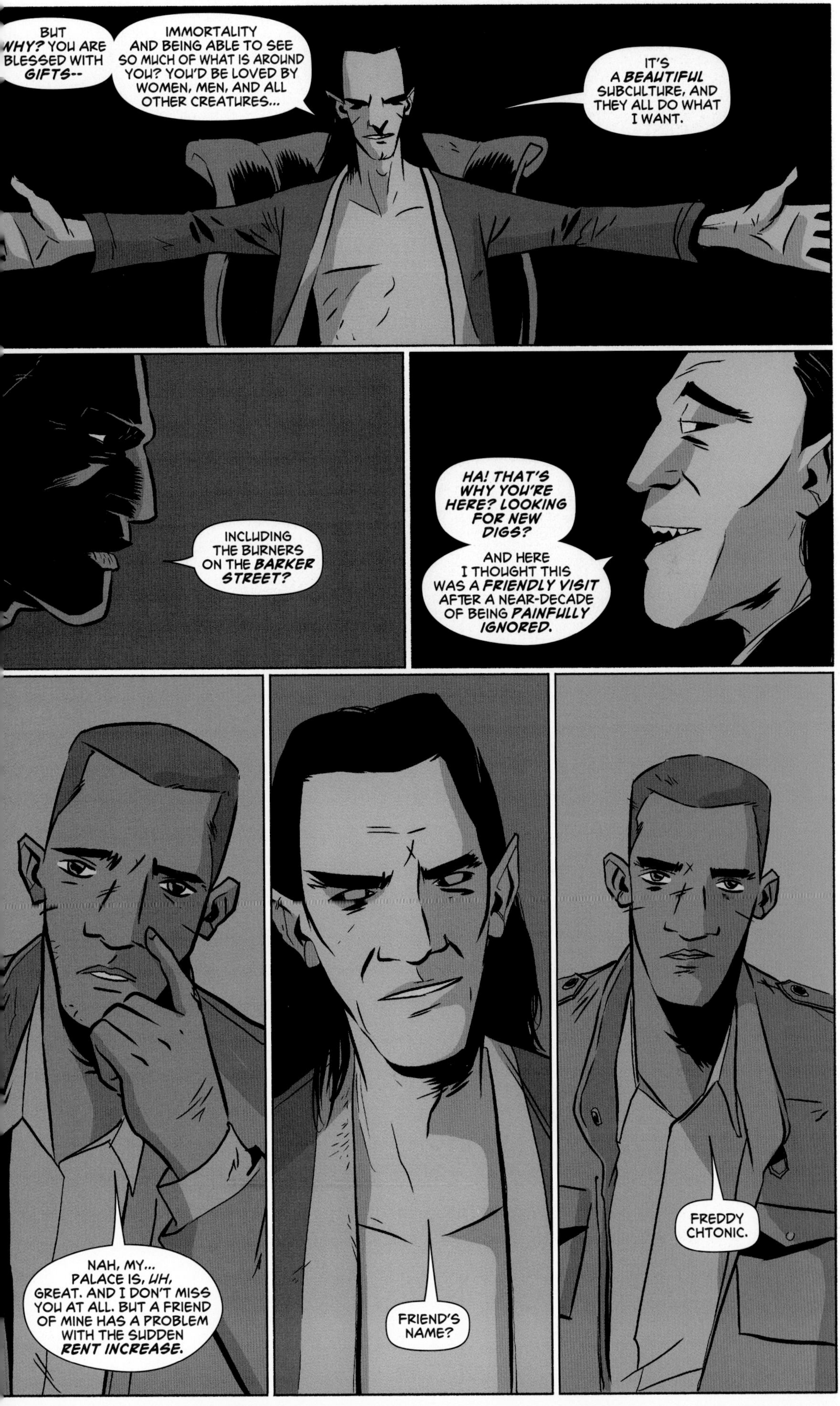
BUT WHY? YOU ARE BLESSED WITH GIFTS--
IMMORTALITY AND BEING ABLE TO SEE SO MUCH OF WHAT IS AROUND YOU? YOU'D BE LOVED BY WOMEN, MEN, AND ALL OTHER CREATURES...
IT'S A BEAUTIFUL SUBCULTURE, AND THEY ALL DO WHAT I WANT.
INCLUDING THE BURNERS ON THE BARKER STREET?
HA! THAT'S WHY YOU'RE HERE? LOOKING FOR NEW DIGS?
AND HERE I THOUGHT THIS WAS A FRIENDLY VISIT AFTER A NEAR-DECADE OF BEING PAINFULLY IGNORED.
NAH, MY... PALACE IS, UH, GREAT. AND I DON'T MISS YOU AT ALL. BUT A FRIEND OF MINE HAS A PROBLEM WITH THE SUDDEN RENT INCREASE.
FRIEND'S NAME?
FREDDY CHTONIC.

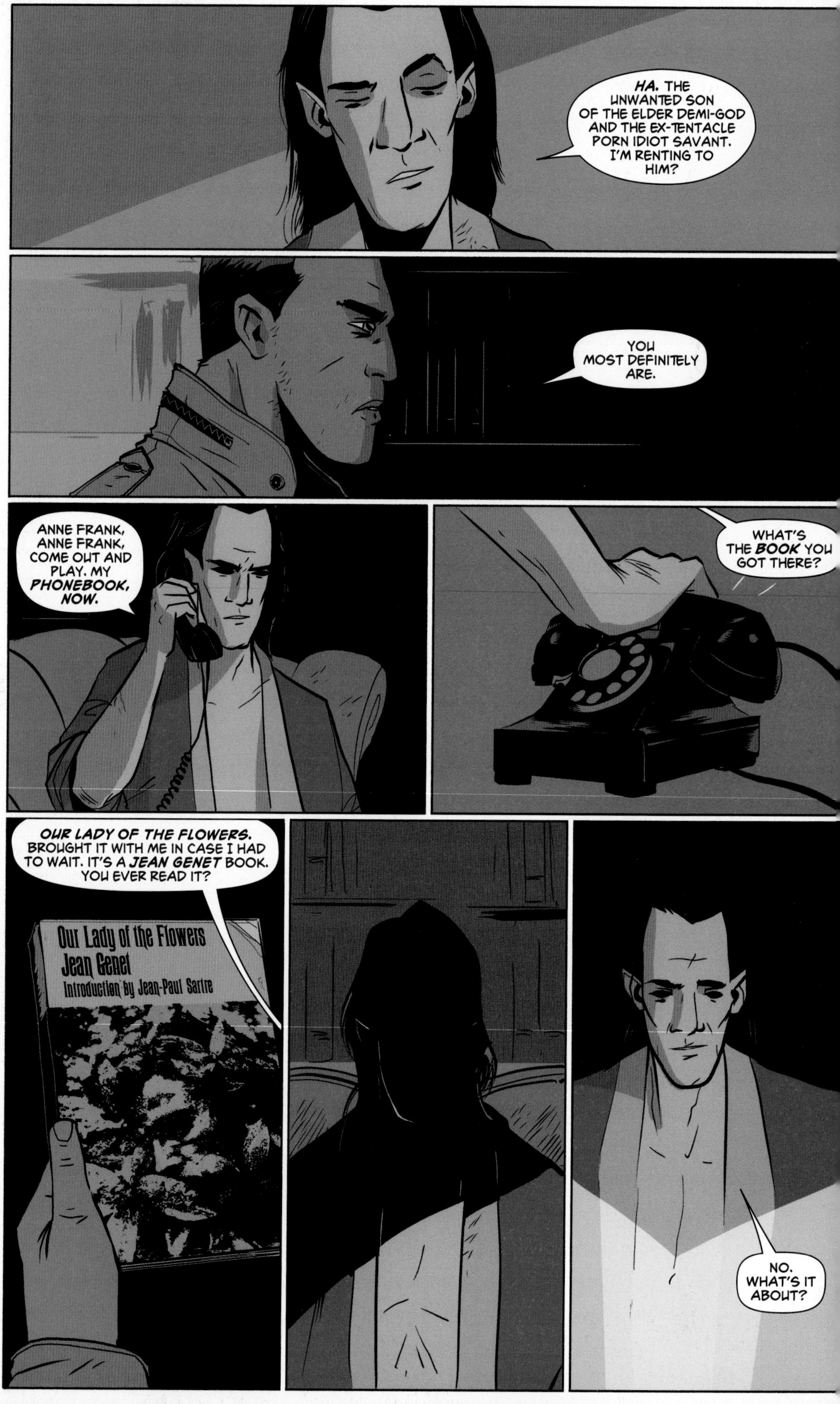
HA. THE UNWANTED SON OF THE ELDER DEMI-GOD AND THE EX-TENTACLE PORN IDIOT SAVANT. I'M RENTING TO HIM?
YOU MOST DEFINITELY ARE.
ANNE FRANK, ANNE FRANK, COME OUT AND PLAY. MY PHONEBOOK, NOW.
WHAT'S THE BOOK YOU GOT THERE?
OUR LADY OF THE FLOWERS. BROUGHT IT WITH ME IN CASE I HAD TO WAIT. IT'S A JEAN GENET BOOK. YOU EVER READ IT?
Our Lady of the Flowers
Jean Genet
Introduction by Jean-Paul Sartre
NO. WHAT'S IT ABOUT?

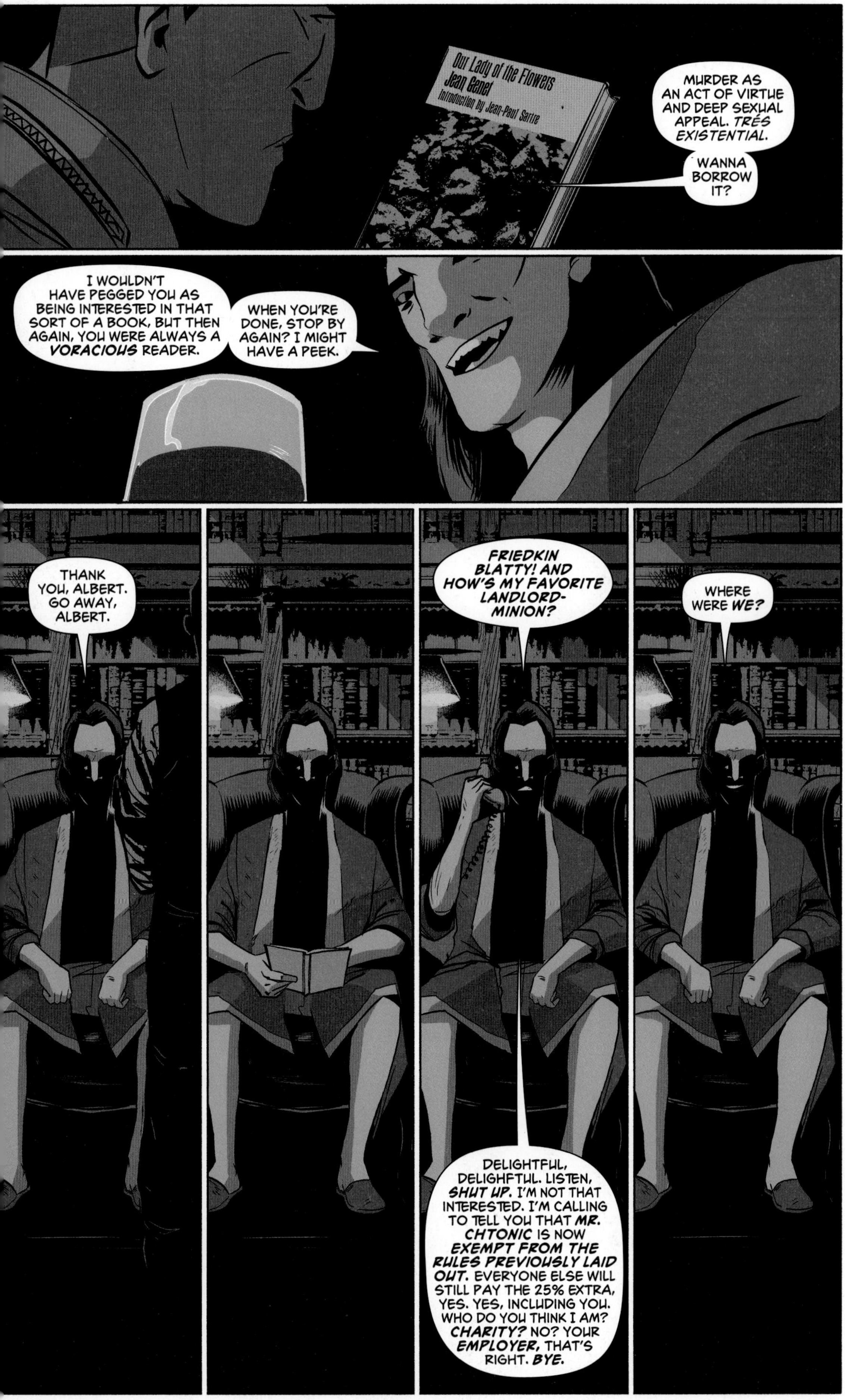
Our Lady of the Flowers
Jean Genet
Introduction by Jean-Paul Sartre
MURDER AS AN ACT OF VIRTUE AND DEEP SEXUAL APPEAL. TRÉS EXISTENTIAL.
WANNA BORROW IT?
I WOULDN'T HAVE PEGGED YOU AS BEING INTERESTED IN THAT SORT OF A BOOK, BUT THEN AGAIN, YOU WERE ALWAYS A VORACIOUS READER.
WHEN YOU'RE DONE, STOP BY AGAIN? I MIGHT HAVE A PEEK.
THANK YOU, ALBERT. GO AWAY, ALBERT.
FRIEDKIN BLATTY! AND HOW'S MY FAVORITE LANDLORD-MINION?
DELIGHTFUL, DELIGHTFUL. LISTEN, SHUT UP. I'M NOT THAT INTERESTED. I'M CALLING TO TELL YOU THAT MR. CHTONIC IS NOW EXEMPT FROM THE RULES PREVIOUSLY LAID OUT. EVERYONE ELSE WILL STILL PAY THE 25% EXTRA, YES. YES, INCLUDING YOU. WHO DO YOU THINK I AM? CHARITY? NO? YOUR EMPLOYER, THAT'S RIGHT. BYE.
WHERE WERE WE?

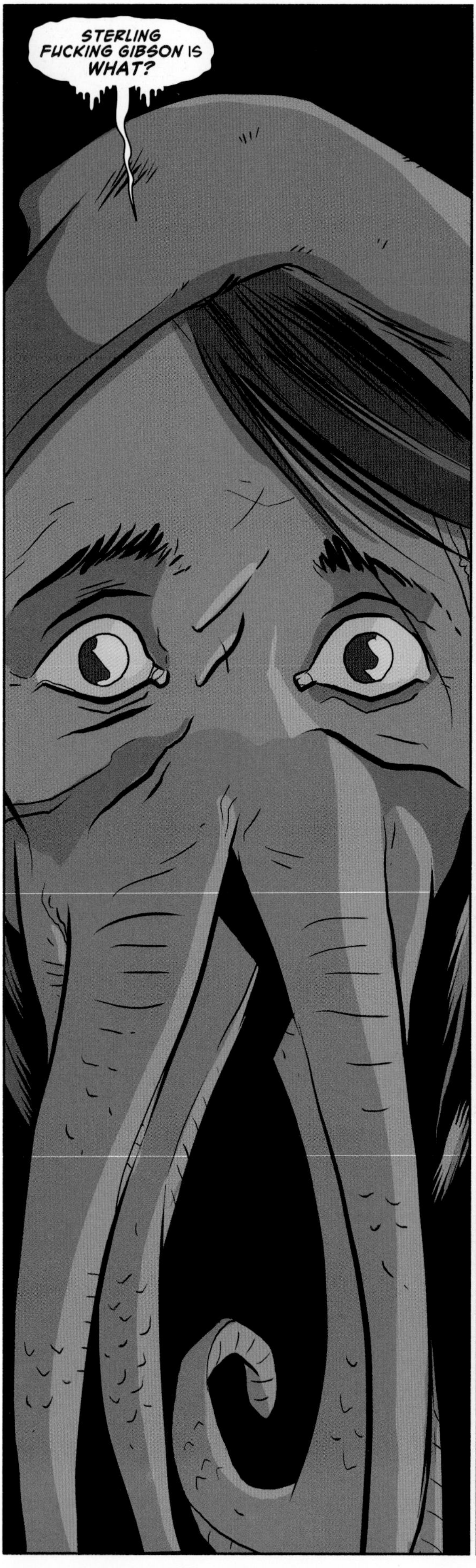
STERLING FUCKING GIBSON IS WHAT?

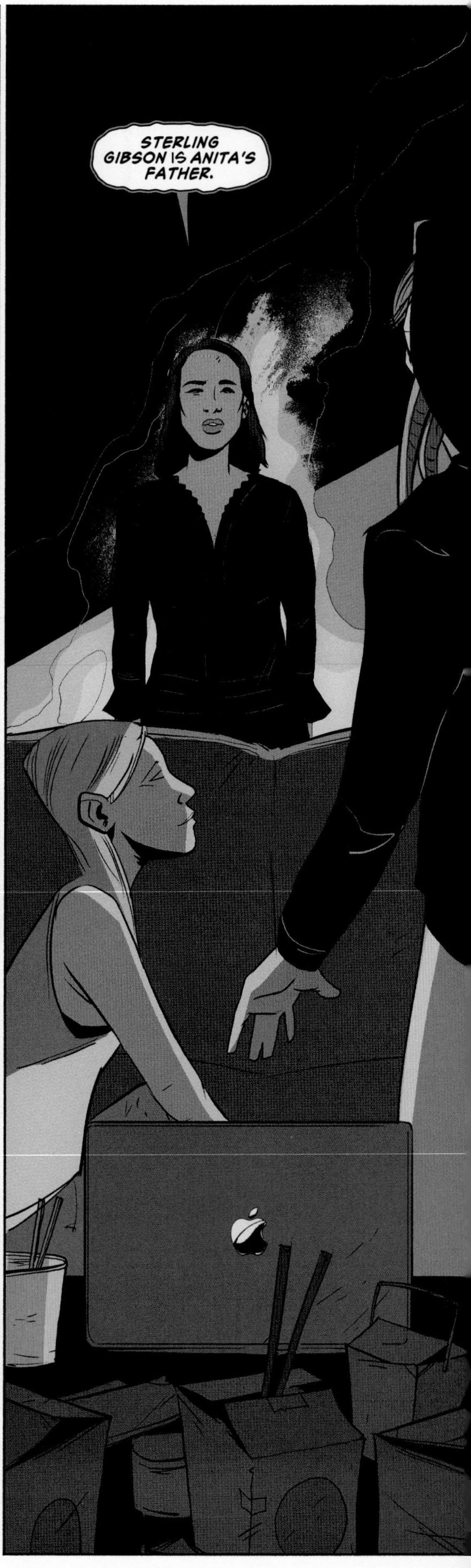
STERLING GIBSON IS ANITA'S FATHER.

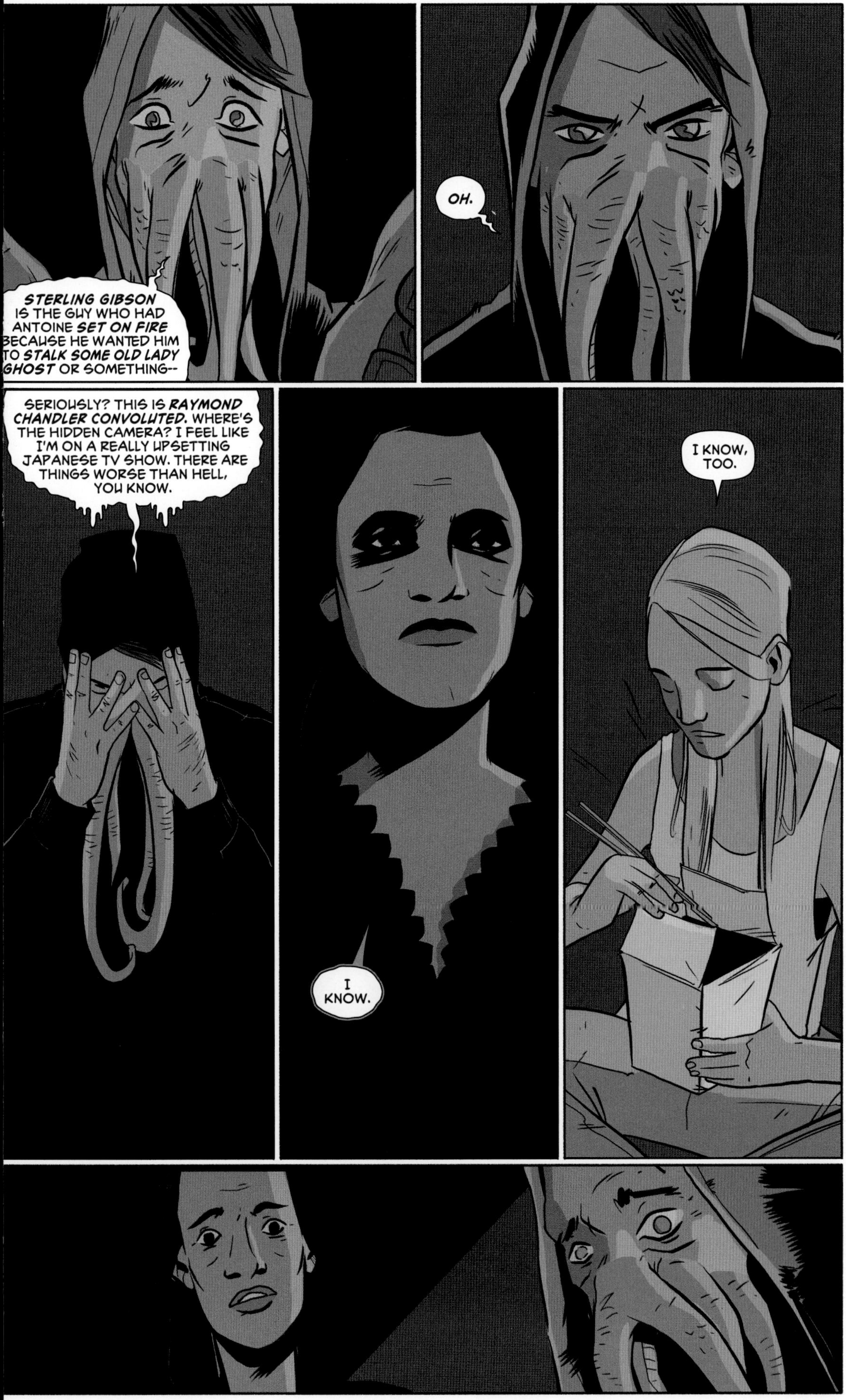
STERLING GIBSON IS THE GUY WHO HAD ANTOINE SET ON FIRE BECAUSE HE WANTED HIM TO STALK SOME OLD LADY GHOST OR SOMETHING--
OH.
SERIOUSLY? THIS IS RAYMOND CHANDLER CONVOLUTED. WHERE'S THE HIDDEN CAMERA? I FEEL LIKE I'M ON A REALLY UPSETTING JAPANESE TV SHOW. THERE ARE THINGS WORSE THAN HELL, YOU KNOW.
I KNOW.
I KNOW, TOO.

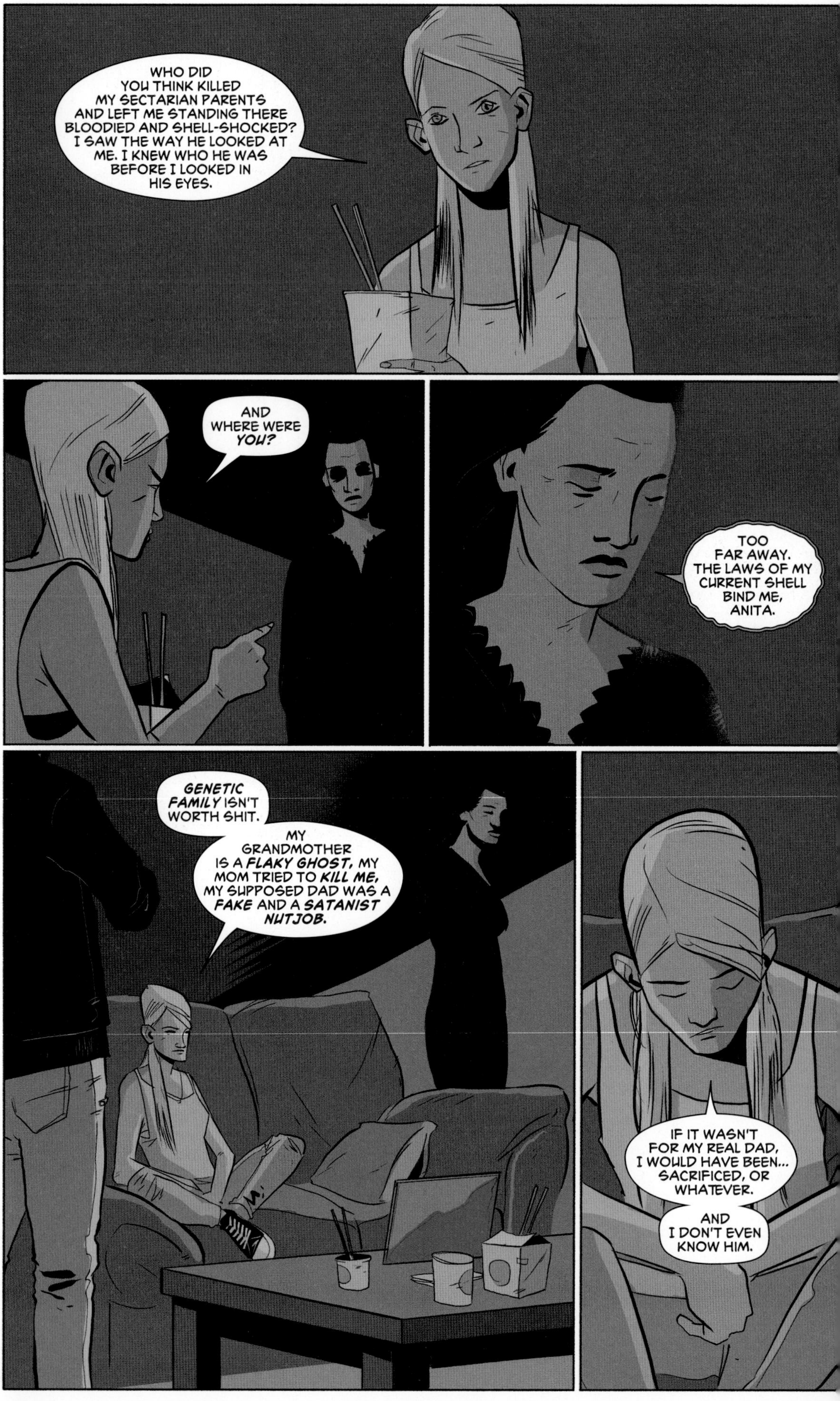
WHO DID YOU THINK KILLED MY SECTARIAN PARENTS AND LEFT ME STANDING THERE BLOODIED AND SHELL-SHOCKED? I SAW THE WAY HE LOOKED AT ME. I KNEW WHO HE WAS BEFORE I LOOKED IN HIS EYES.
AND WHERE WERE *YOU?*
TOO FAR AWAY. THE LAWS OF MY CURRENT SHELL BIND ME, ANITA.
GENETIC FAMILY ISN'T WORTH SHIT.
MY GRANDMOTHER IS A ***FLAKY GHOST,*** MY MOM TRIED TO ***KILL ME,*** MY SUPPOSED DAD WAS A ***FAKE*** AND A ***SATANIST NUTJOB.***
IF IT WASN'T FOR MY REAL DAD, I WOULD HAVE BEEN... SACRIFICED, OR WHATEVER.
AND I DON'T EVEN KNOW HIM.

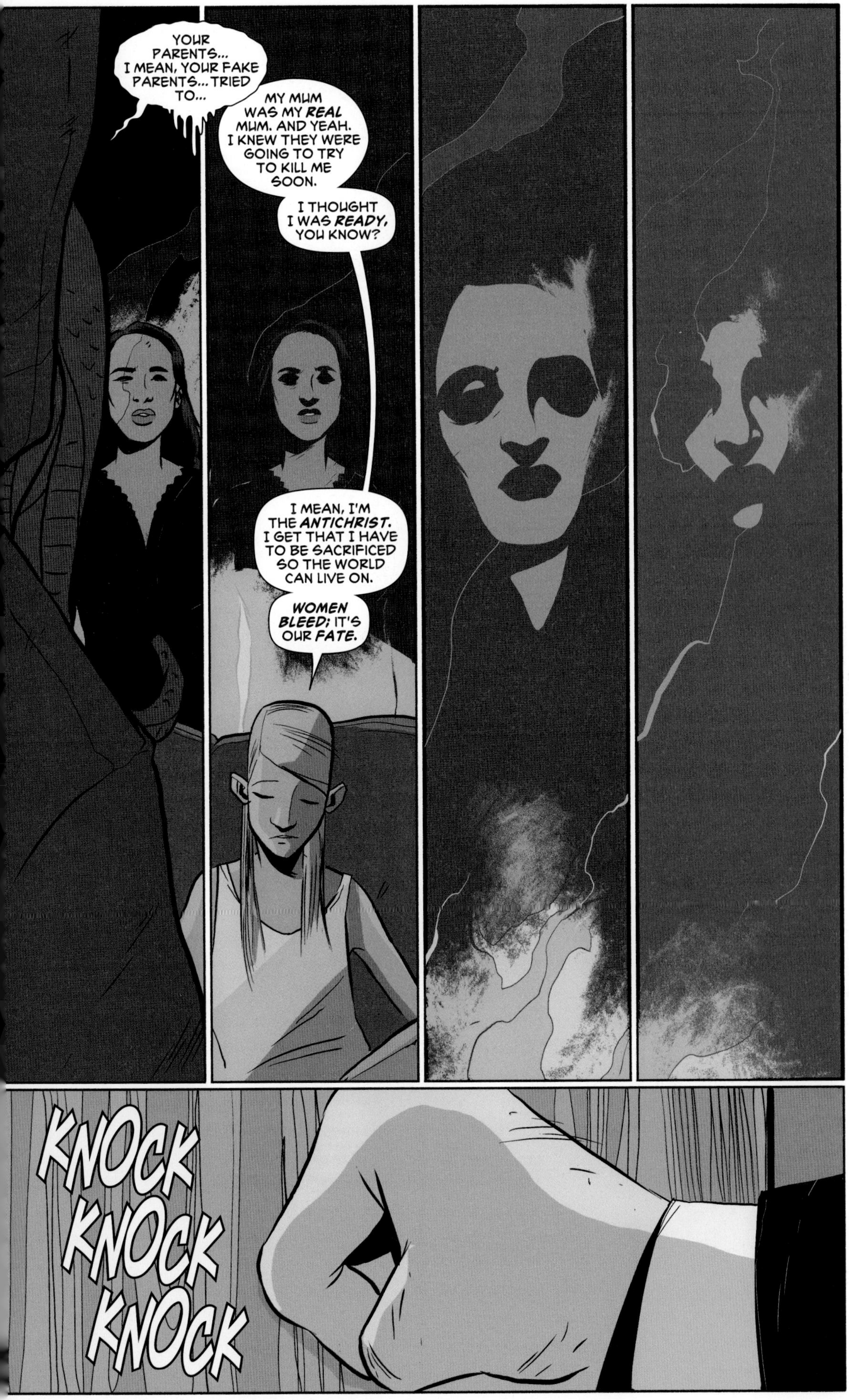

YOUR PARENTS... I MEAN, YOUR FAKE PARENTS... TRIED TO...
MY MUM WAS MY *REAL* MUM. AND YEAH. I KNEW THEY WERE GOING TO TRY TO KILL ME SOON.
I THOUGHT I WAS *READY,* YOU KNOW?
I MEAN, I'M THE *ANTICHRIST.* I GET THAT I HAVE TO BE SACRIFICED SO THE WORLD CAN LIVE ON.
WOMEN BLEED; IT'S OUR *FATE.*
KNOCK KNOCK KNOCK

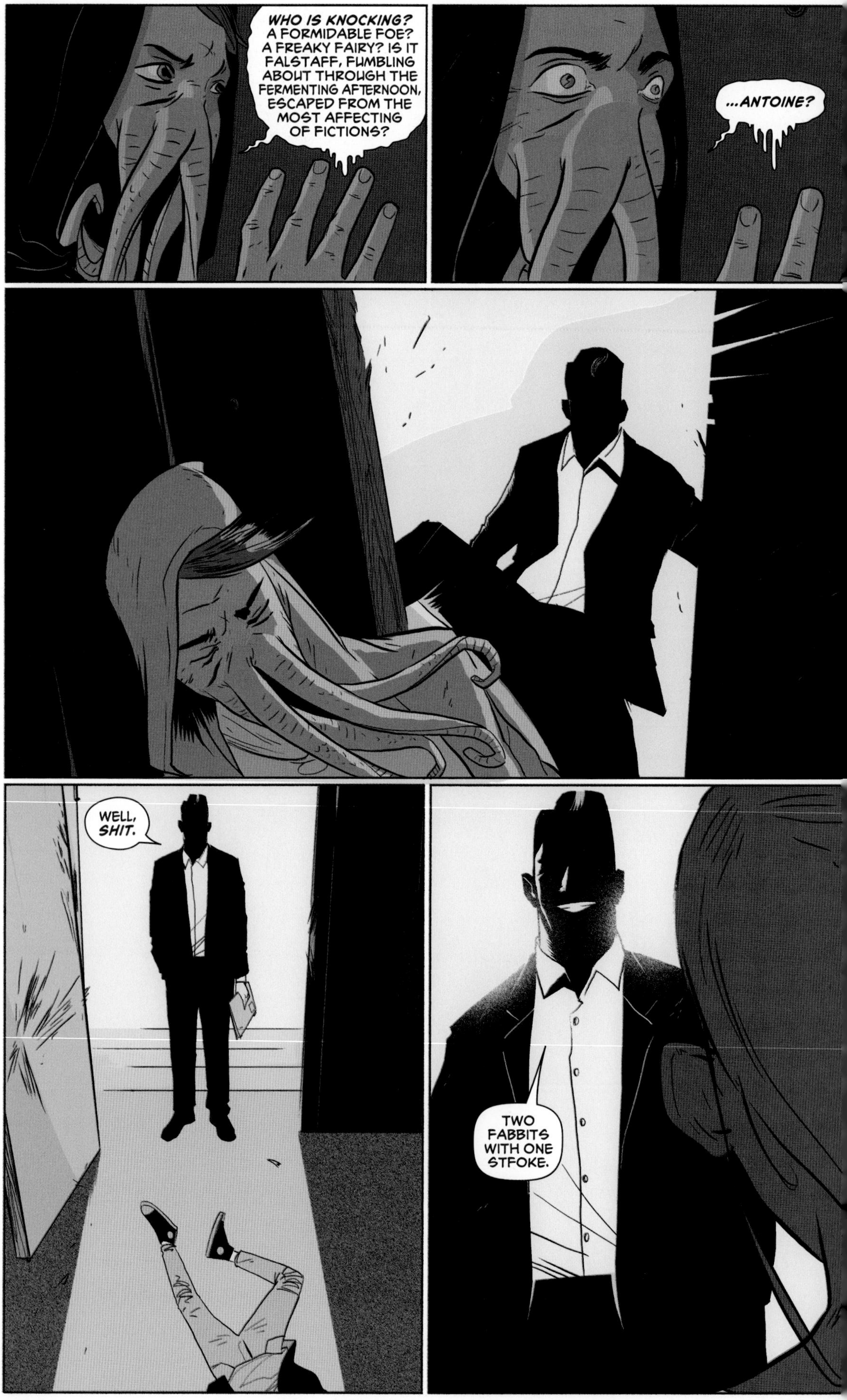
WHO IS KNOCKING? A FORMIDABLE FOE? A FREAKY FAIRY? IS IT FALSTAFF, FUMBLING ABOUT THROUGH THE FERMENTING AFTERNOON, ESCAPED FROM THE MOST AFFECTING OF FICTIONS?
...ANTOINE?
WELL, SHIT.
TWO FABBITS WITH ONE STFOKE.

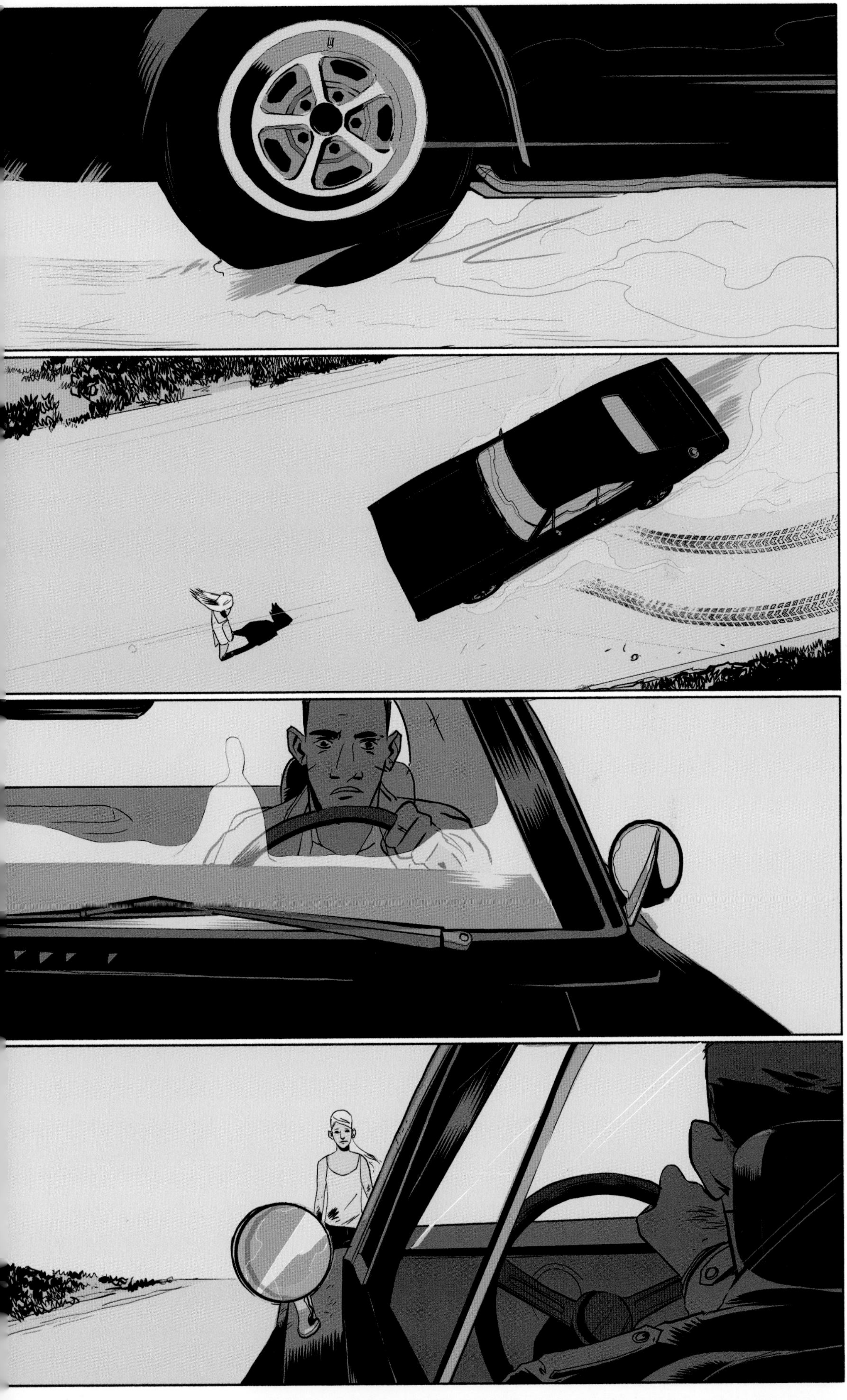

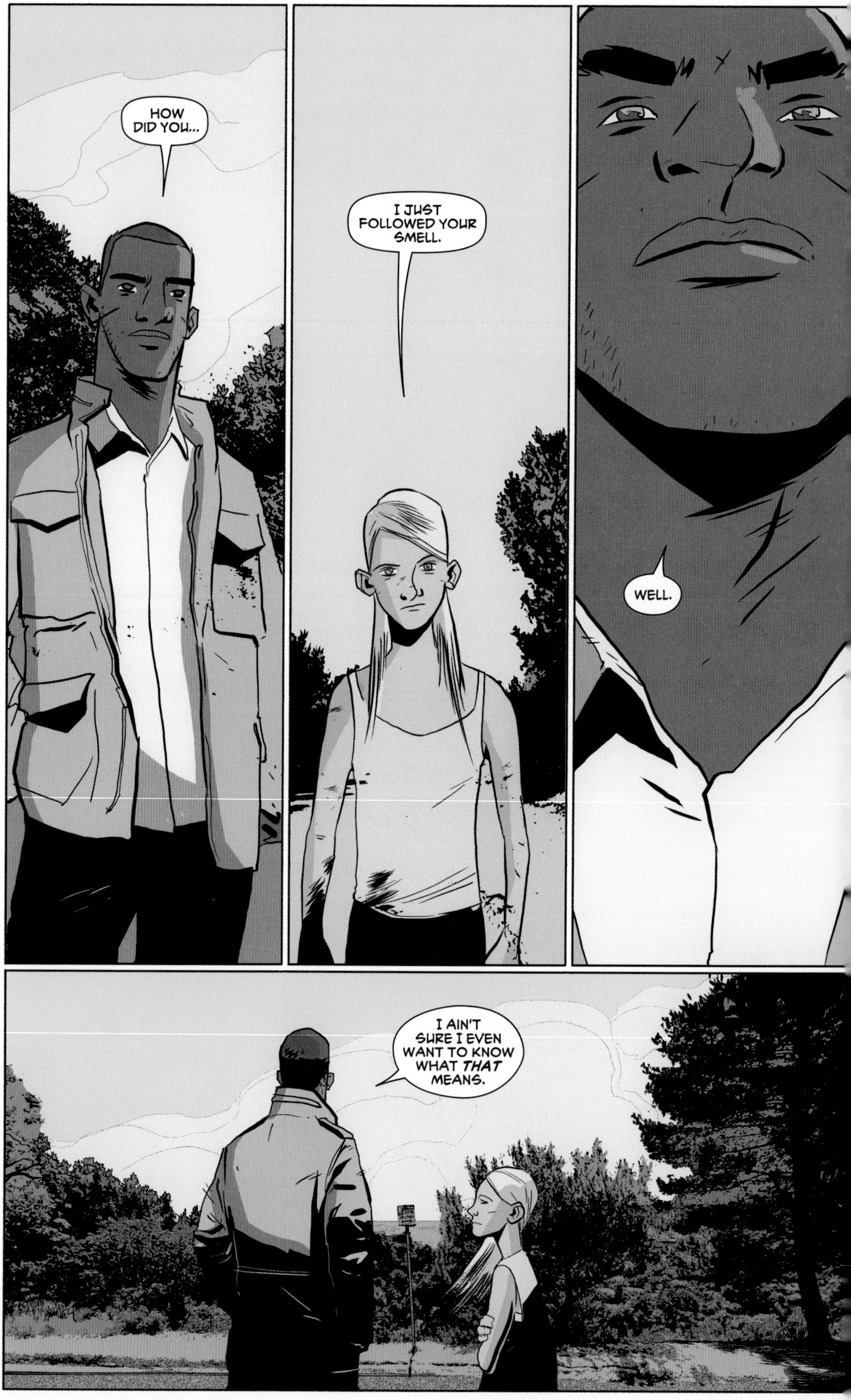
HOW DID YOU...
I JUST FOLLOWED YOUR SMELL.
WELL.
I AIN'T SURE I EVEN WANT TO KNOW WHAT *THAT* MEANS.

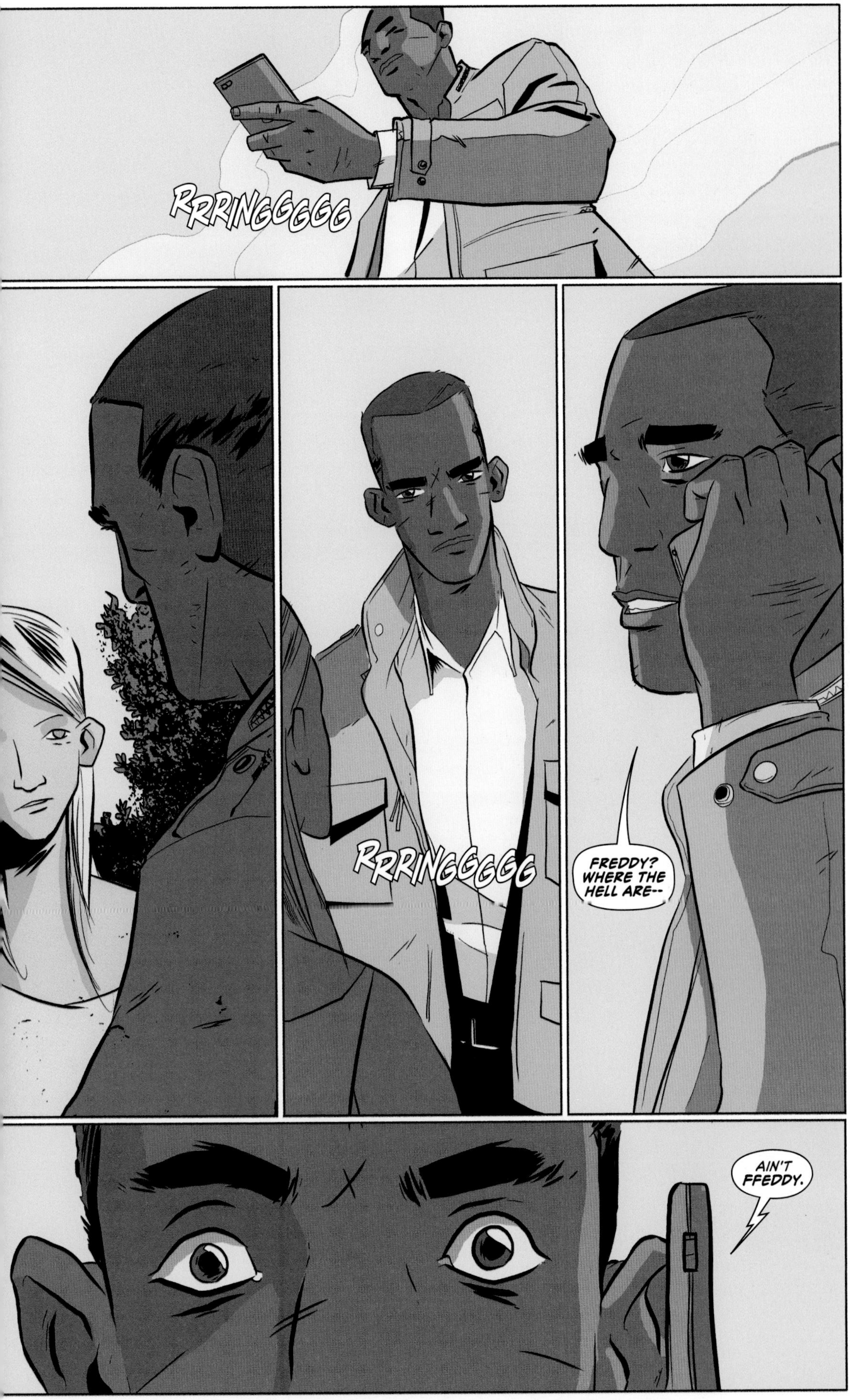
RRRINGGGGG
RRRINGGGGG
FREDDY? WHERE THE HELL ARE--
AIN'T FFEDDY.

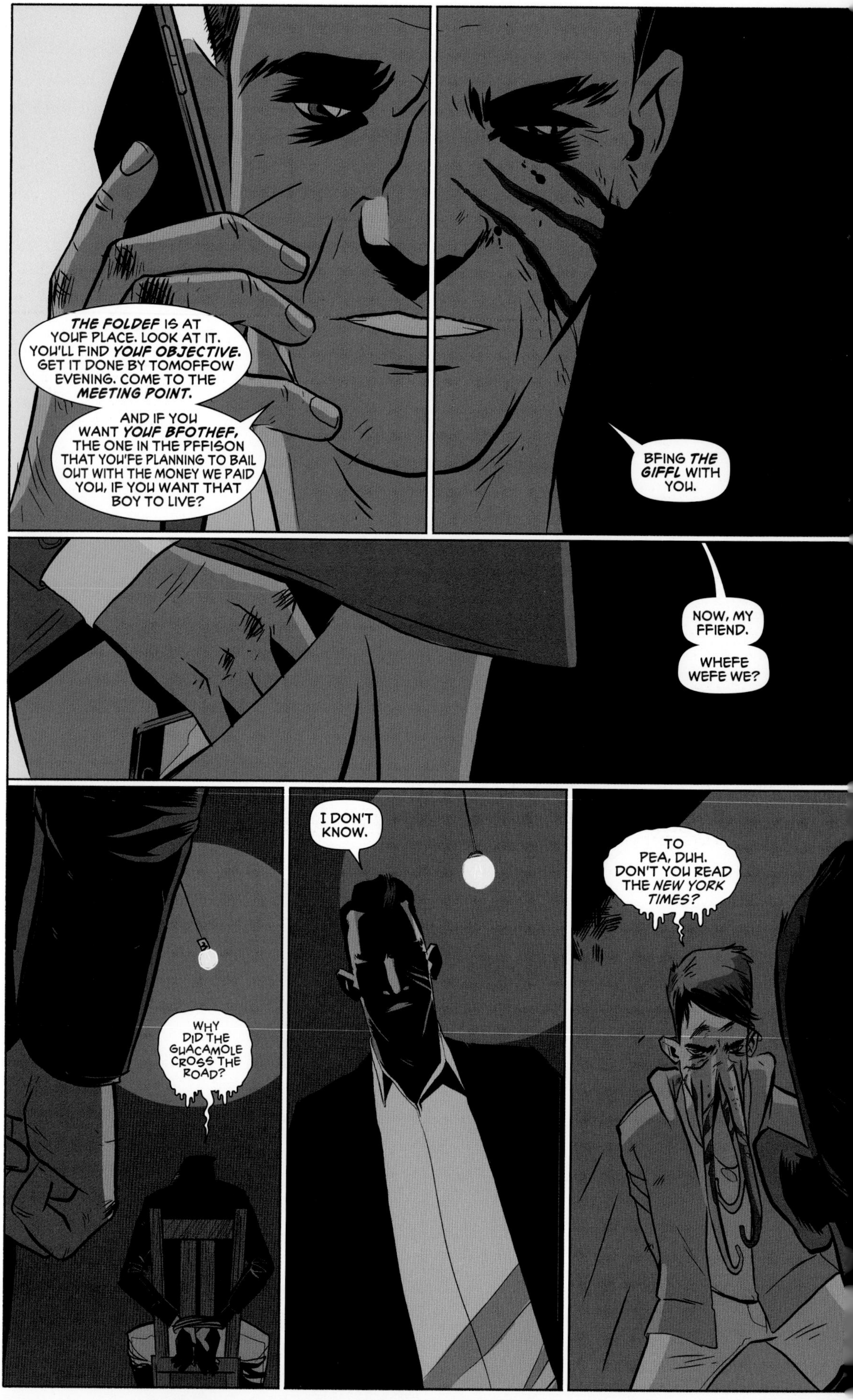
THE FOLDEF IS AT YOUF PLACE. LOOK AT IT. YOU'LL FIND YOUF OBJECTIVE. GET IT DONE BY TOMOFFOW EVENING. COME TO THE MEETING POINT.
AND IF YOU WANT YOUF BFOTHEF, THE ONE IN THE PFFISON THAT YOU'FE PLANNING TO BAIL OUT WITH THE MONEY WE PAID YOU, IF YOU WANT THAT BOY TO LIVE?
BFING THE GIFFL WITH YOU.
NOW, MY FFIEND.
WHEFE WEFE WE?
WHY DID THE GUACAMOLE CROSS THE ROAD?
I DON'T KNOW.
TO PEA, DUH. DON'T YOU READ THE NEW YORK TIMES?

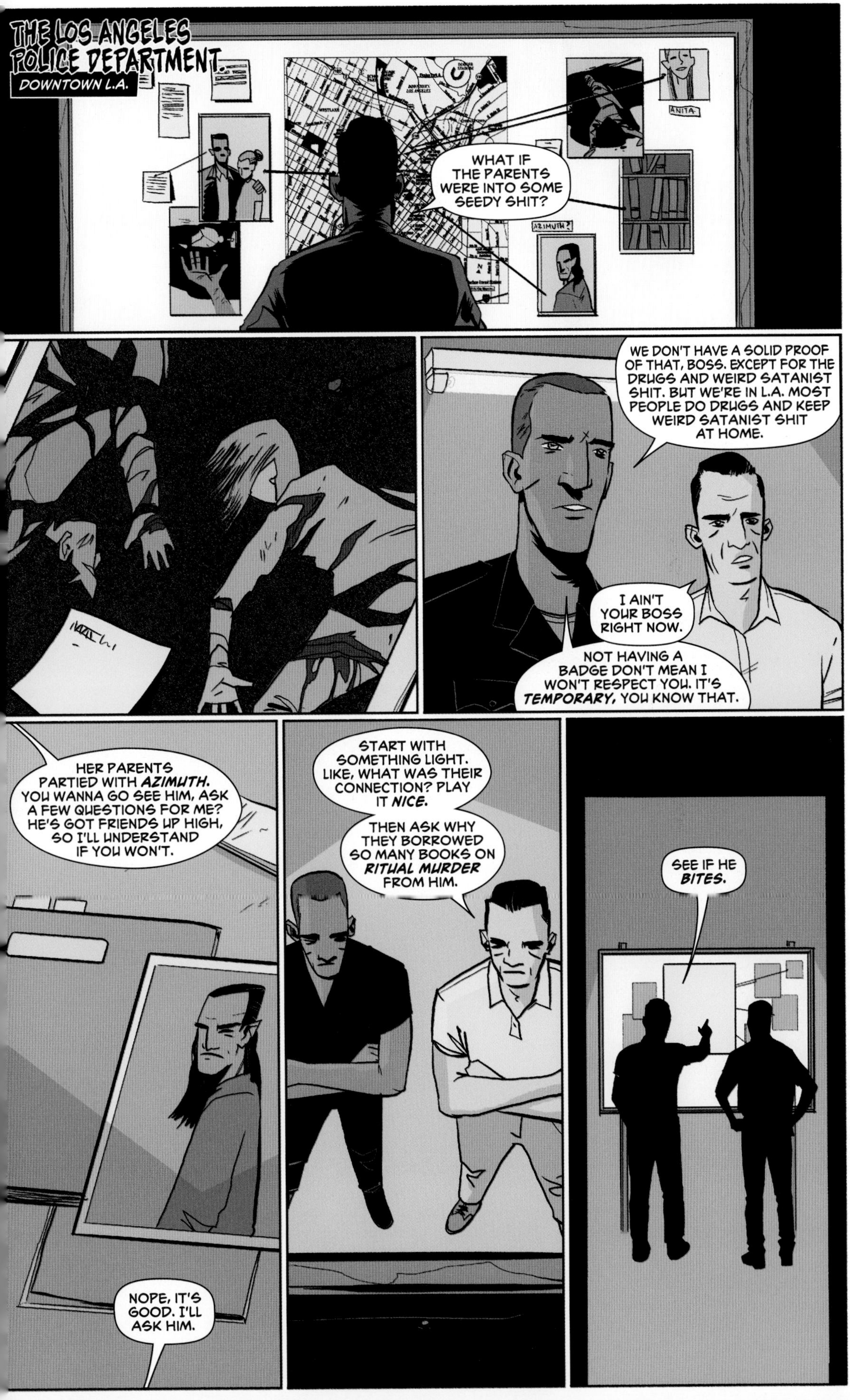
THE LOS ANGELES POLICE DEPARTMENT.
DOWNTOWN L.A.
ANITA
AZIMUTH?
WHAT IF THE PARENTS WERE INTO SOME SEEDY SHIT?
WE DON'T HAVE A SOLID PROOF OF THAT, BOSS. EXCEPT FOR THE DRUGS AND WEIRD SATANIST SHIT. BUT WE'RE IN L.A. MOST PEOPLE DO DRUGS AND KEEP WEIRD SATANIST SHIT AT HOME.
I AIN'T YOUR BOSS RIGHT NOW.
NOT HAVING A BADGE DON'T MEAN I WON'T RESPECT YOU. IT'S *TEMPORARY,* YOU KNOW THAT.
HER PARENTS PARTIED WITH *AZIMUTH.* YOU WANNA GO SEE HIM, ASK A FEW QUESTIONS FOR ME? HE'S GOT FRIENDS UP HIGH, SO I'LL UNDERSTAND IF YOU WON'T.
NOPE, IT'S GOOD. I'LL ASK HIM.
START WITH SOMETHING LIGHT. LIKE, WHAT WAS THEIR CONNECTION? PLAY IT *NICE.*
THEN ASK WHY THEY BORROWED SO MANY BOOKS ON *RITUAL MURDER* FROM HIM.
SEE IF HE *BITES.*

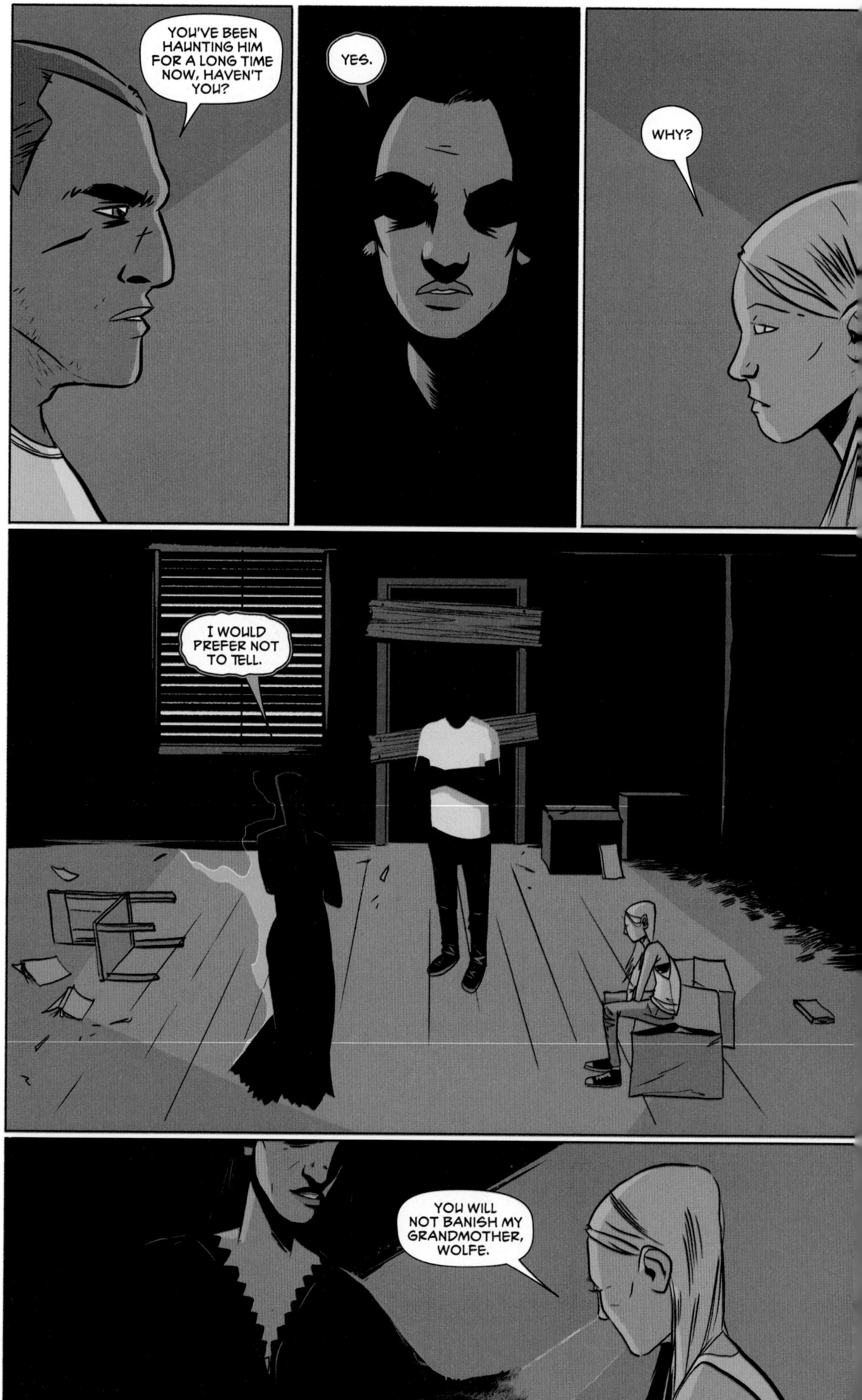
YOU'VE BEEN HAUNTING HIM FOR A LONG TIME NOW, HAVEN'T YOU?
YES.
WHY?
I WOULD PREFER NOT TO TELL.
YOU WILL NOT BANISH MY GRANDMOTHER, WOLFE.

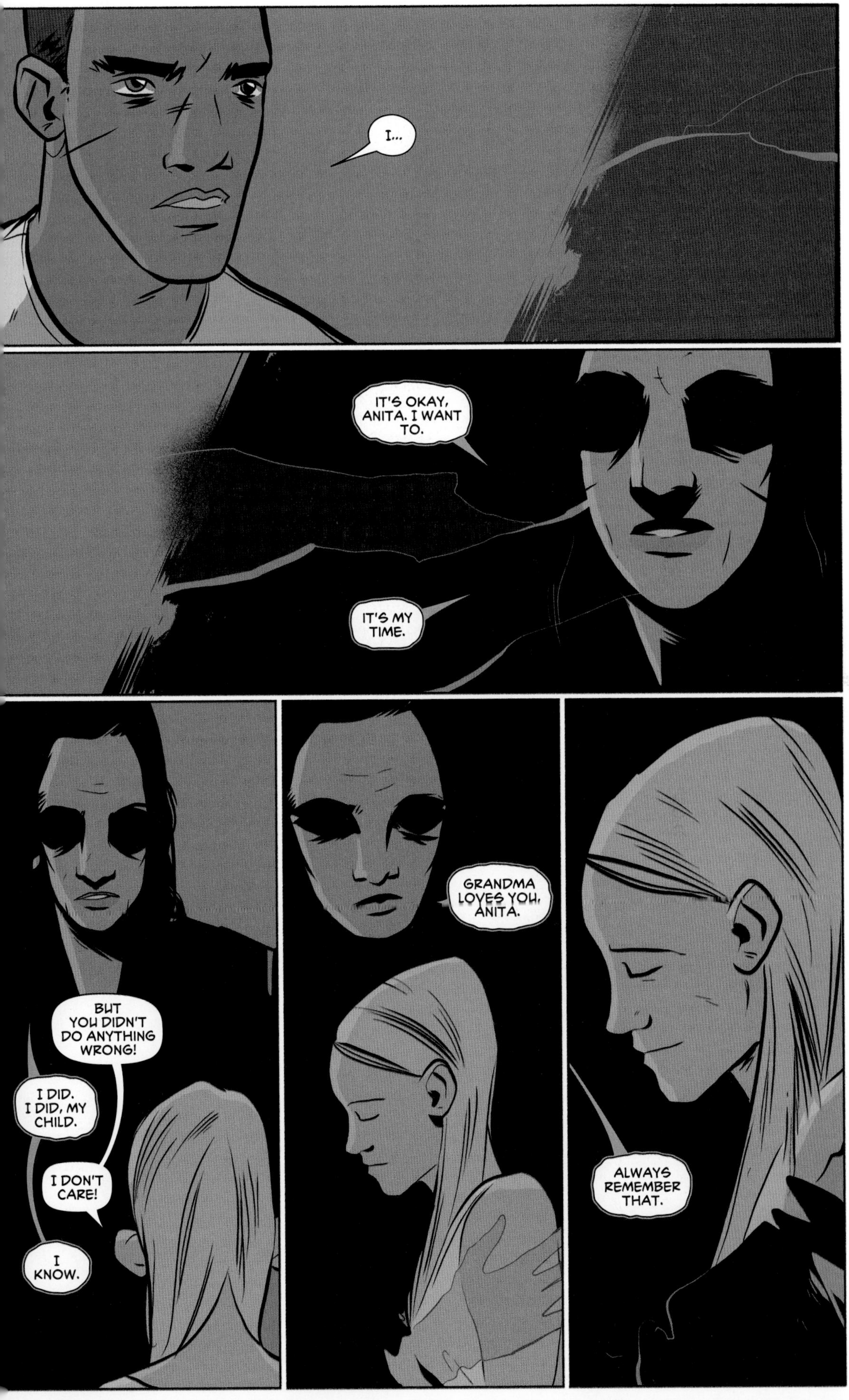
I...
IT'S OKAY, ANITA. I WANT TO.
IT'S MY TIME.
BUT YOU DIDN'T DO ANYTHING WRONG!
I DID. I DID, MY CHILD.
I DON'T CARE!
I KNOW.
GRANDMA LOVES YOU, ANITA.
ALWAYS REMEMBER THAT.

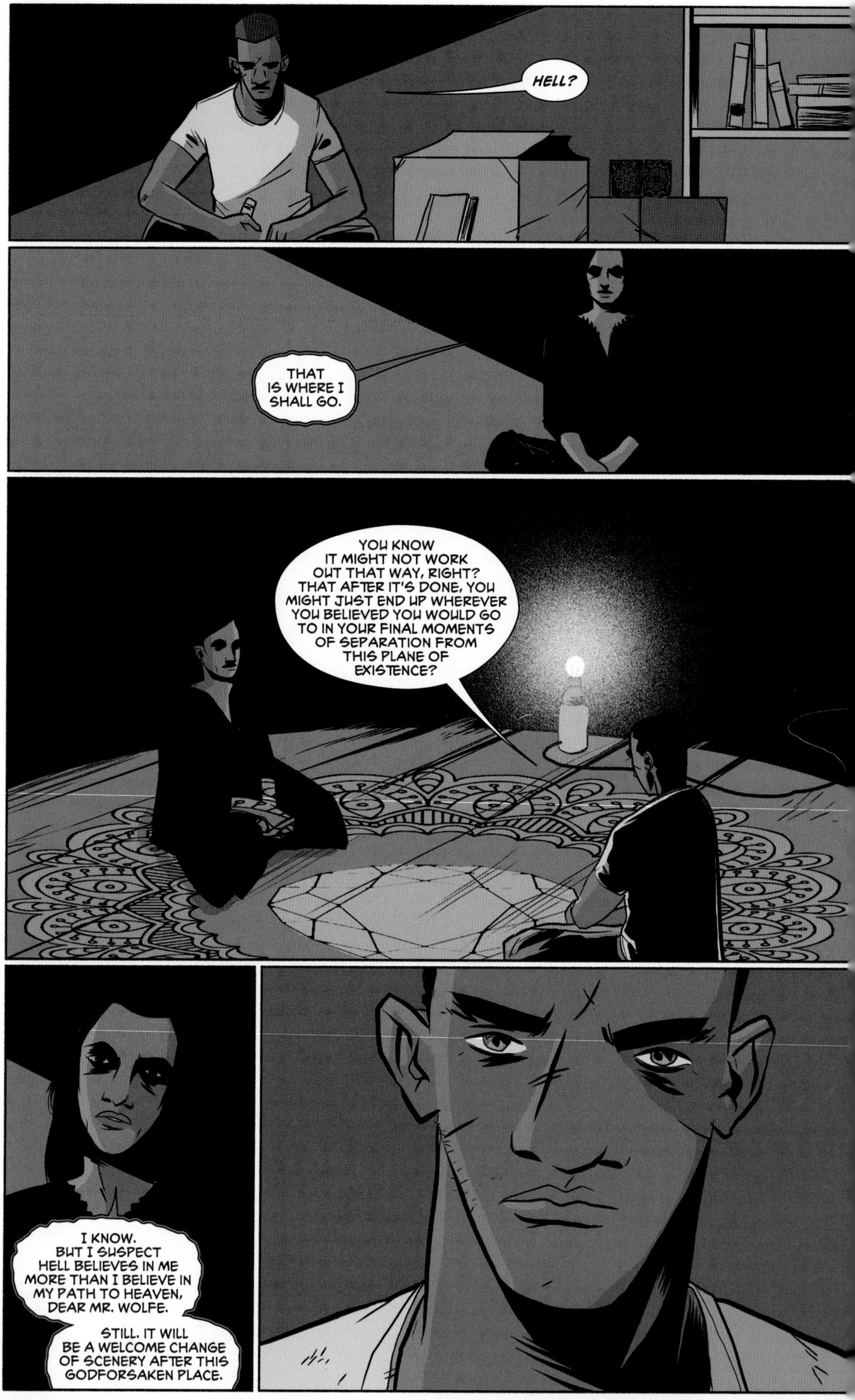
HELL?
THAT IS WHERE I SHALL GO.
YOU KNOW IT MIGHT NOT WORK OUT THAT WAY, RIGHT? THAT AFTER IT'S DONE, YOU MIGHT JUST END UP WHEREVER YOU BELIEVED YOU WOULD GO TO IN YOUR FINAL MOMENTS OF SEPARATION FROM THIS PLANE OF EXISTENCE?
I KNOW. BUT I SUSPECT HELL BELIEVES IN ME MORE THAN I BELIEVE IN MY PATH TO HEAVEN, DEAR MR. WOLFE.
STILL. IT WILL BE A WELCOME CHANGE OF SCENERY AFTER THIS GODFORSAKEN PLACE.

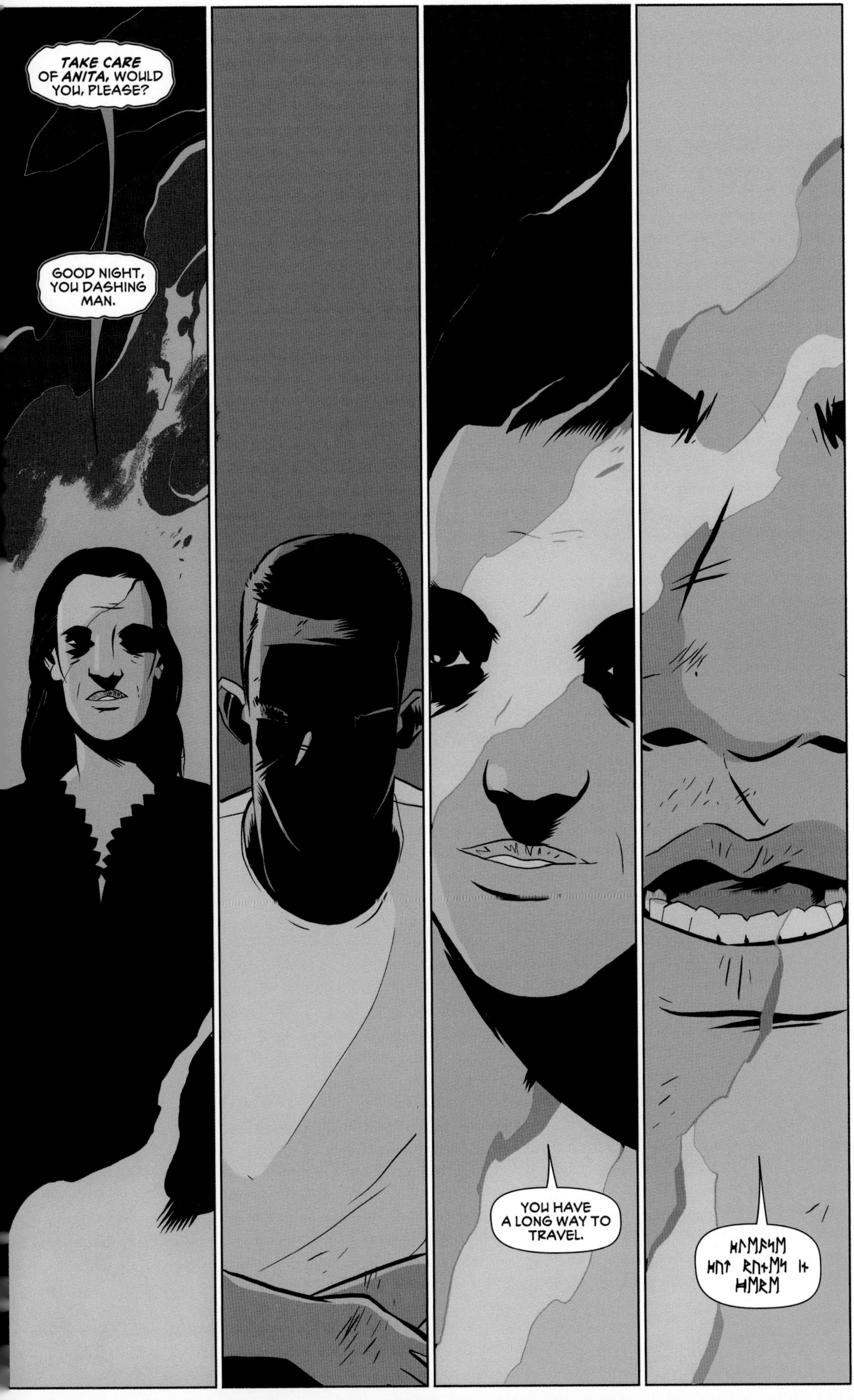
TAKE CARE OF ANITA, WOULD YOU, PLEASE?
GOOD NIGHT, YOU DASHING MAN.
YOU HAVE A LONG WAY TO TRAVEL.

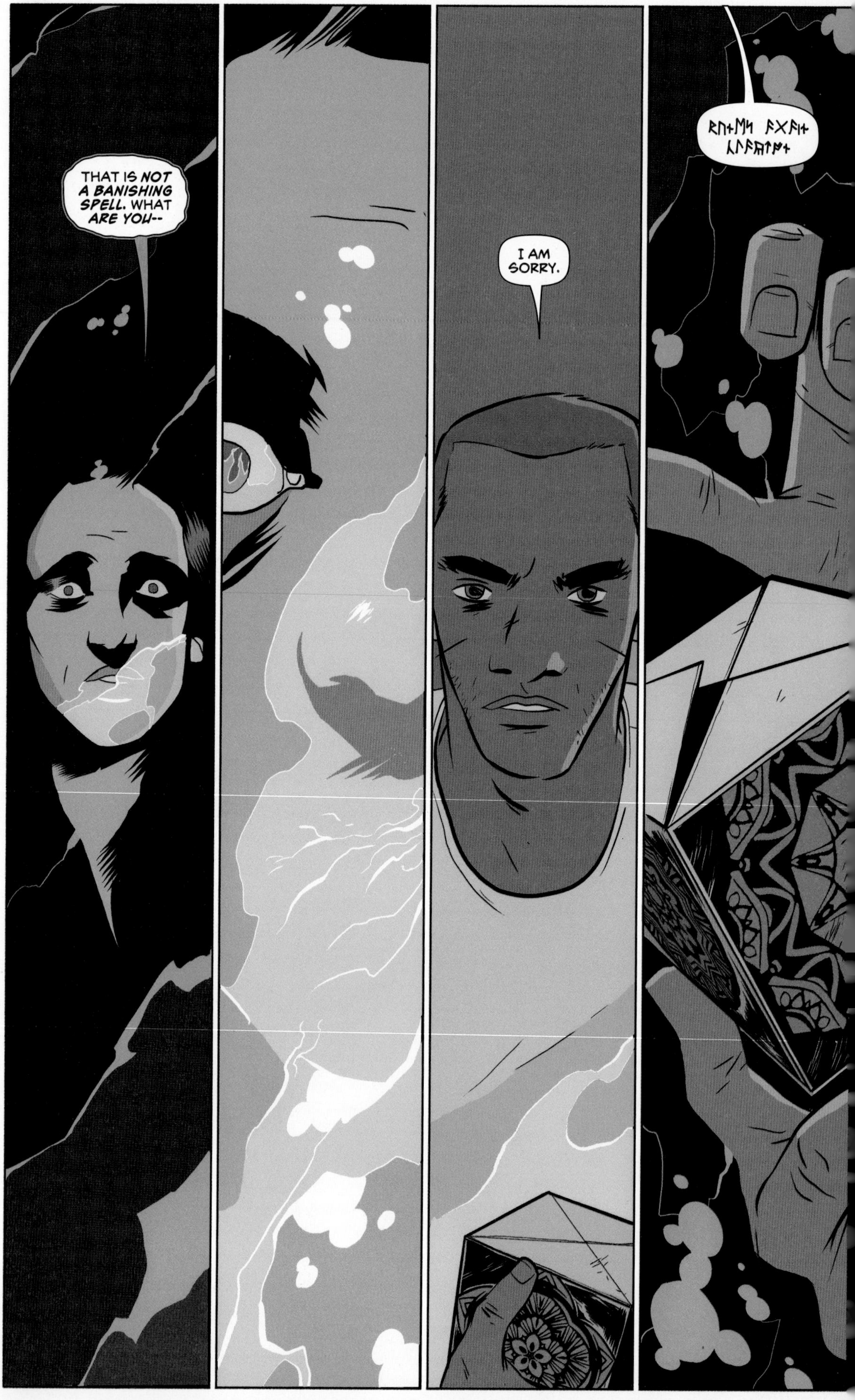
THAT IS NOT A BANISHING SPELL. WHAT ARE YOU--
I AM SORRY.

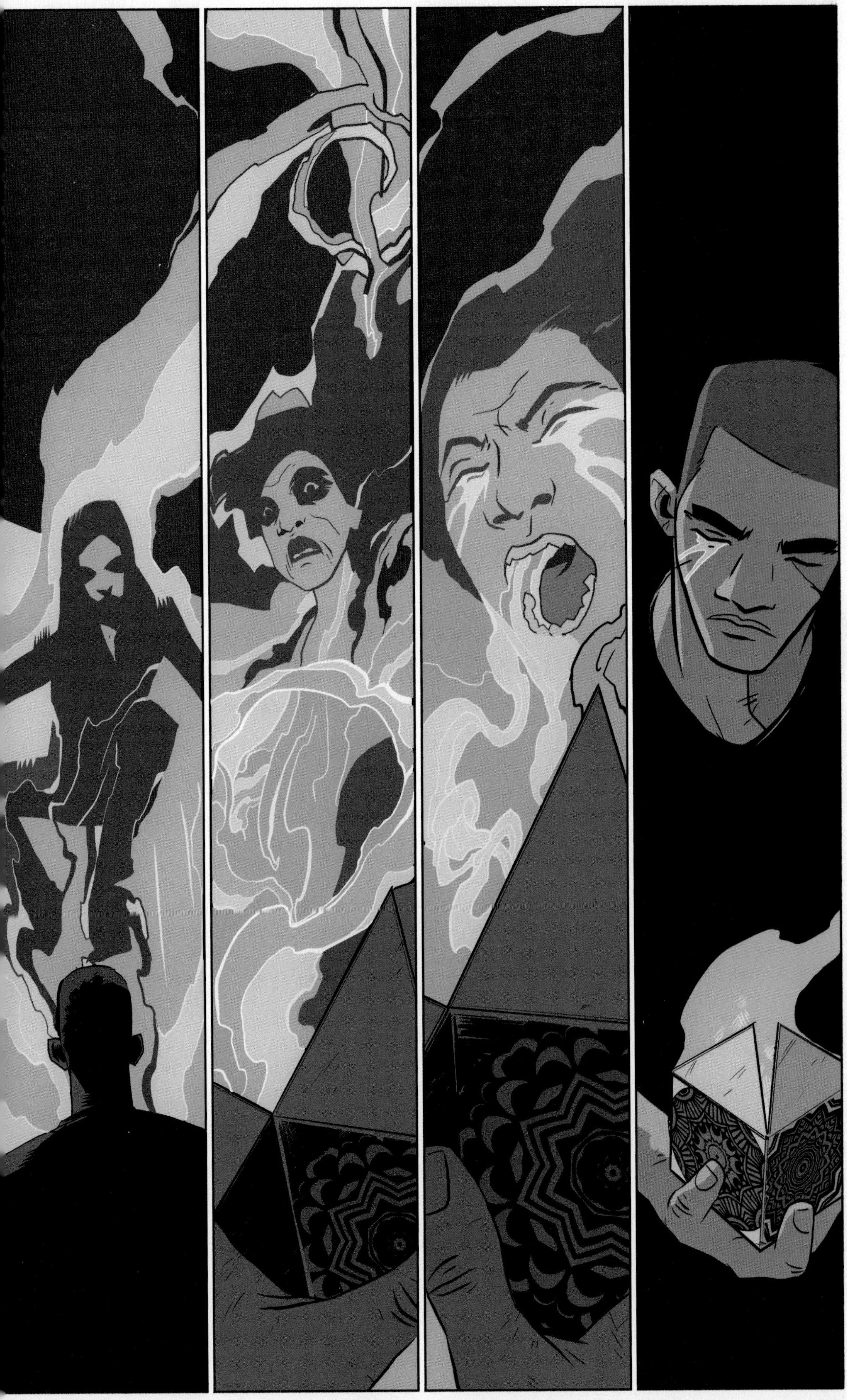

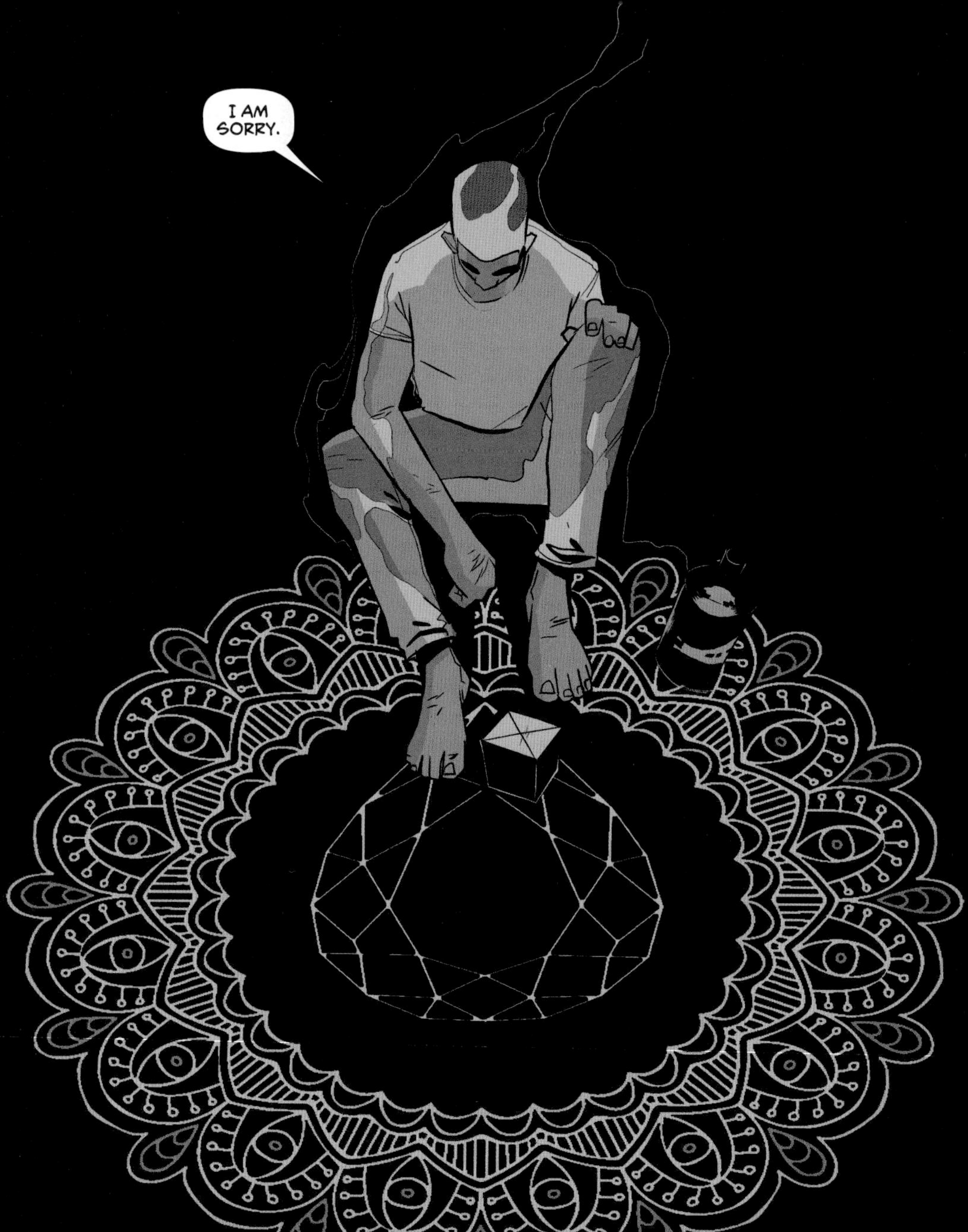
I AM SORRY.

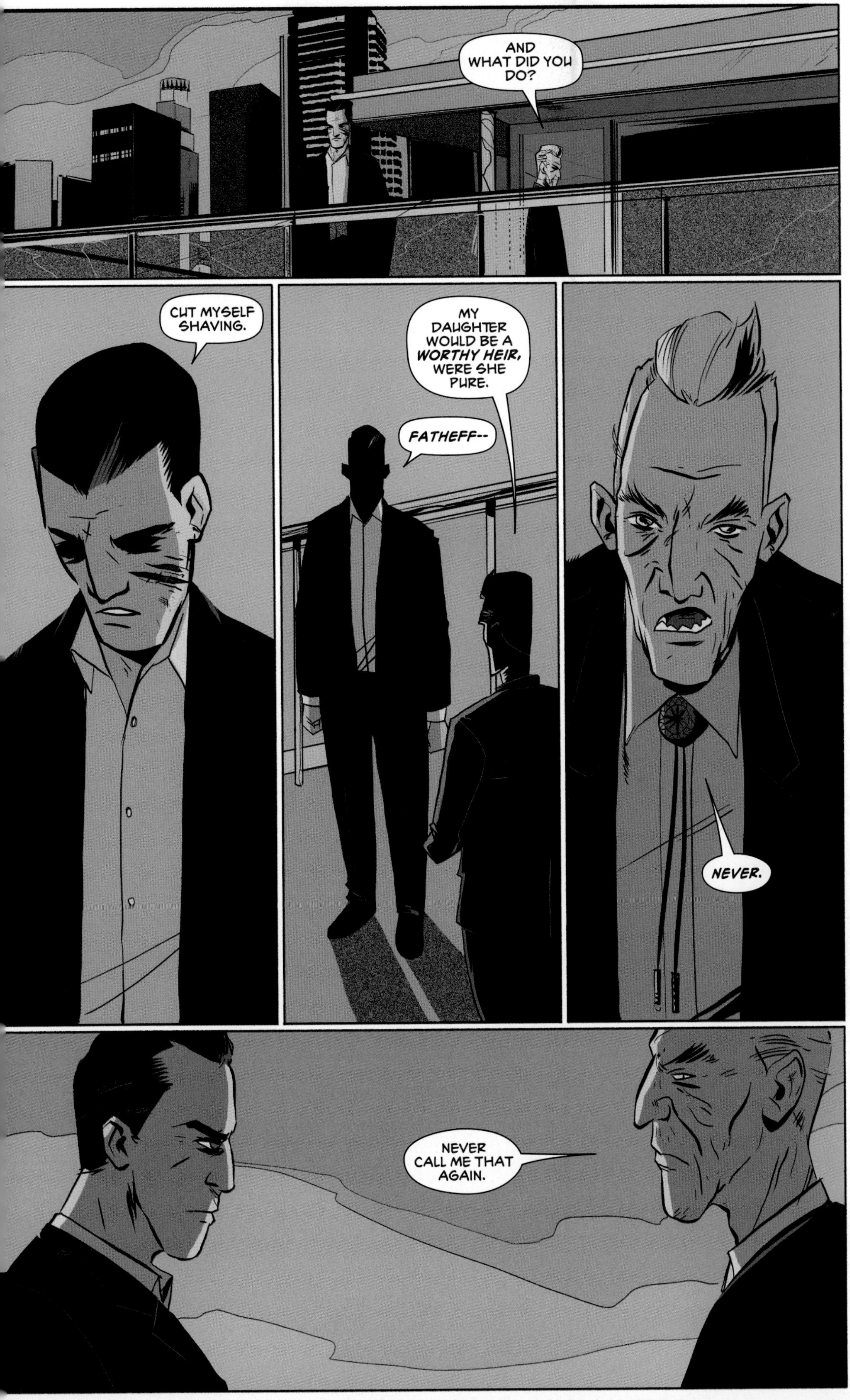
AND WHAT DID YOU DO?
CUT MYSELF SHAVING.
MY DAUGHTER WOULD BE A WORTHY HEIR, WERE SHE PURE.
FATHEFF--
NEVER.
NEVER CALL ME THAT AGAIN.

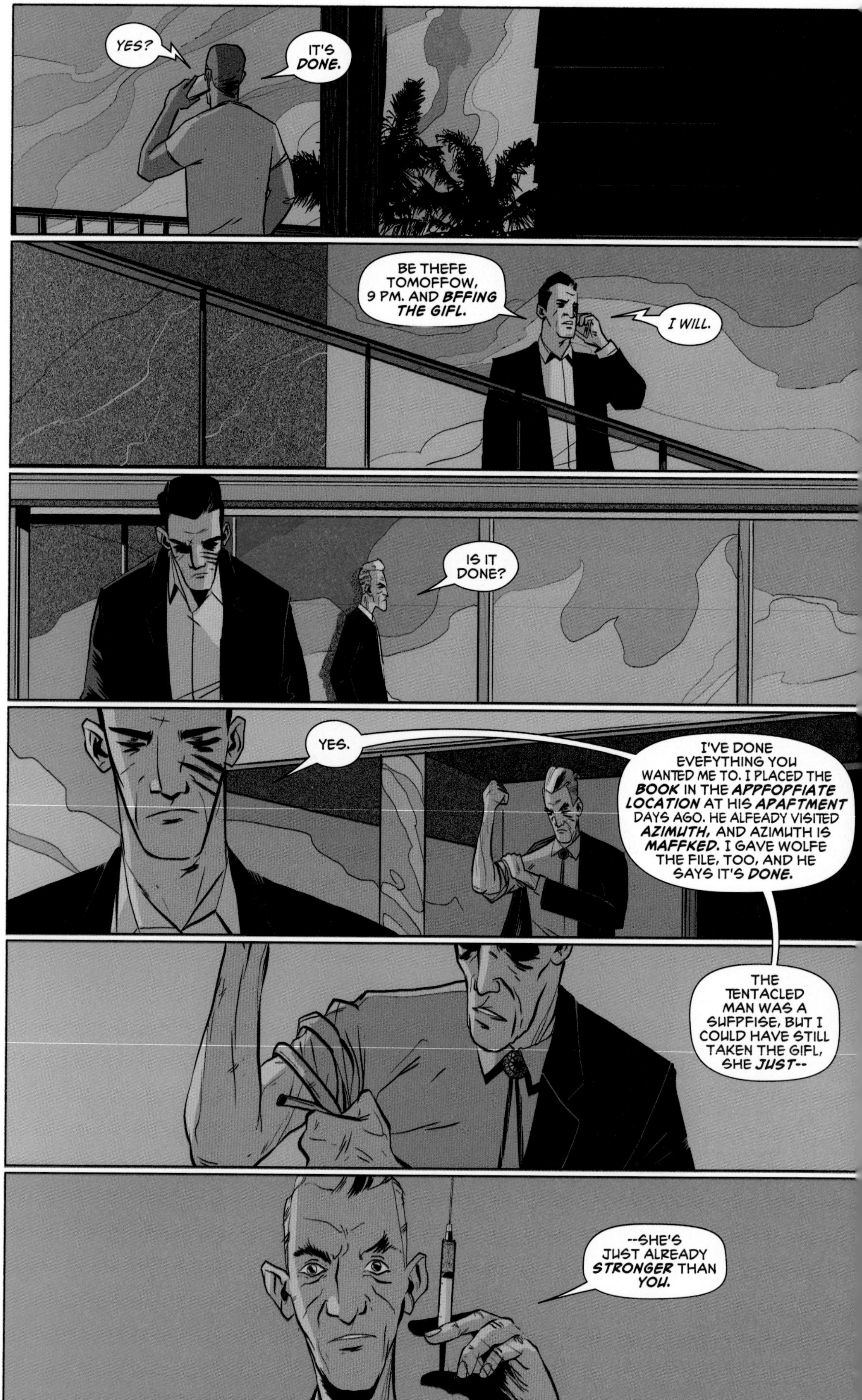
YES?
IT'S DONE.
BE THEFE TOMOFFOW, 9 PM. AND BFFING THE GIFL.
I WILL.
IS IT DONE?
YES.
I'VE DONE EVEFYTHING YOU WANTED ME TO. I PLACED THE BOOK IN THE APPFOPFIATE LOCATION AT HIS APAFTMENT DAYS AGO. HE ALFEADY VISITED AZIMUTH, AND AZIMUTH IS MAFFKED. I GAVE WOLFE THE FILE, TOO, AND HE SAYS IT'S DONE.
THE TENTACLED MAN WAS A SUFPFISE, BUT I COULD HAVE STILL TAKEN THE GIFL, SHE JUST--
--SHE'S JUST ALREADY STRONGER THAN YOU.

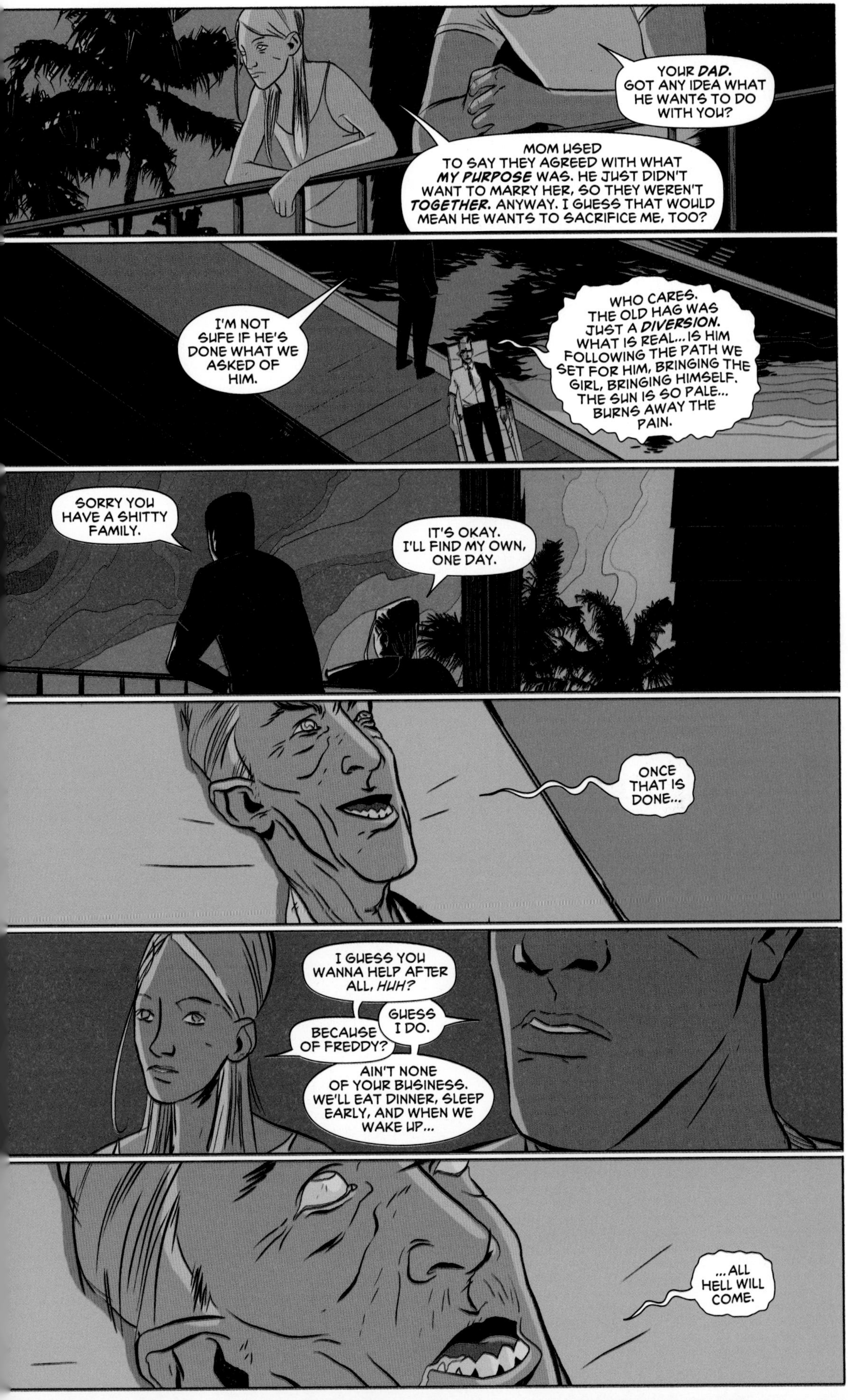

YOUR *DAD.* GOT ANY IDEA WHAT HE WANTS TO DO WITH YOU?
MOM USED TO SAY THEY AGREED WITH WHAT *MY PURPOSE* WAS. HE JUST DIDN'T WANT TO MARRY HER, SO THEY WEREN'T *TOGETHER.* ANYWAY. I GUESS THAT WOULD MEAN HE WANTS TO SACRIFICE ME, TOO?
I'M NOT SUFE IF HE'S DONE WHAT WE ASKED OF HIM.
WHO CARES. THE OLD HAG WAS JUST A *DIVERSION.* WHAT IS REAL... IS HIM FOLLOWING THE PATH WE SET FOR HIM, BRINGING THE GIRL, BRINGING HIMSELF. THE SUN IS SO PALE... BURNS AWAY THE PAIN.
SORRY YOU HAVE A SHITTY FAMILY.
IT'S OKAY. I'LL FIND MY OWN, ONE DAY.
ONCE THAT IS DONE...
I GUESS YOU WANNA HELP AFTER ALL, *HUH?*
GUESS I DO.
BECAUSE OF FREDDY?
AIN'T NONE OF YOUR BUSINESS. WE'LL EAT DINNER, SLEEP EARLY, AND WHEN WE WAKE UP...
...ALL HELL WILL COME.

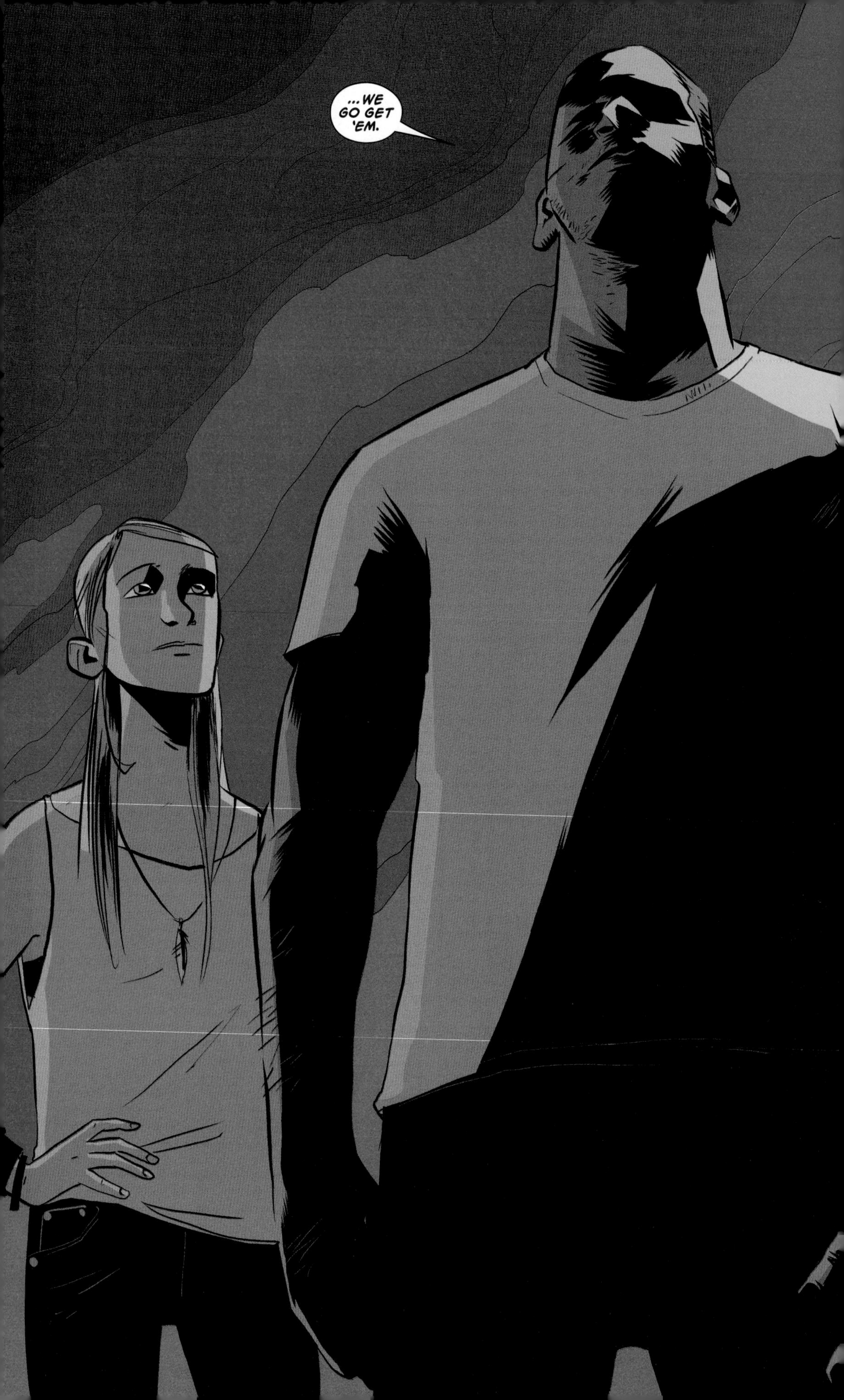
...WE GO GET 'EM.

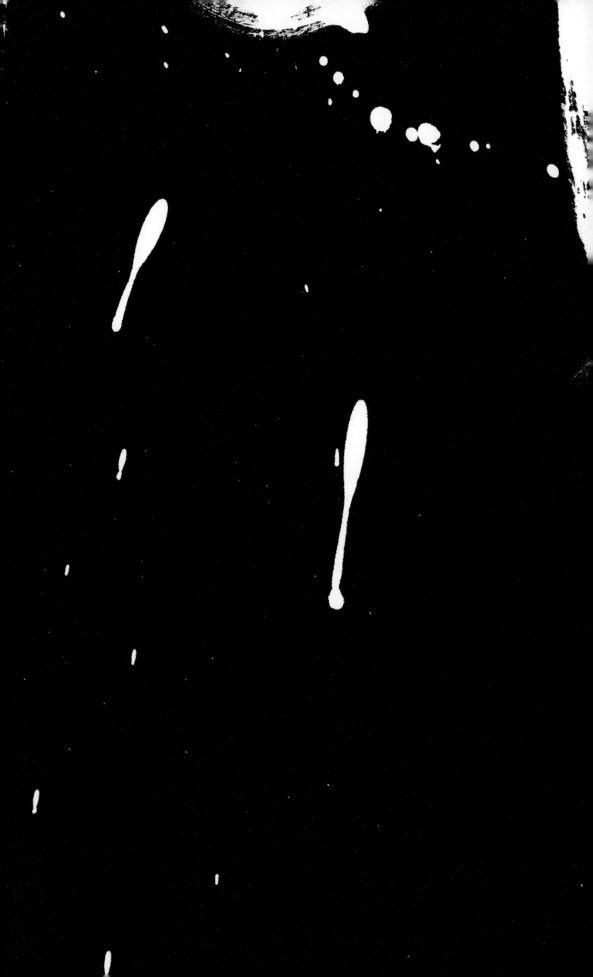

Chapter 4

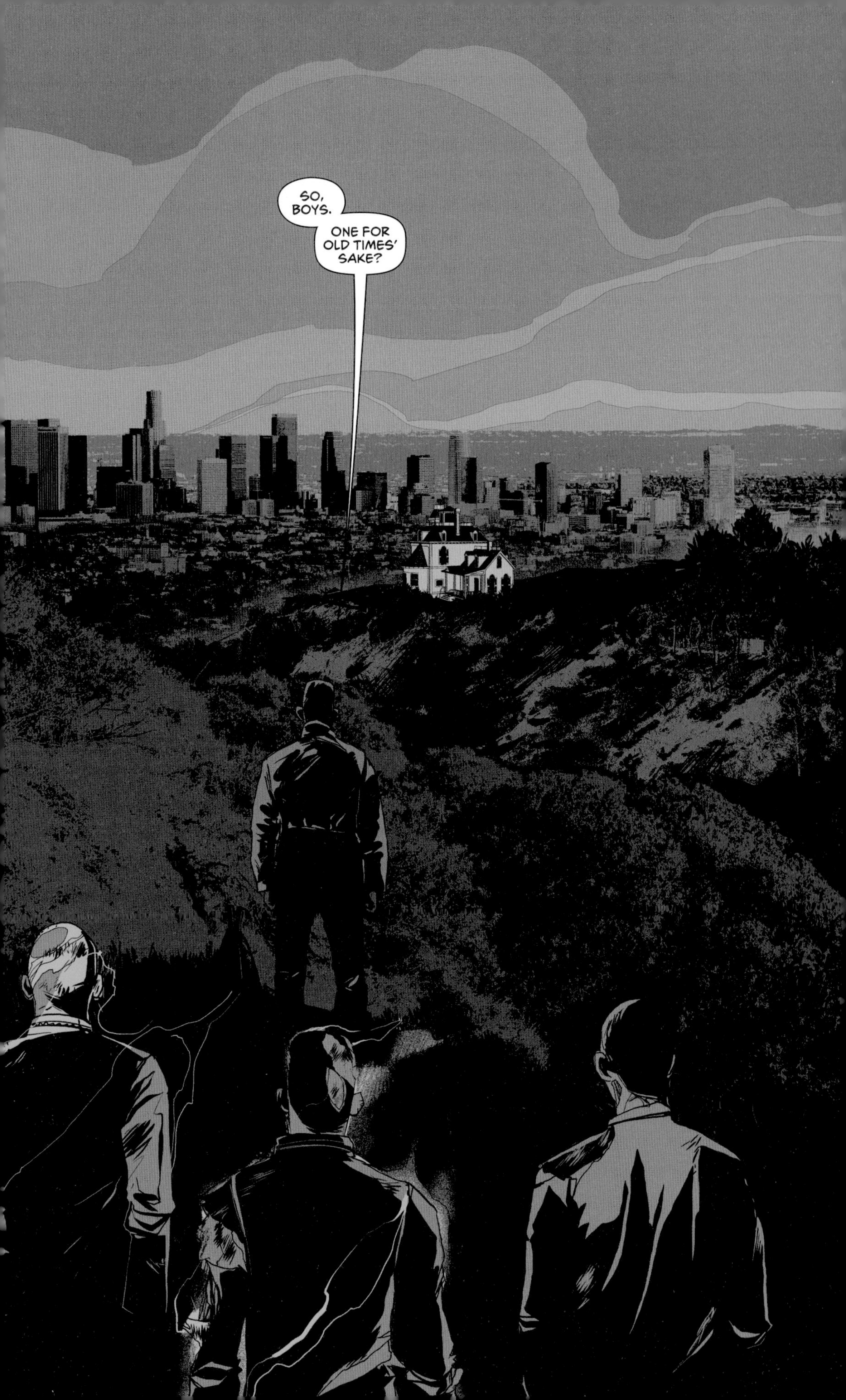
SO, BOYS.
ONE FOR OLD TIMES' SAKE?

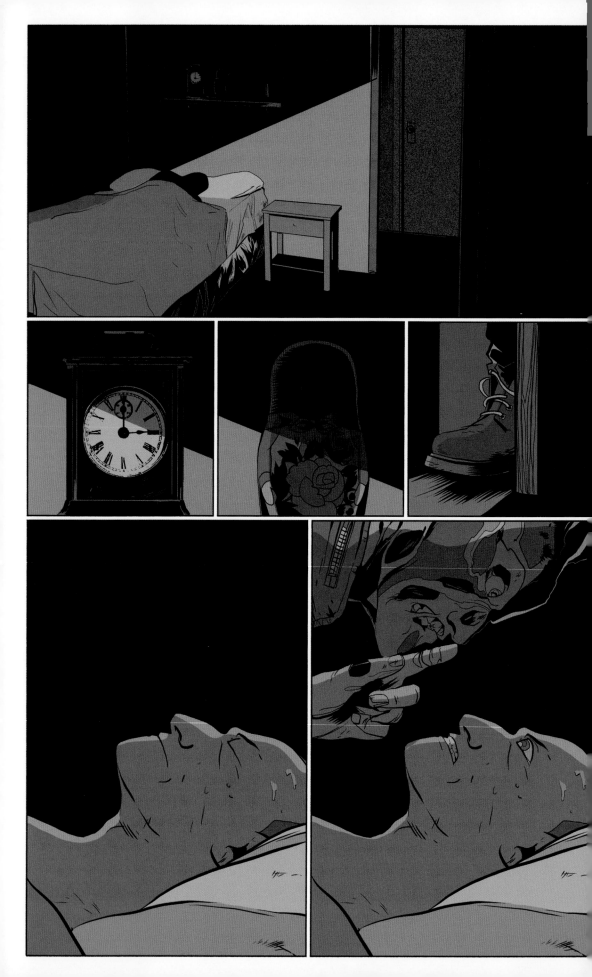

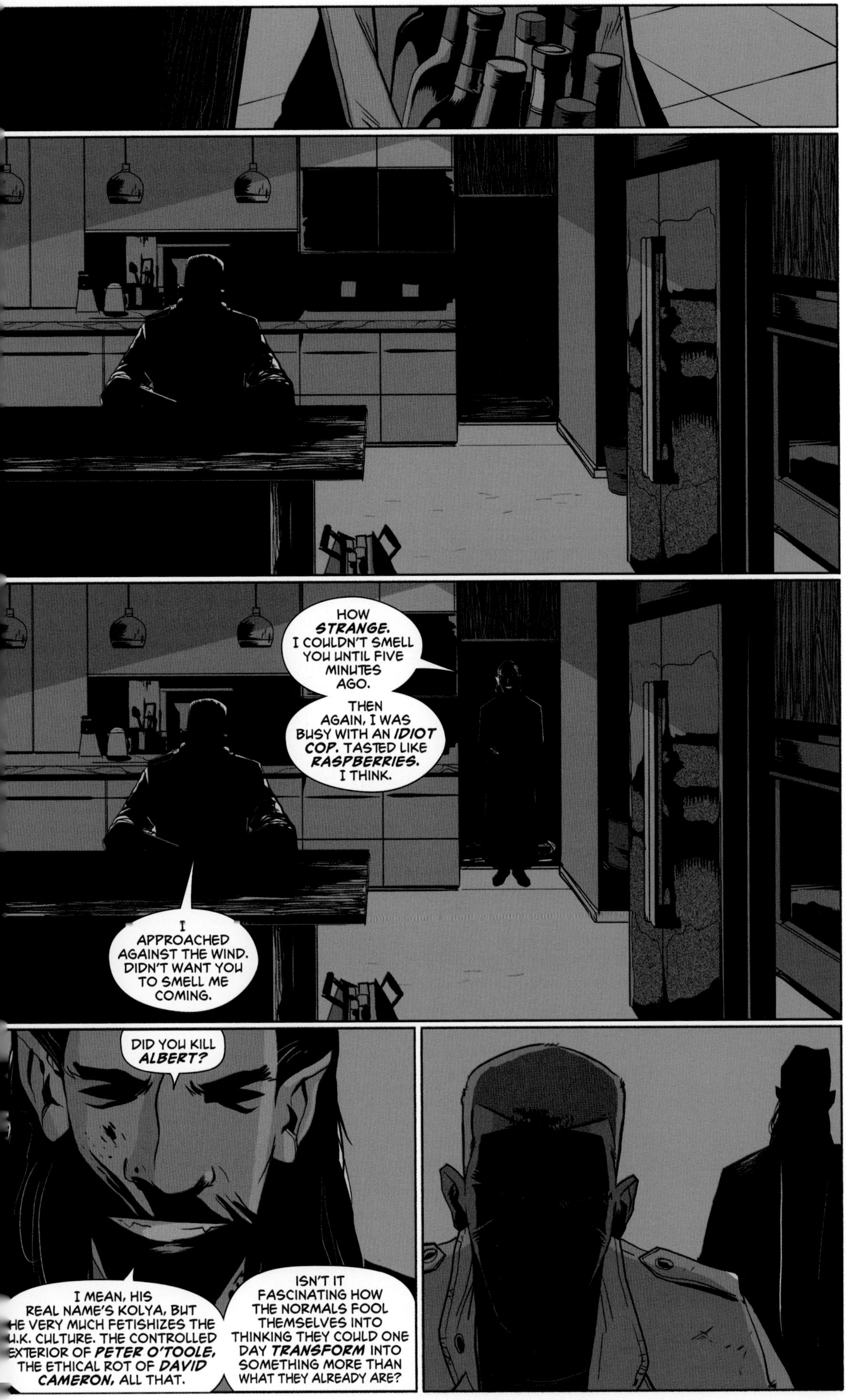
HOW STRANGE. I COULDN'T SMELL YOU UNTIL FIVE MINUTES AGO.
THEN AGAIN, I WAS BUSY WITH AN IDIOT COP. TASTED LIKE RASPBERRIES. I THINK.
I APPROACHED AGAINST THE WIND. DIDN'T WANT YOU TO SMELL ME COMING.
DID YOU KILL ALBERT?
I MEAN, HIS REAL NAME'S KOLYA, BUT HE VERY MUCH FETISHIZES THE U.K. CULTURE. THE CONTROLLED EXTERIOR OF PETER O'TOOLE, THE ETHICAL ROT OF DAVID CAMERON, ALL THAT.
ISN'T IT FASCINATING HOW THE NORMALS FOOL THEMSELVES INTO THINKING THEY COULD ONE DAY TRANSFORM INTO SOMETHING MORE THAN WHAT THEY ALREADY ARE?

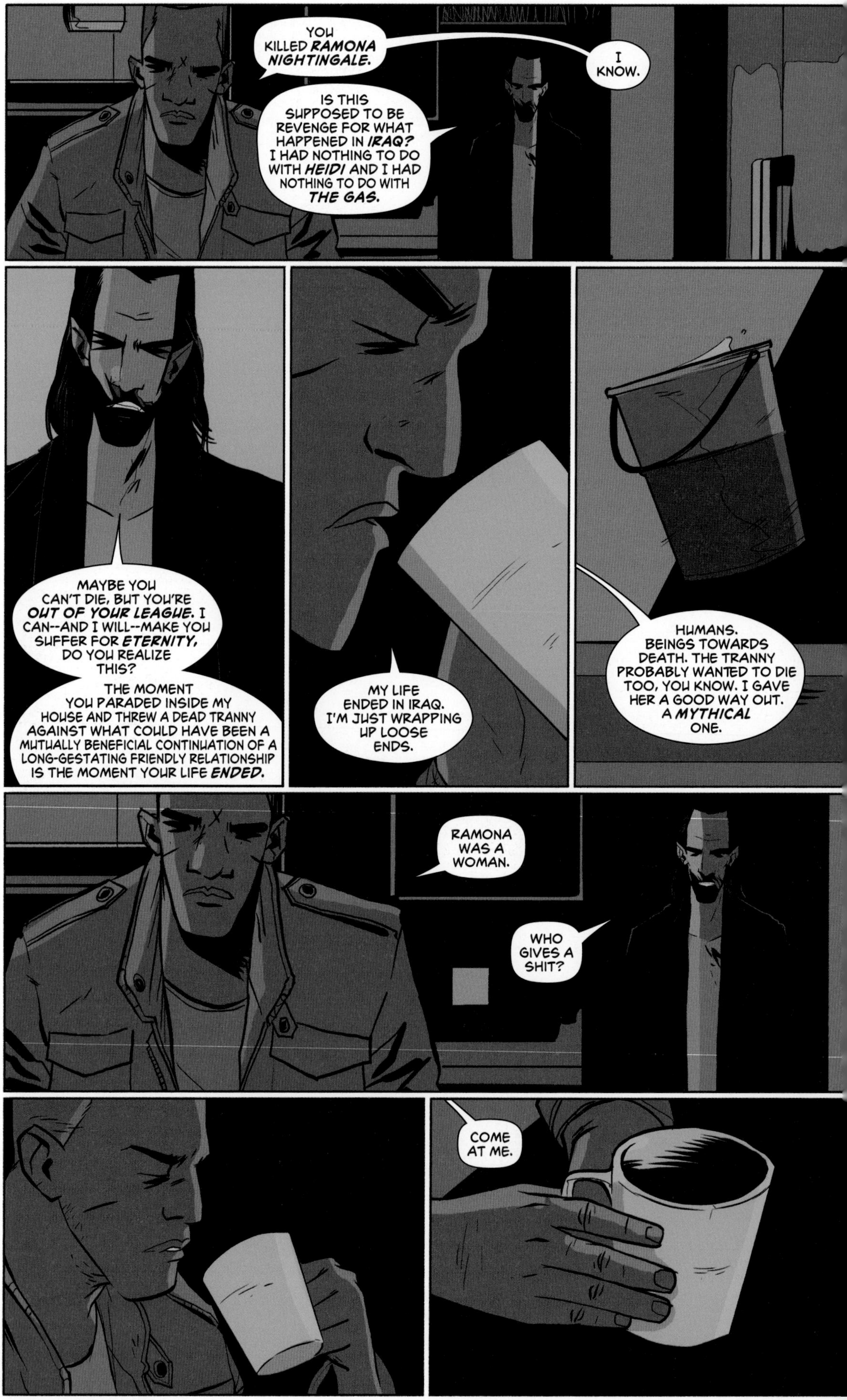
YOU KILLED RAMONA NIGHTINGALE.
I KNOW.
IS THIS SUPPOSED TO BE REVENGE FOR WHAT HAPPENED IN IRAQ? I HAD NOTHING TO DO WITH HEIDI AND I HAD NOTHING TO DO WITH THE GAS.
MAYBE YOU CAN'T DIE, BUT YOU'RE OUT OF YOUR LEAGUE. I CAN--AND I WILL--MAKE YOU SUFFER FOR ETERNITY, DO YOU REALIZE THIS?
THE MOMENT YOU PARADED INSIDE MY HOUSE AND THREW A DEAD TRANNY AGAINST WHAT COULD HAVE BEEN A MUTUALLY BENEFICIAL CONTINUATION OF A LONG-GESTATING FRIENDLY RELATIONSHIP IS THE MOMENT YOUR LIFE ENDED.
MY LIFE ENDED IN IRAQ. I'M JUST WRAPPING UP LOOSE ENDS.
HUMANS. BEINGS TOWARDS DEATH. THE TRANNY PROBABLY WANTED TO DIE TOO, YOU KNOW. I GAVE HER A GOOD WAY OUT. A MYTHICAL ONE.
RAMONA WAS A WOMAN.
WHO GIVES A SHIT?
COME AT ME.

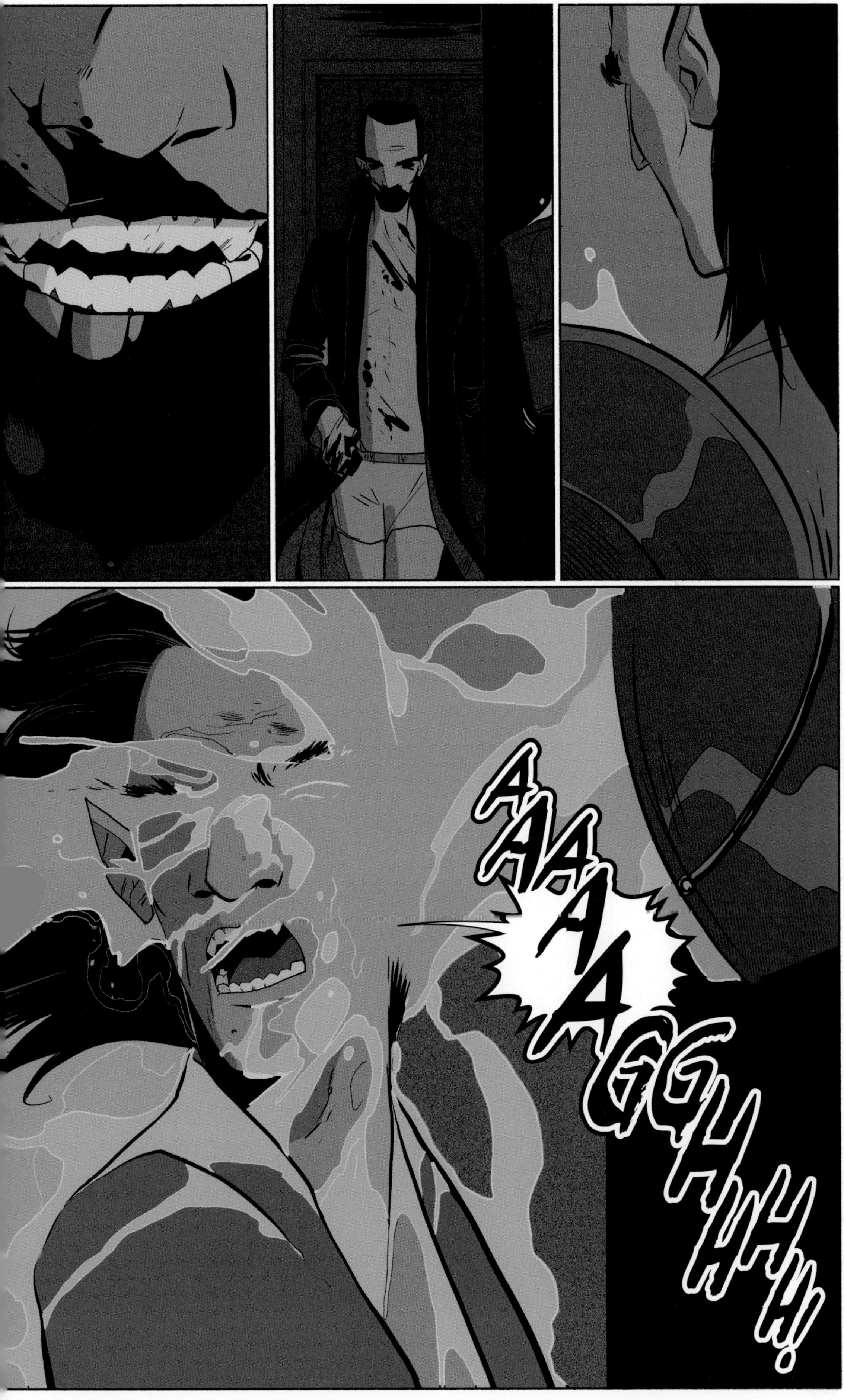
AAAAAGGHHHH!

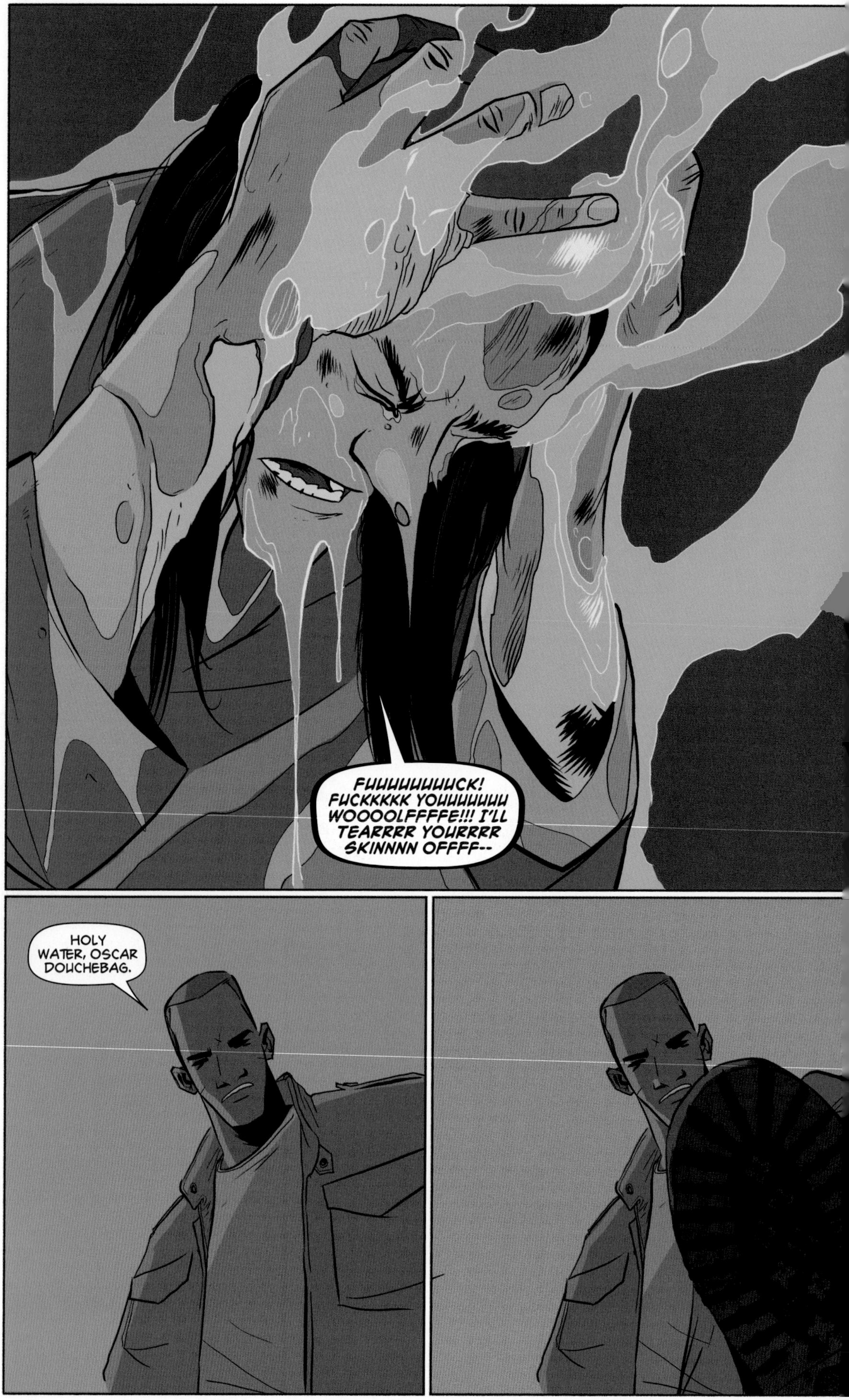
FUUUUUUUUCK! FUCKKKKK YOUUUUUUU WOOOOLFFFFE!!! I'LL TEARRRR YOURRRR SKINNNN OFFFF--
HOLY WATER, OSCAR DOUCHEBAG.

IDIOT. NO IDEA WHAT YOU WALKED INTO.

YOU'LL LEARN SOON ENOUGH.

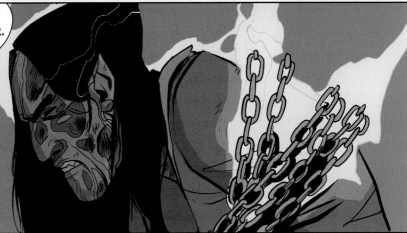

I HOPED THAT WHAT HAPPENED DURING THE WAR TAUGHT YOU A THING OR TWO ABOUT *SURVIVAL*. I MEAN, YOU KNEW AT THE TIME, AND YOU DIDN'T STOP US.

AND NOW ALL OF A SUDDEN YOU'RE *MR. FIXIT L.A. COMMUNITY STANDUP GUY?*

YOU STUPID FUCK. I'M AN APEX PREDATOR. THIS IS MY NATURE.

WHO SENT YOU? *GIBSON* SENT YOU? OR *BACHMAN?*

SYNCHRONICITY SENT ME. *FLOWERS, CYCLES, APOCALYPSE...* ALL AROUND ME ALL DAY LONG. REMINDERS OF SOMETHIN'.

I KNOW THERE'S A TRAP WAITING. HAD NO IDEA Y'ALL WORKING TOGETHER, THOUGH.

NOT AS FUNNY AS THE LOOK ON YOUR FACE WHEN THEY'RE DONE WITH YOU.

THEY'VE BEEN TALKING WITH HEIDI, YOU KNOW? YOU FUCKING IDIOT. YOU HAVE NO IDEA HOW DEEP IN YOU ARE.

ATLANTIS WILL FALL AGAIN AND YOU'LL BE SCREAMING FOR ETERNITY.

ATLANTIS. *HMH.* INTERESTING.

THERE'S A THING I DON'T TELL PEOPLE. *A TRADE SECRET.* YOU WANNA KNOW WHAT IT IS?

I DON'T FUCKING CARE.

OKAY, I'LL TELL YOU.

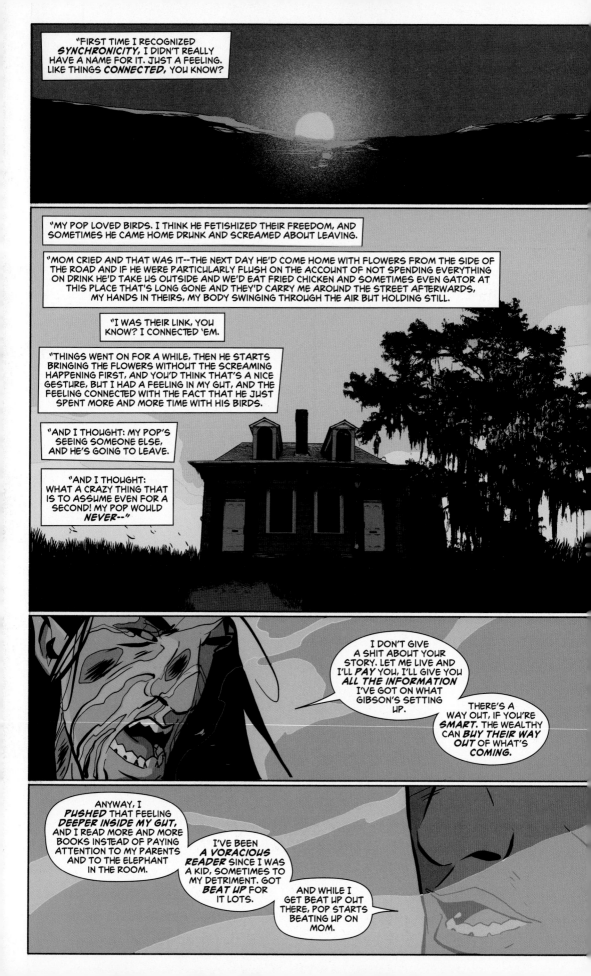

"FIRST TIME I RECOGNIZED *SYNCHRONICITY*, I DIDN'T REALLY HAVE A NAME FOR IT. JUST A FEELING. LIKE THINGS *CONNECTED*, YOU KNOW?

"MY POP LOVED BIRDS. I THINK HE FETISHIZED THEIR FREEDOM, AND SOMETIMES HE CAME HOME DRUNK AND SCREAMED ABOUT LEAVING.

"MOM CRIED AND THAT WAS IT--THE NEXT DAY HE'D COME HOME WITH FLOWERS FROM THE SIDE OF THE ROAD AND IF HE WERE PARTICULARLY FLUSH ON THE ACCOUNT OF NOT SPENDING EVERYTHING ON DRINK HE'D TAKE US OUTSIDE AND WE'D EAT FRIED CHICKEN AND SOMETIMES EVEN GATOR AT THIS PLACE THAT'S LONG GONE AND THEY'D CARRY ME AROUND THE STREET AFTERWARDS, MY HANDS IN THEIRS, MY BODY SWINGING THROUGH THE AIR BUT HOLDING STILL.

"I WAS THEIR LINK, YOU KNOW? I CONNECTED 'EM.

"THINGS WENT ON FOR A WHILE, THEN HE STARTS BRINGING THE FLOWERS WITHOUT THE SCREAMING HAPPENING FIRST, AND YOU'D THINK THAT'S A NICE GESTURE, BUT I HAD A FEELING IN MY GUT, AND THE FEELING CONNECTED WITH THE FACT THAT HE JUST SPENT MORE AND MORE TIME WITH HIS BIRDS.

"AND I THOUGHT: MY POP'S SEEING SOMEONE ELSE, AND HE'S GOING TO LEAVE.

"AND I THOUGHT: WHAT A CRAZY THING THAT IS TO ASSUME EVEN FOR A SECOND! MY POP WOULD *NEVER*--"

I DON'T GIVE A SHIT ABOUT YOUR STORY. LET ME LIVE AND I'LL *PAY* YOU, I'LL GIVE YOU *ALL THE INFORMATION* I'VE GOT ON WHAT GIBSON'S SETTING UP.

THERE'S A WAY OUT, IF YOU'RE *SMART*. THE WEALTHY CAN *BUY THEIR WAY OUT* OF WHAT'S COMING.

ANYWAY, I *PUSHED* THAT FEELING *DEEPER INSIDE MY GUT*, AND I READ MORE AND MORE BOOKS INSTEAD OF PAYING ATTENTION TO MY PARENTS AND TO THE ELEPHANT IN THE ROOM.

I'VE BEEN *A VORACIOUS READER* SINCE I WAS A KID, SOMETIMES TO MY DETRIMENT. GOT *BEAT UP* FOR IT LOTS.

AND WHILE I GET BEAT UP OUT THERE, POP STARTS BEATING UP ON MOM.

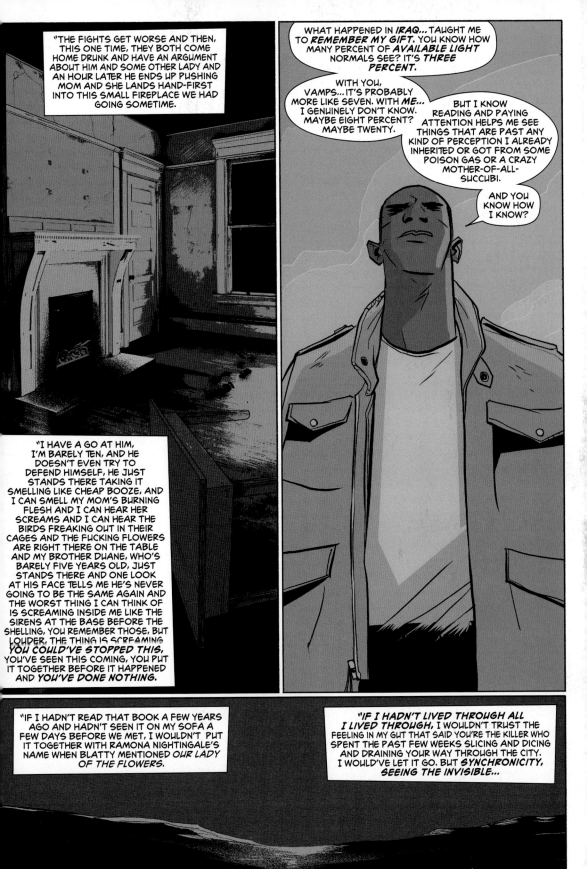

"THE FIGHTS GET WORSE AND THEN, THIS ONE TIME, THEY BOTH COME HOME DRUNK AND HAVE AN ARGUMENT ABOUT HIM AND SOME OTHER LADY AND AN HOUR LATER HE ENDS UP PUSHING MOM AND SHE LANDS HAND-FIRST INTO THIS SMALL FIREPLACE WE HAD GOING SOMETIME.

WHAT HAPPENED IN *IRAQ*... TAUGHT ME TO *REMEMBER MY GIFT*. YOU KNOW HOW MANY PERCENT OF *AVAILABLE LIGHT* NORMALS SEE? IT'S *THREE PERCENT*.

WITH YOU, VAMPS... IT'S PROBABLY MORE LIKE SEVEN. WITH *ME*... I GENUINELY DON'T KNOW. MAYBE EIGHT PERCENT? MAYBE TWENTY.

BUT I KNOW READING AND PAYING ATTENTION HELPS ME SEE THINGS THAT ARE PAST ANY KIND OF PERCEPTION I ALREADY INHERITED OR GOT FROM SOME POISON GAS OR A CRAZY MOTHER-OF-ALL-SUCCUBI.

AND YOU KNOW HOW I KNOW?

"I HAVE A GO AT HIM, I'M BARELY TEN, AND HE DOESN'T EVEN TRY TO DEFEND HIMSELF, HE JUST STANDS THERE TAKING IT SMELLING LIKE CHEAP BOOZE, AND I CAN SMELL MY MOM'S BURNING FLESH AND I CAN HEAR HER SCREAMS AND I CAN HEAR THE BIRDS FREAKING OUT IN THEIR CAGES AND THE FUCKING FLOWERS ARE RIGHT THERE ON THE TABLE AND MY BROTHER DUANE, WHO'S BARELY FIVE YEARS OLD, JUST STANDS THERE AND ONE LOOK AT HIS FACE TELLS ME HE'S NEVER GOING TO BE THE SAME AGAIN AND THE WORST THING I CAN THINK OF IS SCREAMING INSIDE ME LIKE THE SIRENS AT THE BASE BEFORE THE SHELLING, YOU REMEMBER THOSE, BUT LOUDER, THE THING IS SCREAMING *YOU COULD'VE STOPPED THIS*, YOU'VE SEEN THIS COMING, YOU PUT IT TOGETHER BEFORE IT HAPPENED AND *YOU'VE DONE NOTHING*.

"IF I HADN'T READ THAT BOOK A FEW YEARS AGO AND HADN'T SEEN IT ON MY SOFA A FEW DAYS BEFORE WE MET, I WOULDN'T PUT IT TOGETHER WITH RAMONA NIGHTINGALE'S NAME WHEN BLATTY MENTIONED *OUR LADY OF THE FLOWERS*.

"*IF I HADN'T LIVED THROUGH ALL I LIVED THROUGH*, I WOULDN'T TRUST THE FEELING IN MY GUT THAT SAID YOU'RE THE KILLER WHO SPENT THE PAST FEW WEEKS SLICING AND DICING AND DRAINING YOUR WAY THROUGH THE CITY. I WOULD'VE LET IT GO. BUT *SYNCHRONICITY, SEEING THE INVISIBLE*...

"...THAT'S WHAT *MAGIC* REALLY IS."

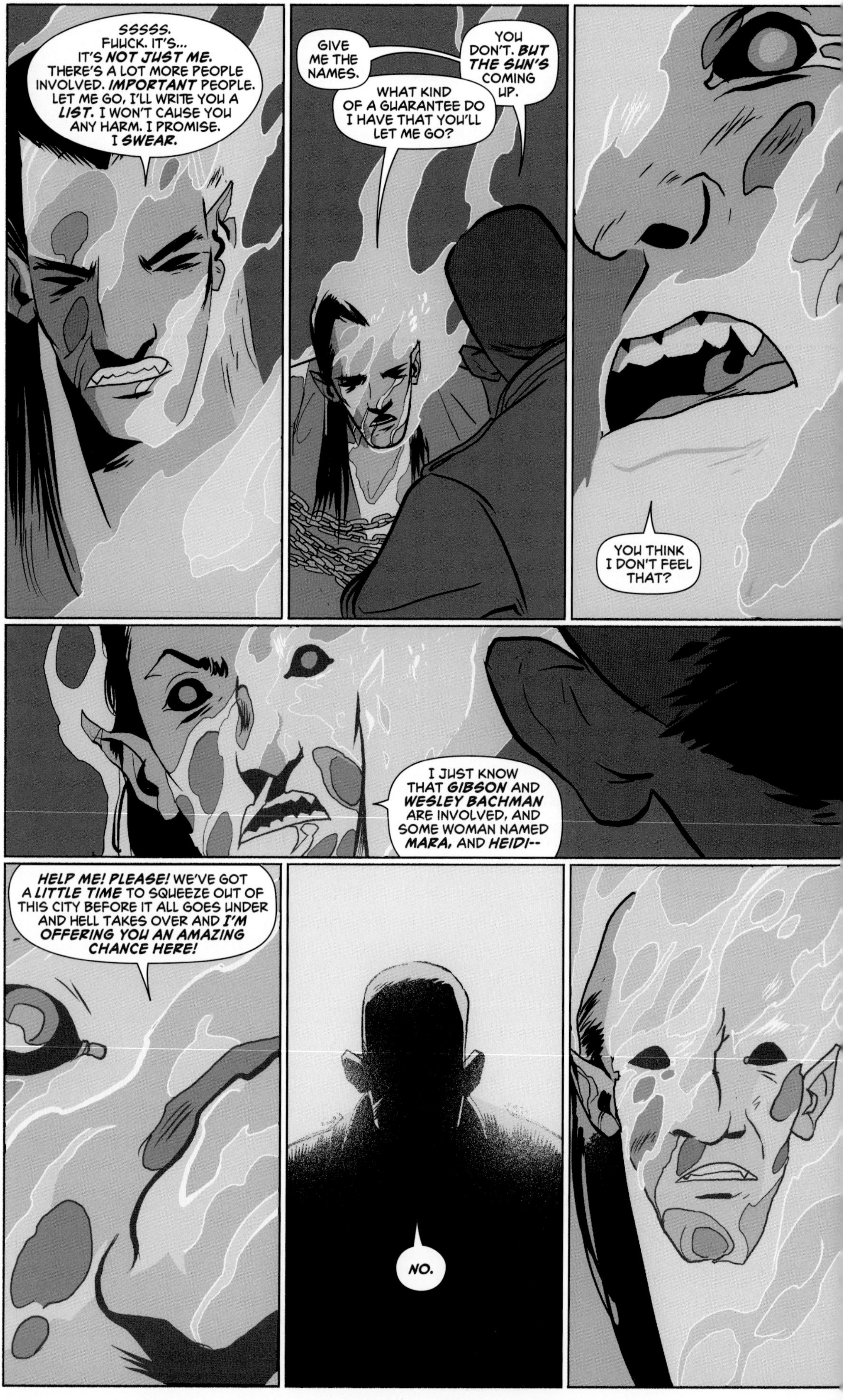
SSSSS. FUUCK. IT'S... IT'S NOT JUST ME. THERE'S A LOT MORE PEOPLE INVOLVED. IMPORTANT PEOPLE. LET ME GO, I'LL WRITE YOU A LIST. I WON'T CAUSE YOU ANY HARM. I PROMISE. I SWEAR.
GIVE ME THE NAMES.
WHAT KIND OF A GUARANTEE DO I HAVE THAT YOU'LL LET ME GO?
YOU DON'T. BUT THE SUN'S COMING UP.
YOU THINK I DON'T FEEL THAT?
I JUST KNOW THAT GIBSON AND WESLEY BACHMAN ARE INVOLVED, AND SOME WOMAN NAMED MARA, AND HEIDI--
HELP ME! PLEASE! WE'VE GOT A LITTLE TIME TO SQUEEZE OUT OF THIS CITY BEFORE IT ALL GOES UNDER AND HELL TAKES OVER AND I'M OFFERING YOU AN AMAZING CHANCE HERE!
NO.

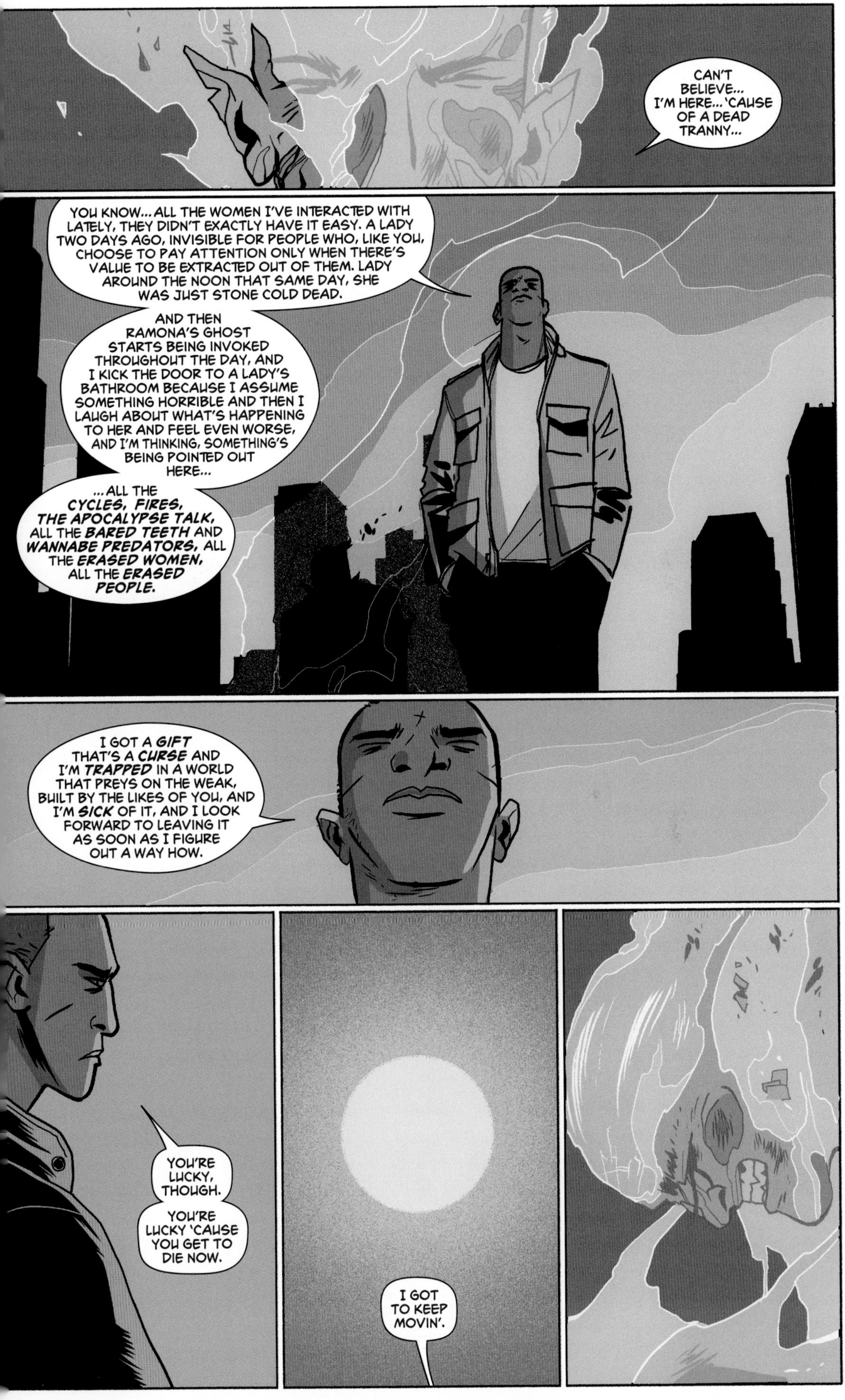
CAN'T BELIEVE... I'M HERE... 'CAUSE OF A DEAD TRANNY...
YOU KNOW... ALL THE WOMEN I'VE INTERACTED WITH LATELY, THEY DIDN'T EXACTLY HAVE IT EASY. A LADY TWO DAYS AGO, INVISIBLE FOR PEOPLE WHO, LIKE YOU, CHOOSE TO PAY ATTENTION ONLY WHEN THERE'S VALUE TO BE EXTRACTED OUT OF THEM. LADY AROUND THE NOON THAT SAME DAY, SHE WAS JUST STONE COLD DEAD.
AND THEN RAMONA'S GHOST STARTS BEING INVOKED THROUGHOUT THE DAY, AND I KICK THE DOOR TO A LADY'S BATHROOM BECAUSE I ASSUME SOMETHING HORRIBLE AND THEN I LAUGH ABOUT WHAT'S HAPPENING TO HER AND FEEL EVEN WORSE, AND I'M THINKING, SOMETHING'S BEING POINTED OUT HERE...
...ALL THE *CYCLES, FIRES, THE APOCALYPSE TALK,* ALL THE *BARED TEETH* AND *WANNABE PREDATORS,* ALL THE *ERASED WOMEN,* ALL THE *ERASED PEOPLE.*
I GOT A *GIFT* THAT'S A *CURSE* AND I'M *TRAPPED* IN A WORLD THAT PREYS ON THE WEAK, BUILT BY THE LIKES OF YOU, AND I'M *SICK* OF IT, AND I LOOK FORWARD TO LEAVING IT AS SOON AS I FIGURE OUT A WAY HOW.
YOU'RE LUCKY, THOUGH.
YOU'RE LUCKY 'CAUSE YOU GET TO DIE NOW.
I GOT TO KEEP MOVIN'.

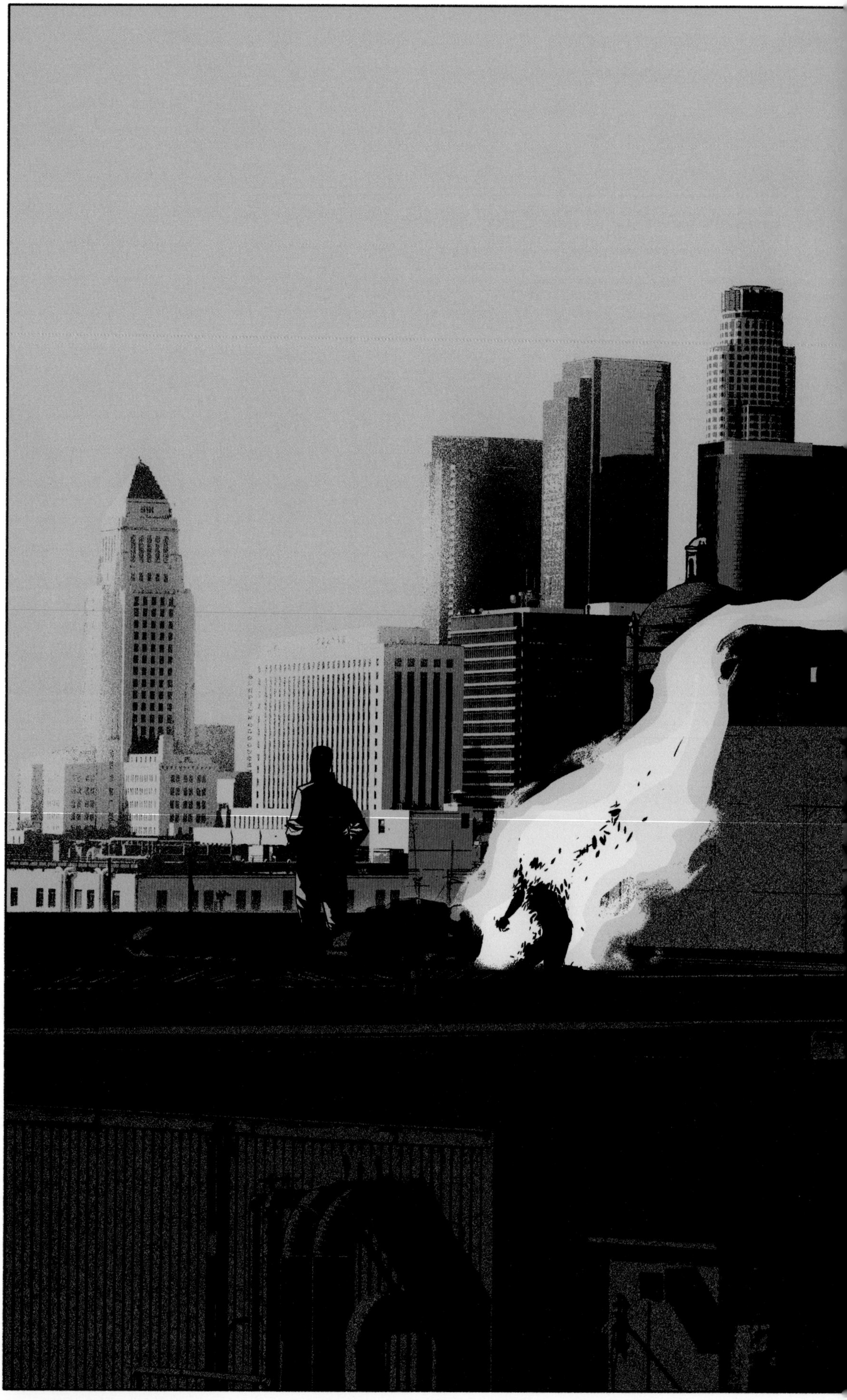

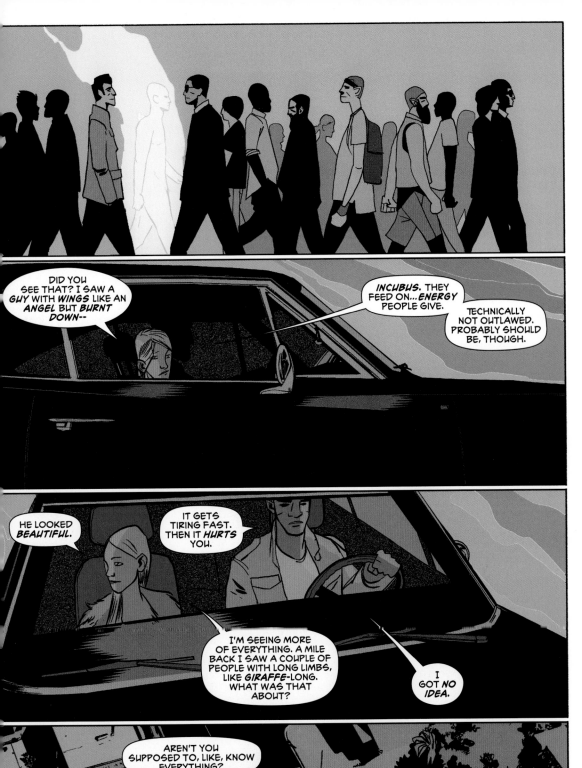

DID YOU SEE THAT? I SAW A GUY WITH *WINGS* LIKE AN ANGEL BUT *BURNT DOWN*--

INCUBUS. THEY FEED ON... *ENERGY* PEOPLE GIVE.

TECHNICALLY NOT OUTLAWED. PROBABLY SHOULD BE, THOUGH.

HE LOOKED *BEAUTIFUL*.

IT GETS TIRING FAST. THEN IT *HURTS* YOU.

I'M SEEING MORE OF EVERYTHING. A MILE BACK I SAW A COUPLE OF PEOPLE WITH LONG LIMBS, LIKE *GIRAFFE*-LONG. WHAT WAS THAT ABOUT?

I GOT *NO* IDEA.

AREN'T YOU SUPPOSED TO, LIKE, KNOW EVERYTHING?

NOBODY KNOWS ANYTHING. FIRST RULE OF HOLLYWOOD AND FIRST RULE OF THE WORLD. PEOPLE JUST CONVINCE THEMSELVES THEY DO, TO VARIOUS DEGREES OF SUCCESS.

BUT REALLY... NOBODY KNOWS ANYTHING.

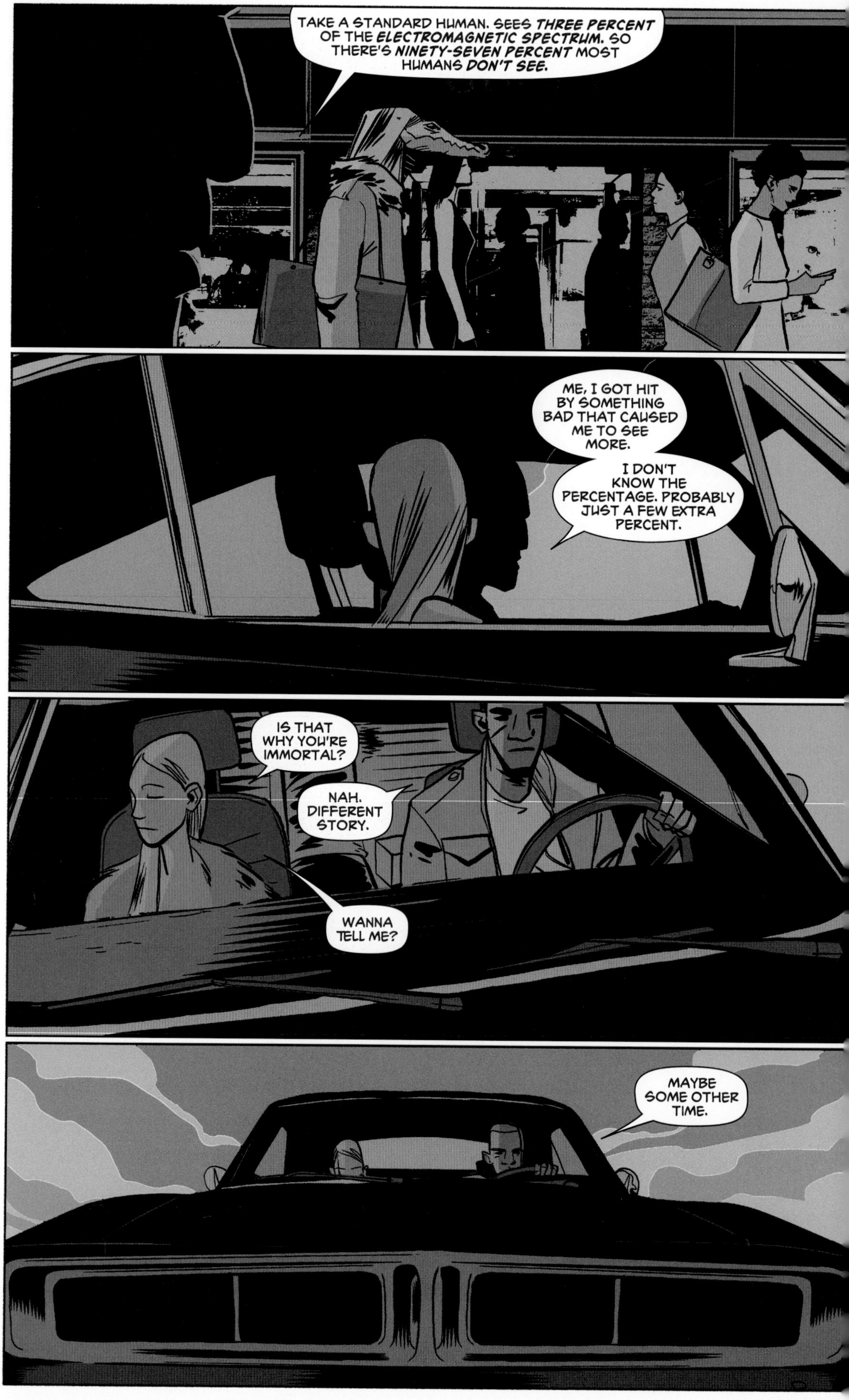
TAKE A STANDARD HUMAN. SEES *THREE PERCENT* OF THE *ELECTROMAGNETIC SPECTRUM.* SO THERE'S *NINETY-SEVEN PERCENT* MOST HUMANS *DON'T SEE.*
ME, I GOT HIT BY SOMETHING BAD THAT CAUSED ME TO SEE MORE.
I DON'T KNOW THE PERCENTAGE. PROBABLY JUST A FEW EXTRA PERCENT.
IS THAT WHY YOU'RE IMMORTAL?
NAH. DIFFERENT STORY.
WANNA TELL ME?
MAYBE SOME OTHER TIME.

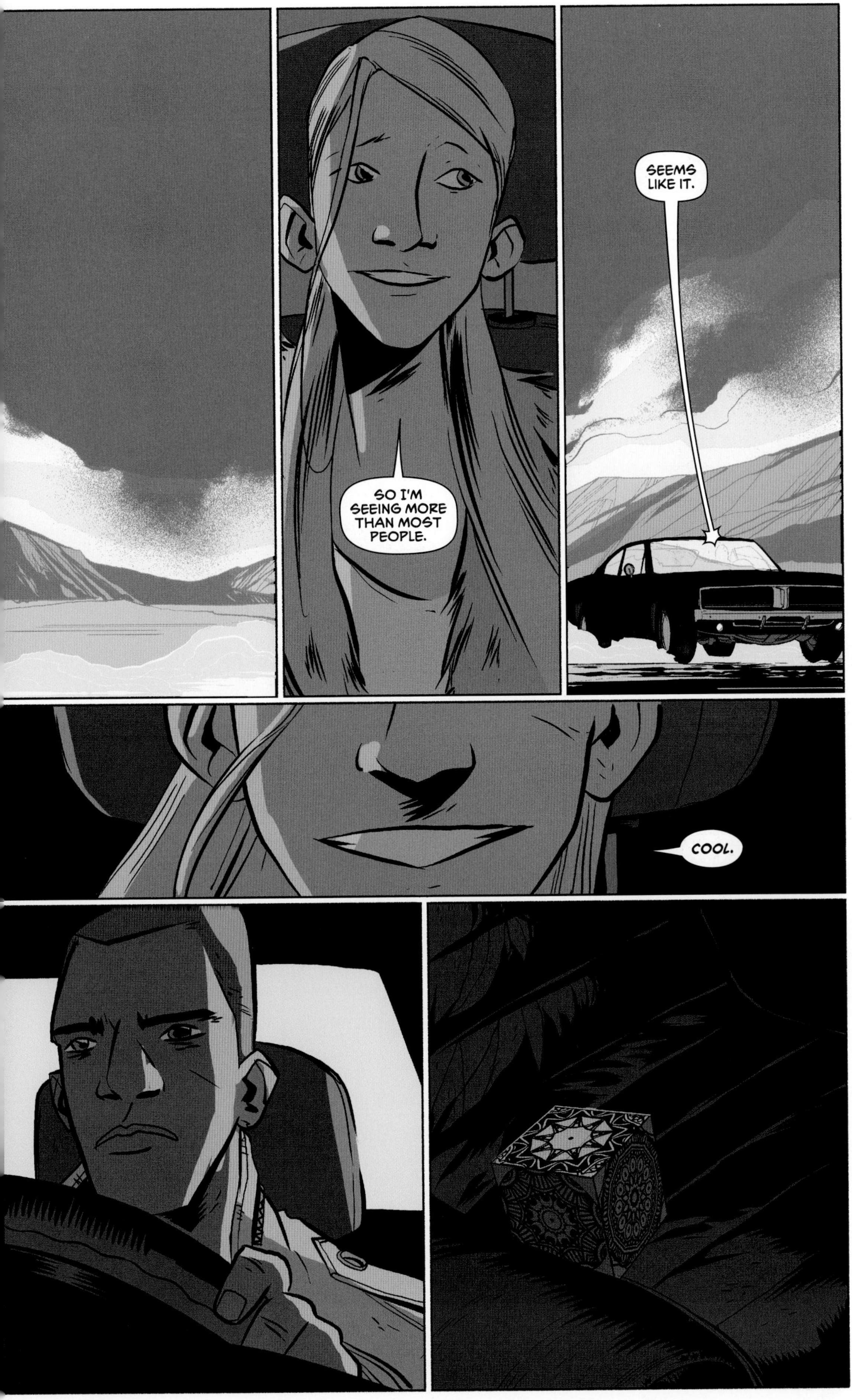
SO I'M SEEING MORE THAN MOST PEOPLE.
SEEMS LIKE IT.
COOL.

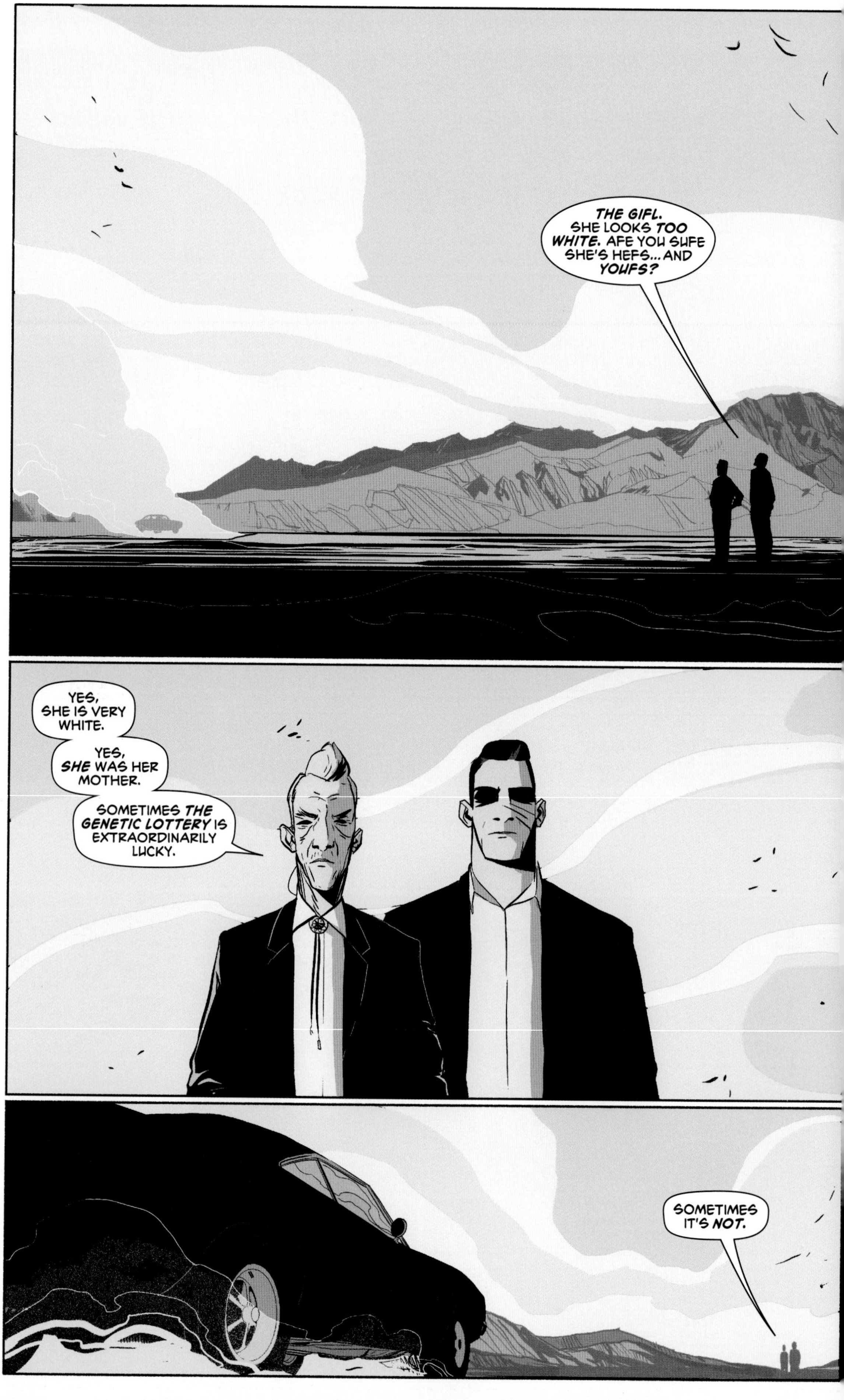
THE GIFL. SHE LOOKS TOO WHITE. AFE YOU SUFE SHE'S HEFS... AND YOUFS?
YES, SHE IS VERY WHITE.
YES, SHE WAS HER MOTHER.
SOMETIMES THE GENETIC LOTTERY IS EXTRAORDINARILY LUCKY.
SOMETIMES IT'S NOT.

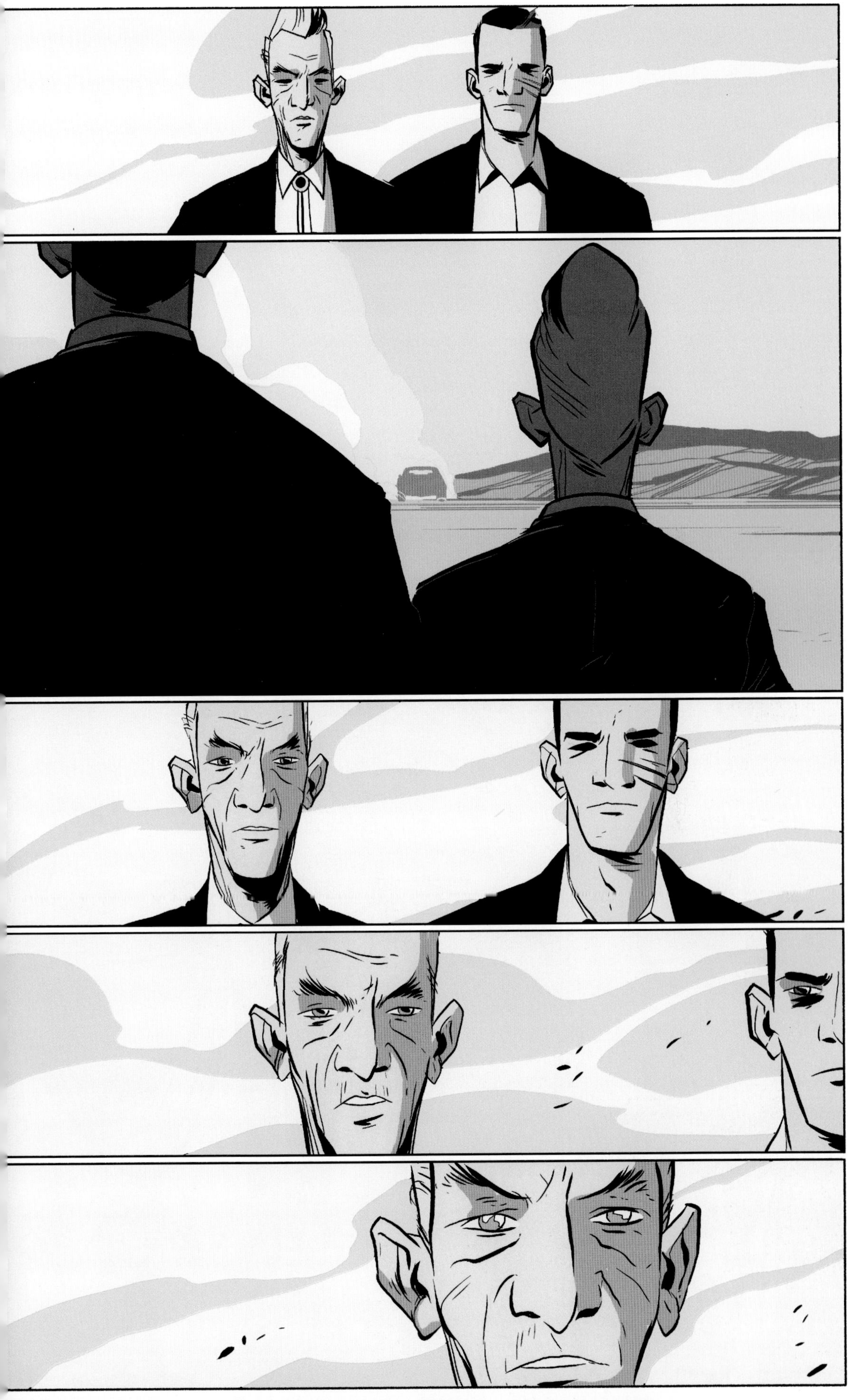

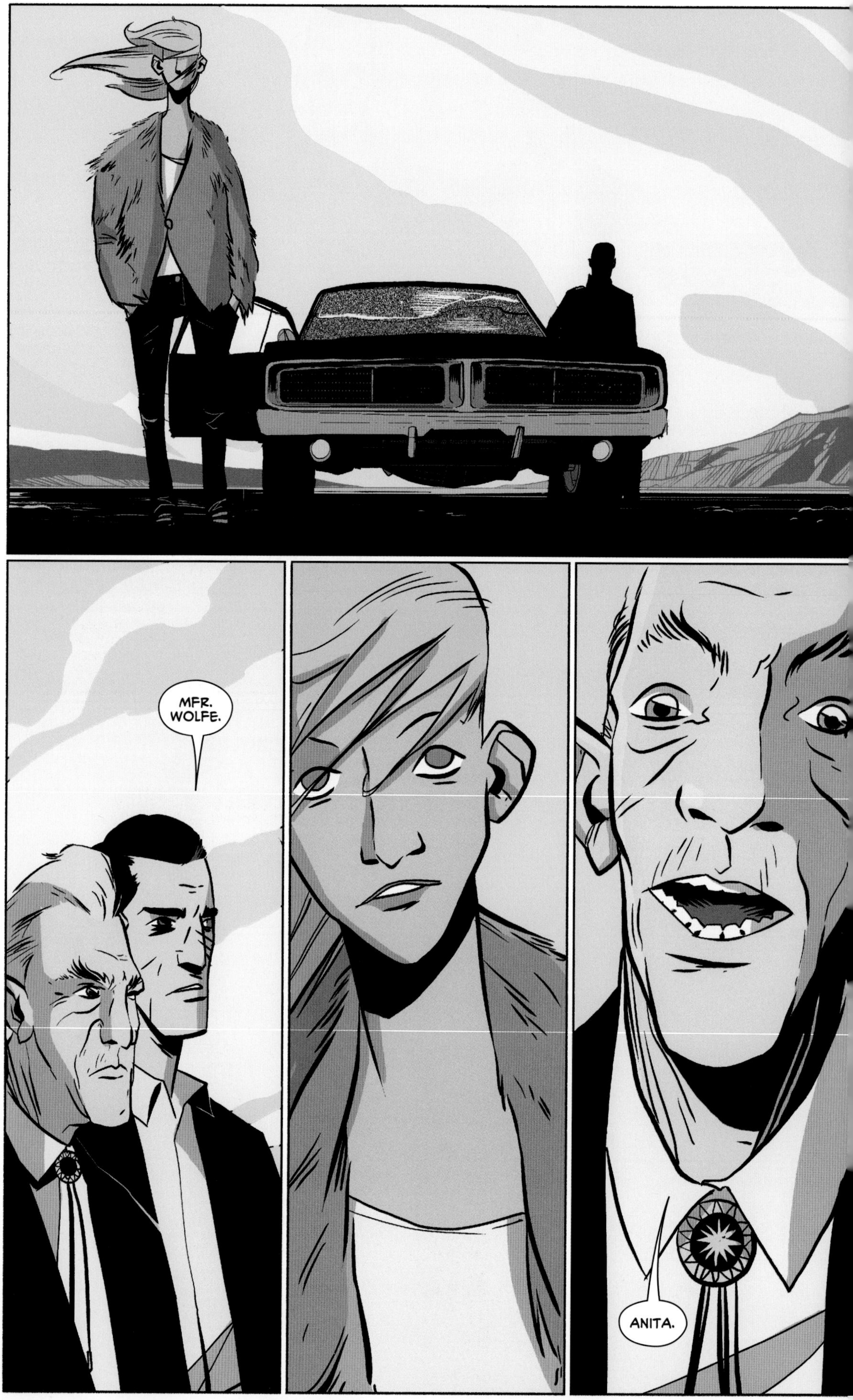
MFR. WOLFE.
ANITA.

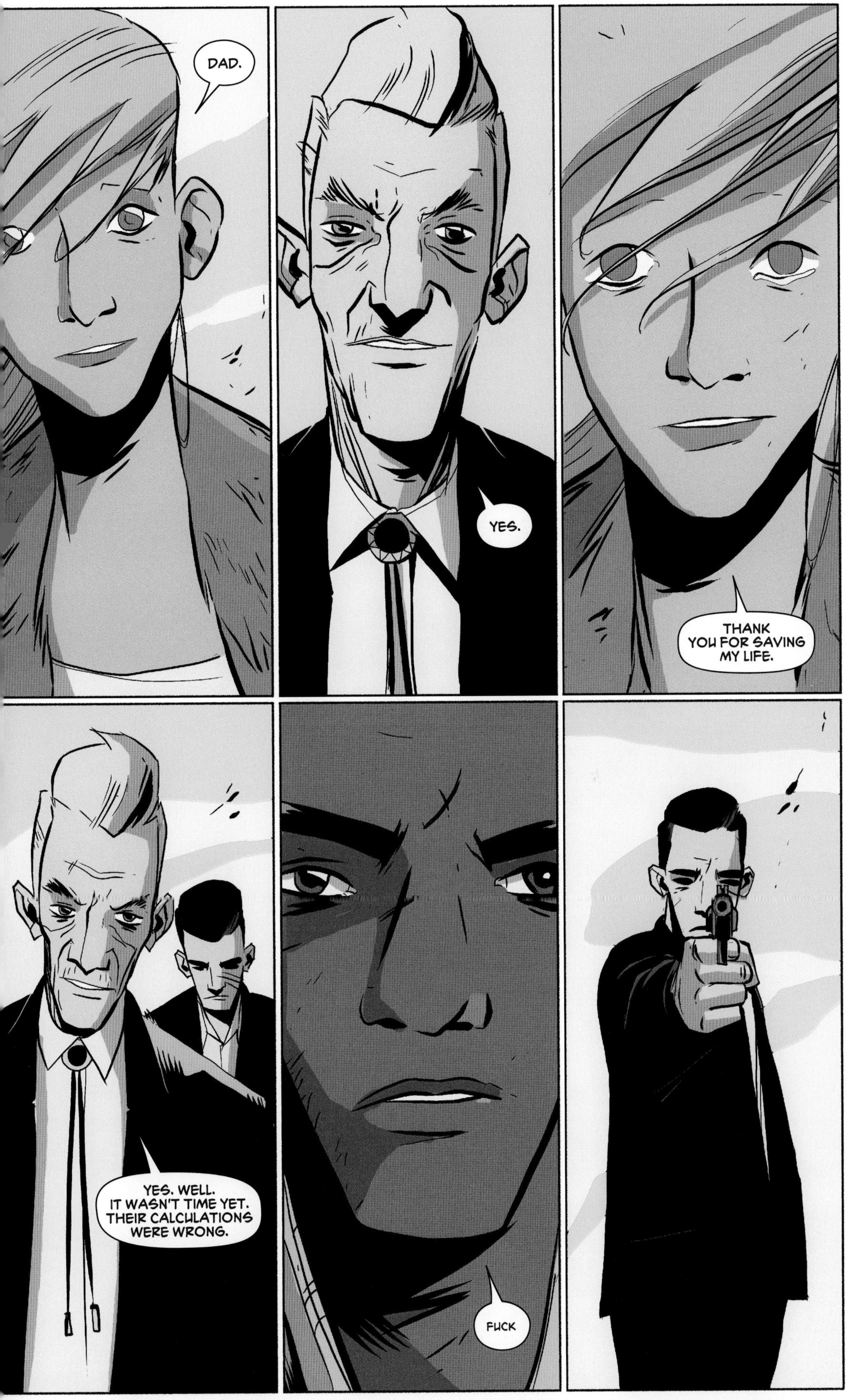
DAD.
YES.
THANK YOU FOR SAVING MY LIFE.
YES. WELL. IT WASN'T TIME YET. THEIR CALCULATIONS WERE WRONG.
FUCK

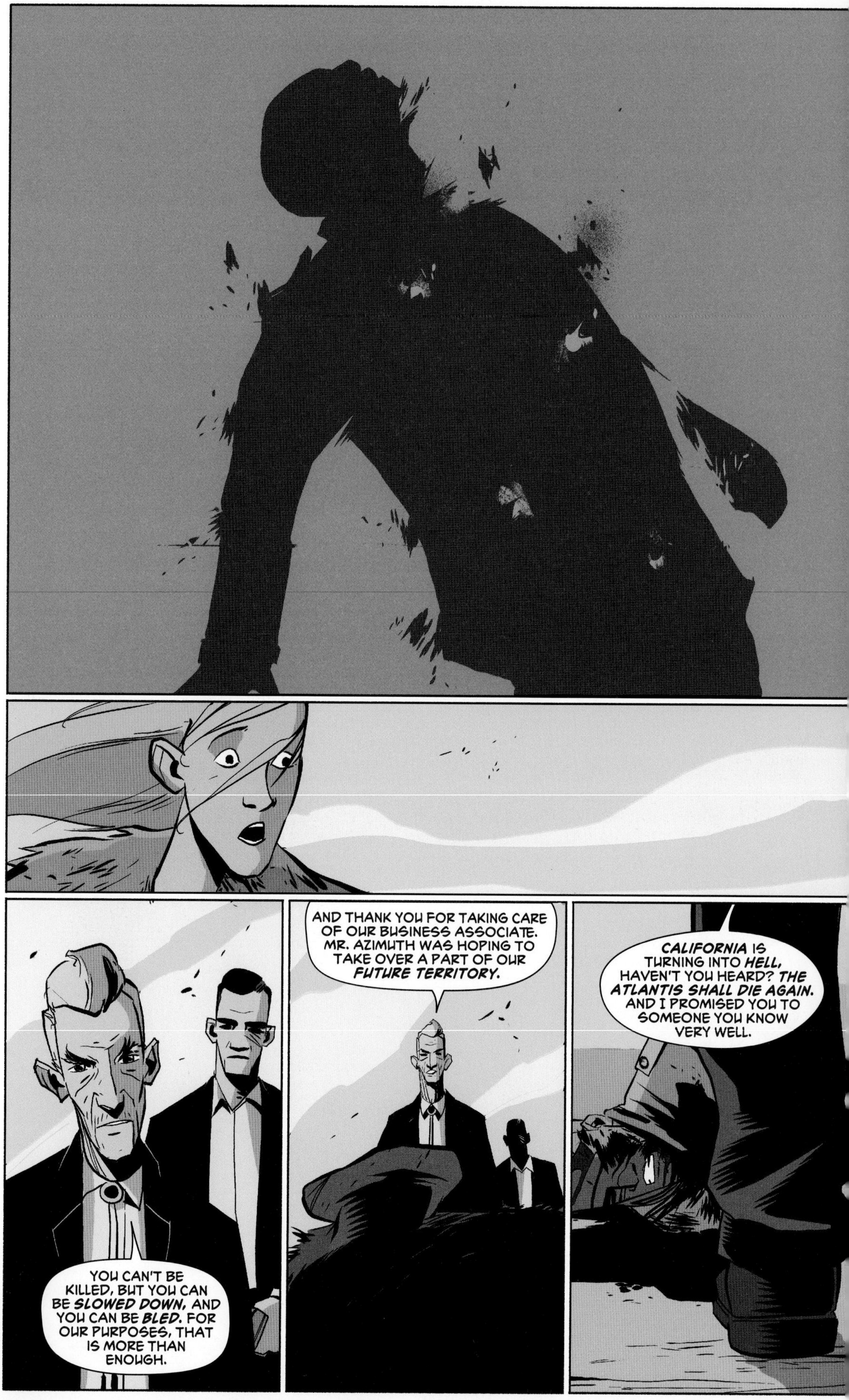
YOU CAN'T BE KILLED, BUT YOU CAN BE SLOWED DOWN, AND YOU CAN BE BLED. FOR OUR PURPOSES, THAT IS MORE THAN ENOUGH.
AND THANK YOU FOR TAKING CARE OF OUR BUSINESS ASSOCIATE. MR. AZIMUTH WAS HOPING TO TAKE OVER A PART OF OUR FUTURE TERRITORY.
CALIFORNIA IS TURNING INTO HELL, HAVEN'T YOU HEARD? THE ATLANTIS SHALL DIE AGAIN. AND I PROMISED YOU TO SOMEONE YOU KNOW VERY WELL.

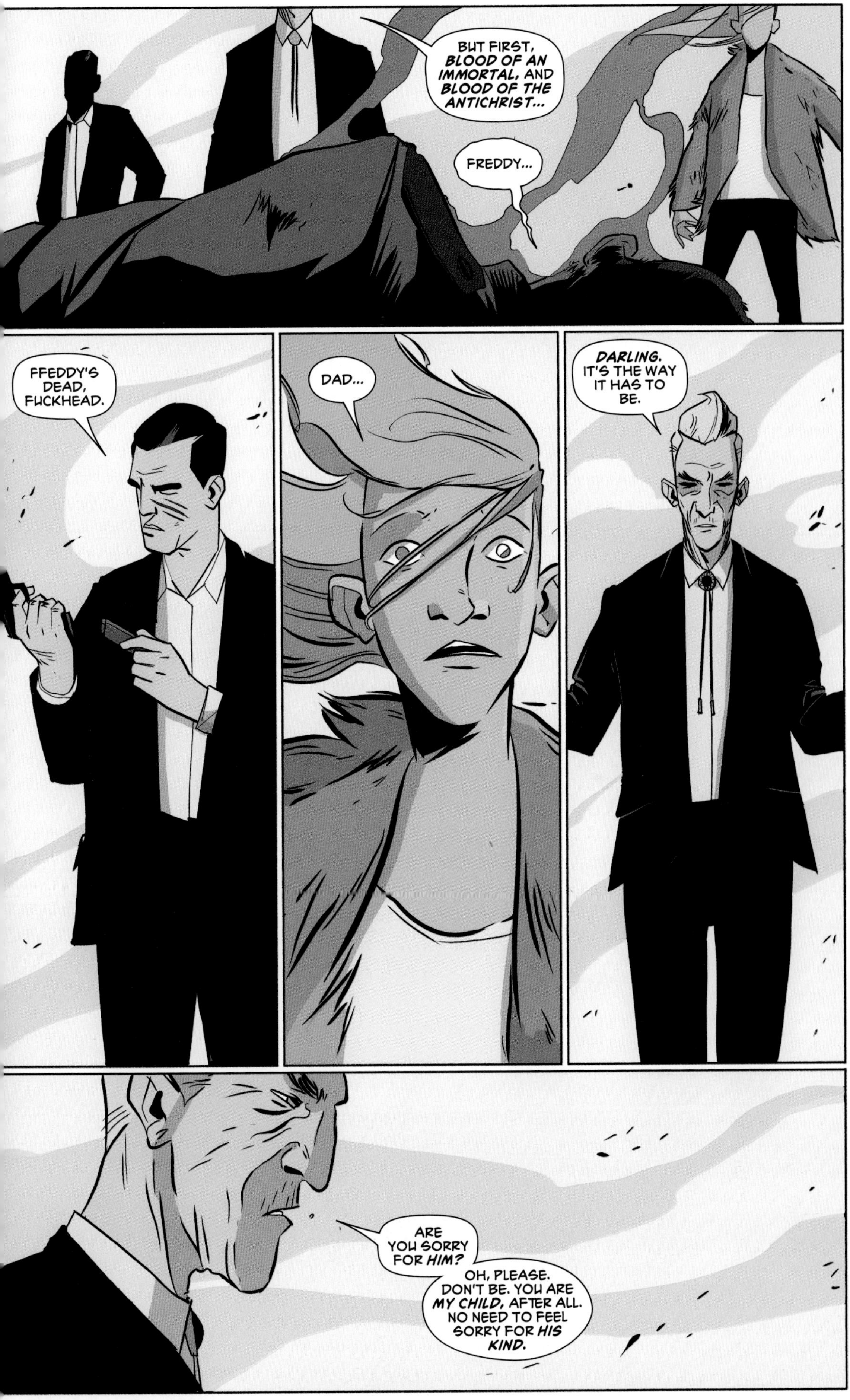
BUT FIRST, BLOOD OF AN IMMORTAL, AND BLOOD OF THE ANTICHRIST...
FREDDY...
FFEDDY'S DEAD, FUCKHEAD.
DAD...
DARLING. IT'S THE WAY IT HAS TO BE.
ARE YOU SORRY FOR HIM?
OH, PLEASE. DON'T BE. YOU ARE MY CHILD, AFTER ALL. NO NEED TO FEEL SORRY FOR HIS KIND.

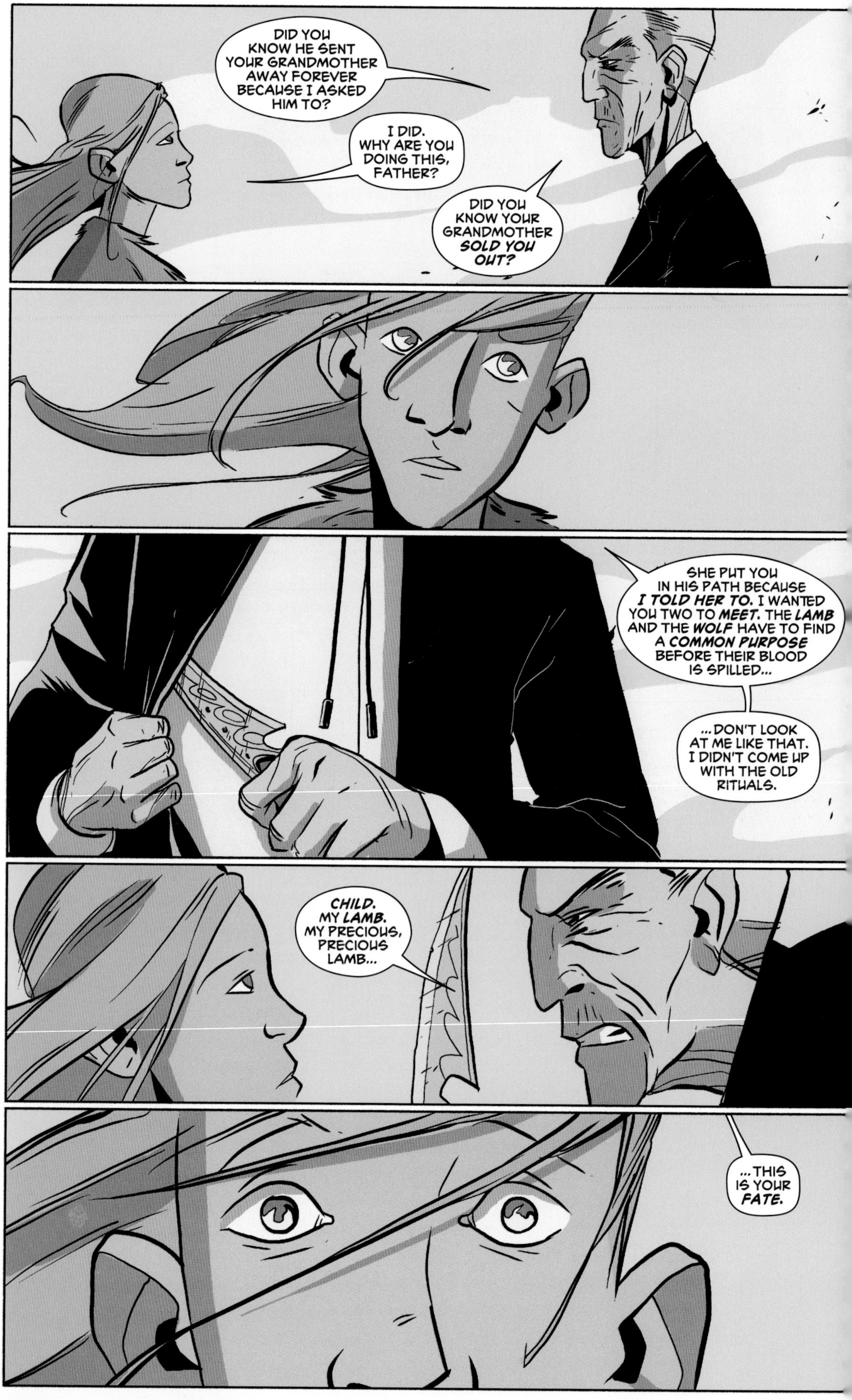
DID YOU KNOW HE SENT YOUR GRANDMOTHER AWAY FOREVER BECAUSE I ASKED HIM TO?
I DID. WHY ARE YOU DOING THIS, FATHER?
DID YOU KNOW YOUR GRANDMOTHER SOLD YOU OUT?
SHE PUT YOU IN HIS PATH BECAUSE I TOLD HER TO. I WANTED YOU TWO TO MEET. THE LAMB AND THE WOLF HAVE TO FIND A COMMON PURPOSE BEFORE THEIR BLOOD IS SPILLED...
...DON'T LOOK AT ME LIKE THAT. I DIDN'T COME UP WITH THE OLD RITUALS.
CHILD. MY LAMB. MY PRECIOUS, PRECIOUS LAMB...
...THIS IS YOUR FATE.

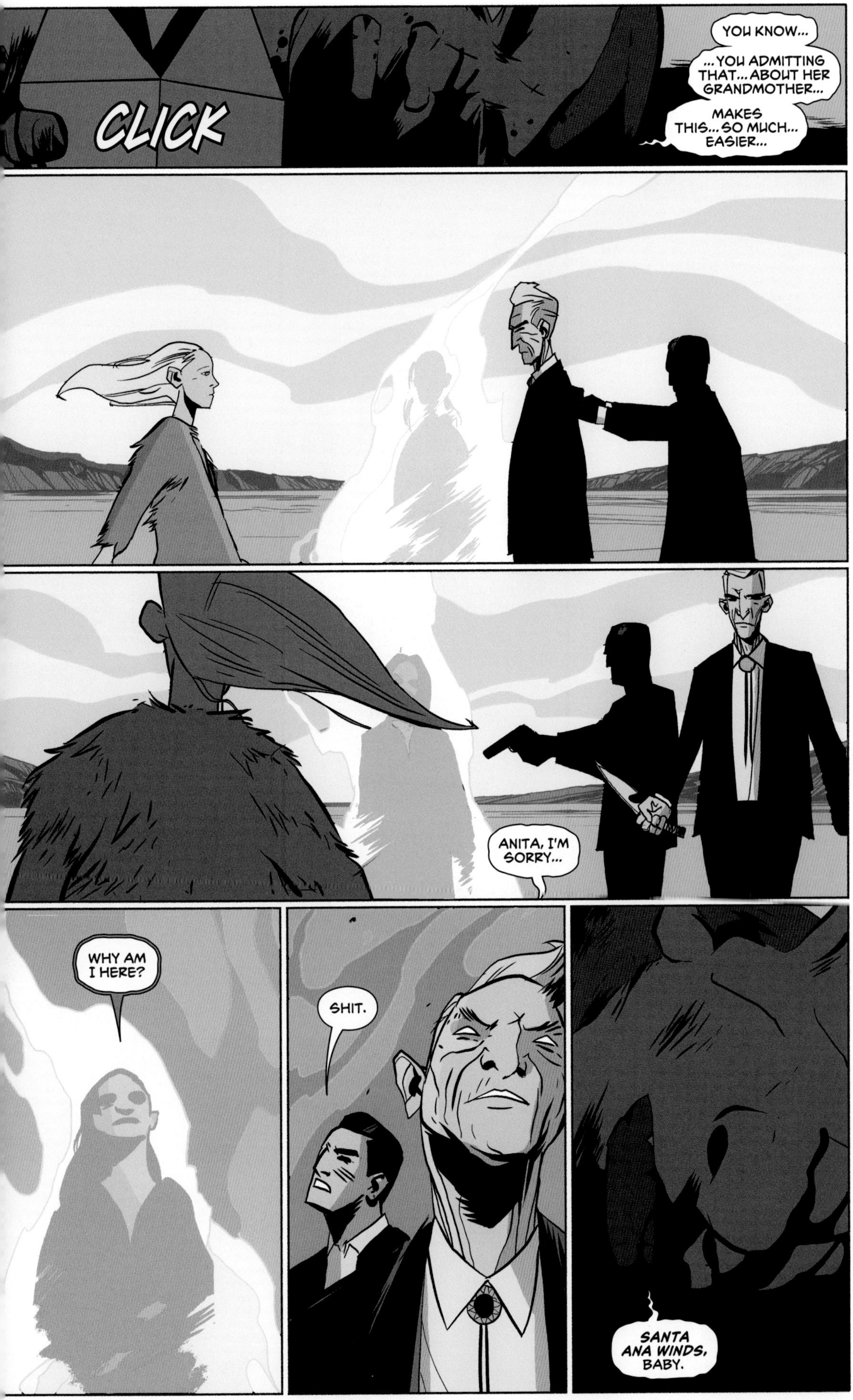
CLICK
YOU KNOW...
...YOU ADMITTING THAT... ABOUT HER GRANDMOTHER...
MAKES THIS... SO MUCH... EASIER...
ANITA, I'M SORRY...
WHY AM I HERE?
SHIT.
SANTA ANA WINDS, BABY.

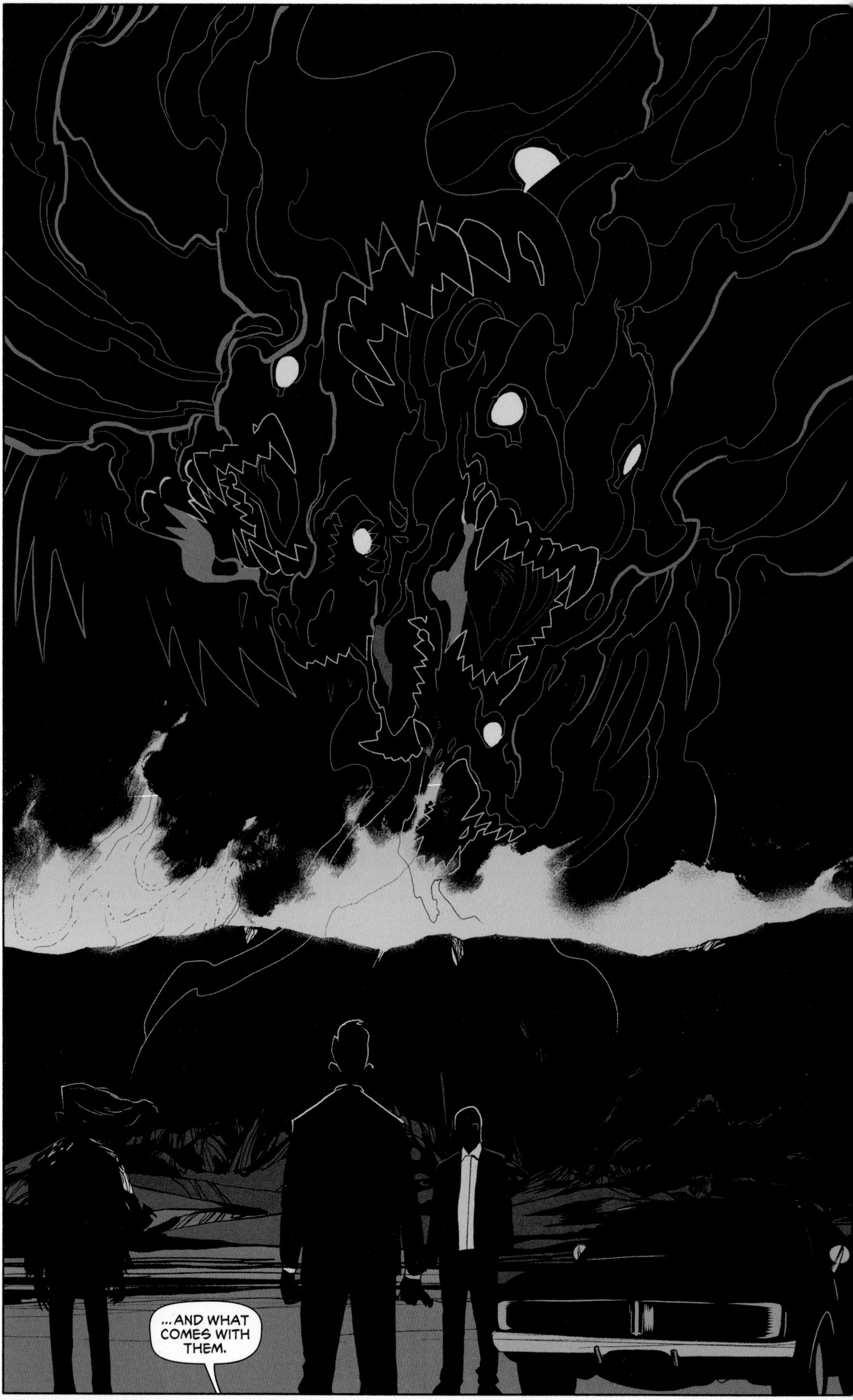
...AND WHAT COMES WITH THEM.

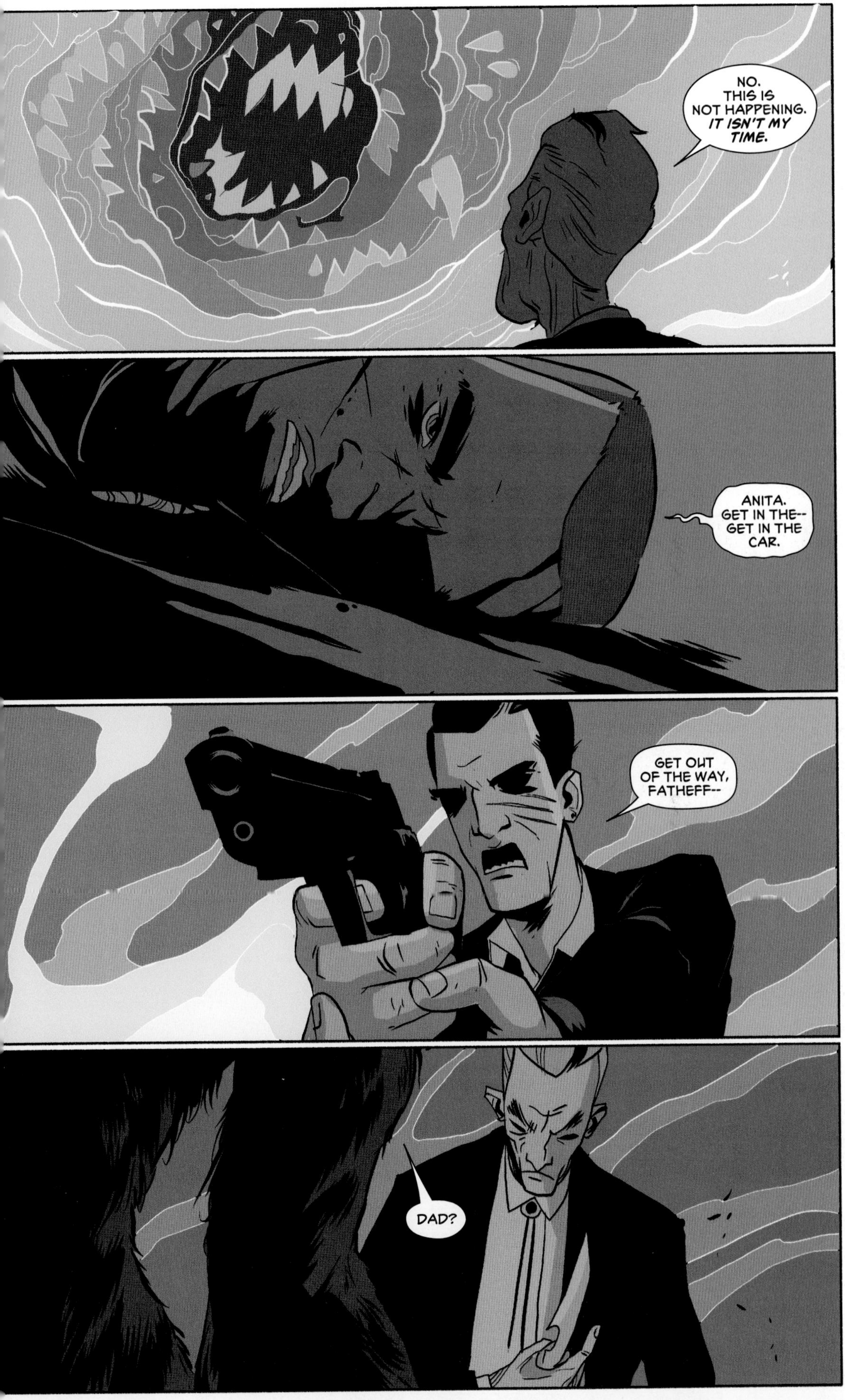
NO. THIS IS NOT HAPPENING. *IT ISN'T MY TIME.*
ANITA. GET IN THE-- GET IN THE CAR.
GET OUT OF THE WAY, FATHEFF--
DAD?

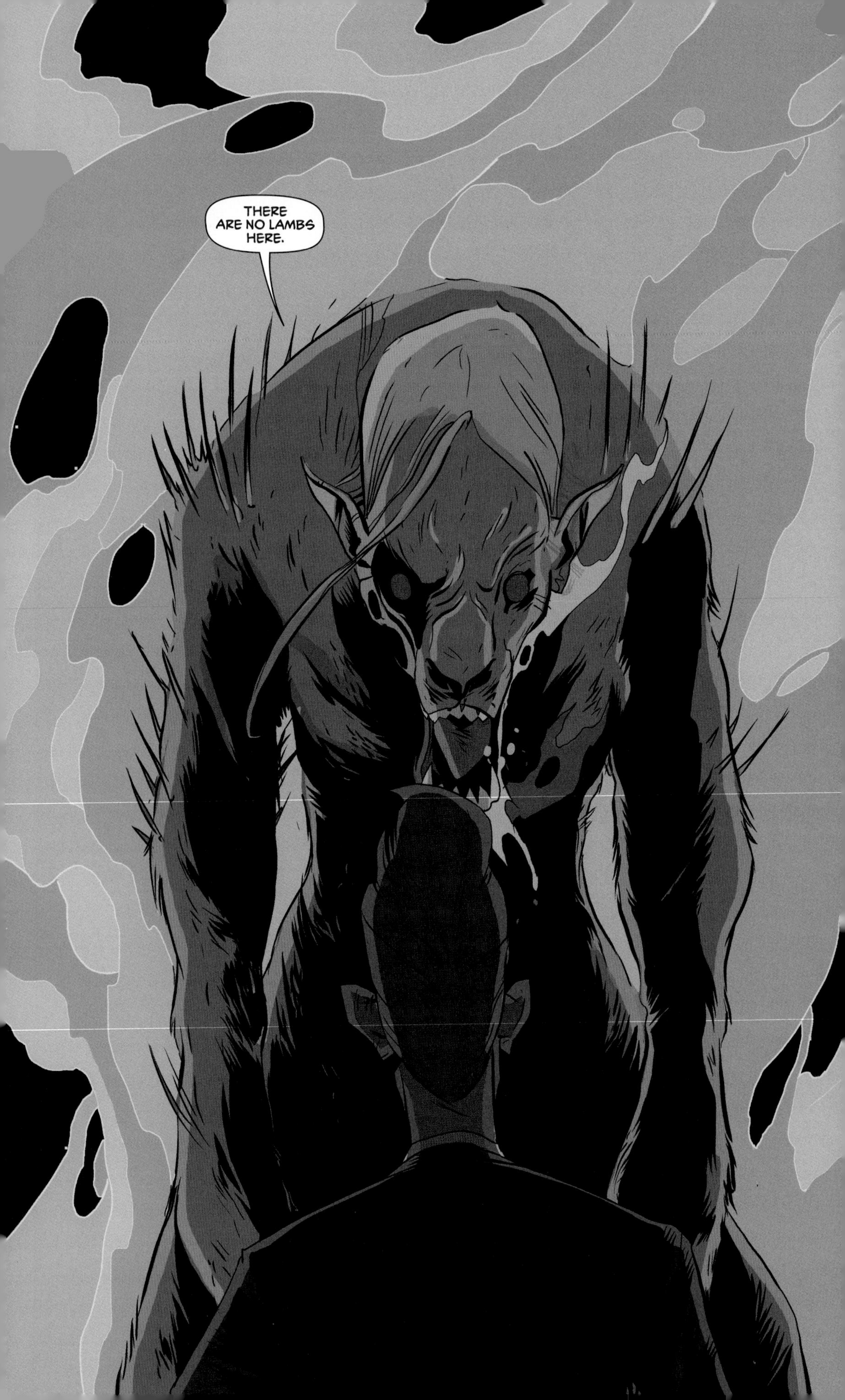
THERE ARE NO LAMBS HERE.

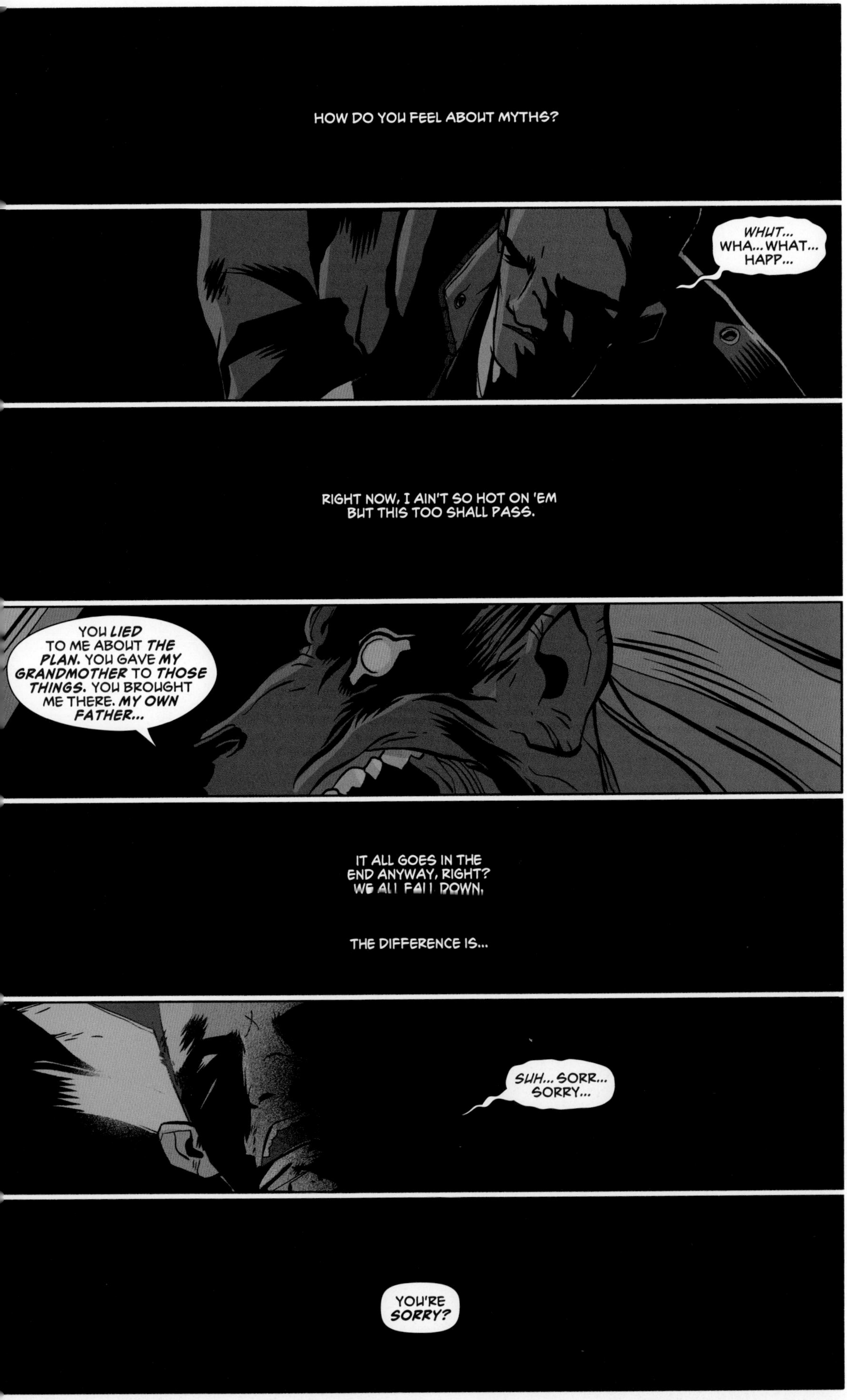
HOW DO YOU FEEL ABOUT MYTHS?
WHUT... WHA... WHAT... HAPP...
RIGHT NOW, I AIN'T SO HOT ON 'EM BUT THIS TOO SHALL PASS.
YOU LIED TO ME ABOUT THE PLAN. YOU GAVE MY GRANDMOTHER TO THOSE THINGS. YOU BROUGHT ME THERE. MY OWN FATHER...
IT ALL GOES IN THE END ANYWAY, RIGHT? WE ALL FALL DOWN.
THE DIFFERENCE IS...
SUH... SORR... SORRY...
YOU'RE SORRY?

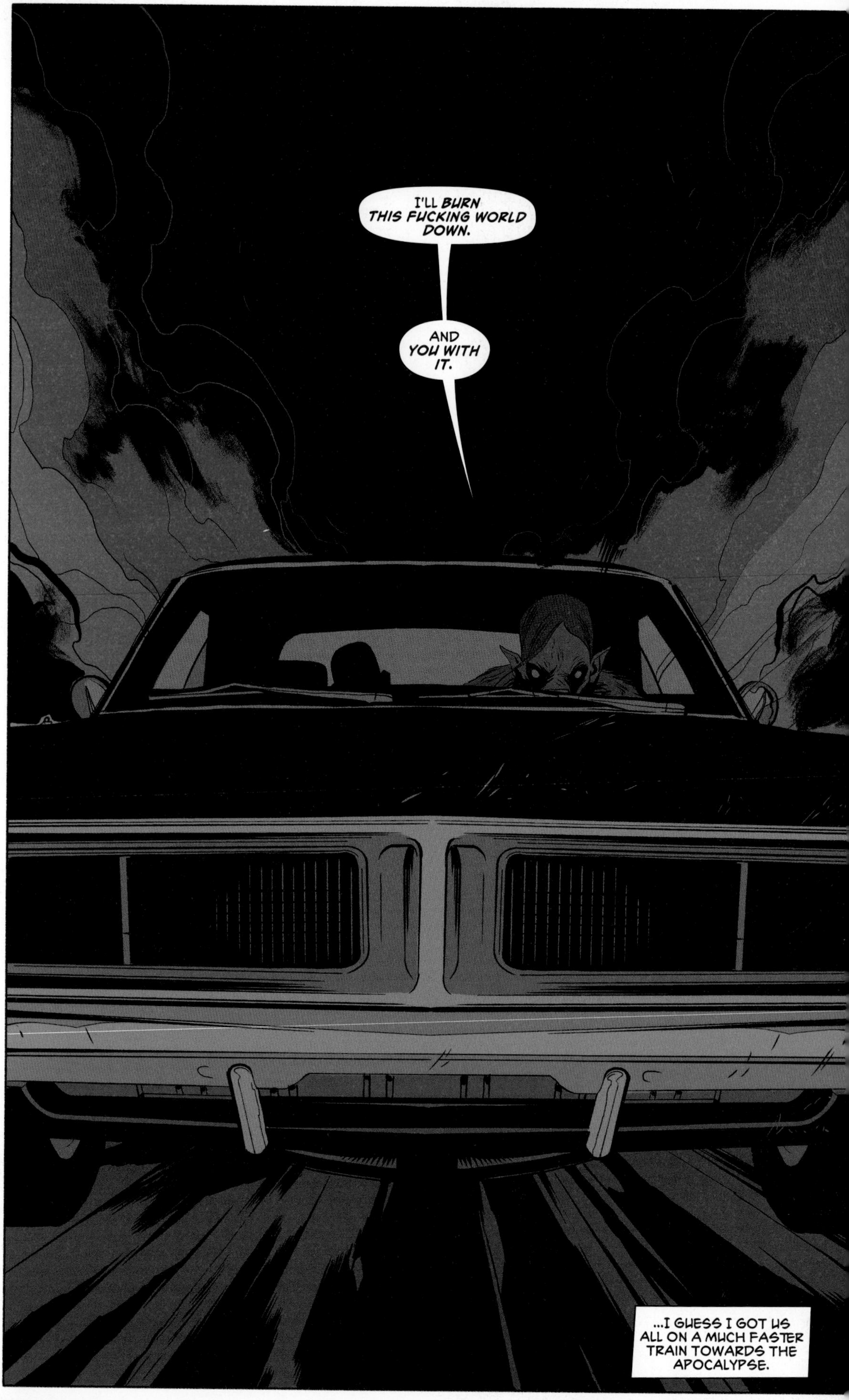
I'LL BURN THIS FUCKING WORLD DOWN.
AND YOU WITH IT.
...I GUESS I GOT US ALL ON A MUCH FASTER TRAIN TOWARDS THE APOCALYPSE.

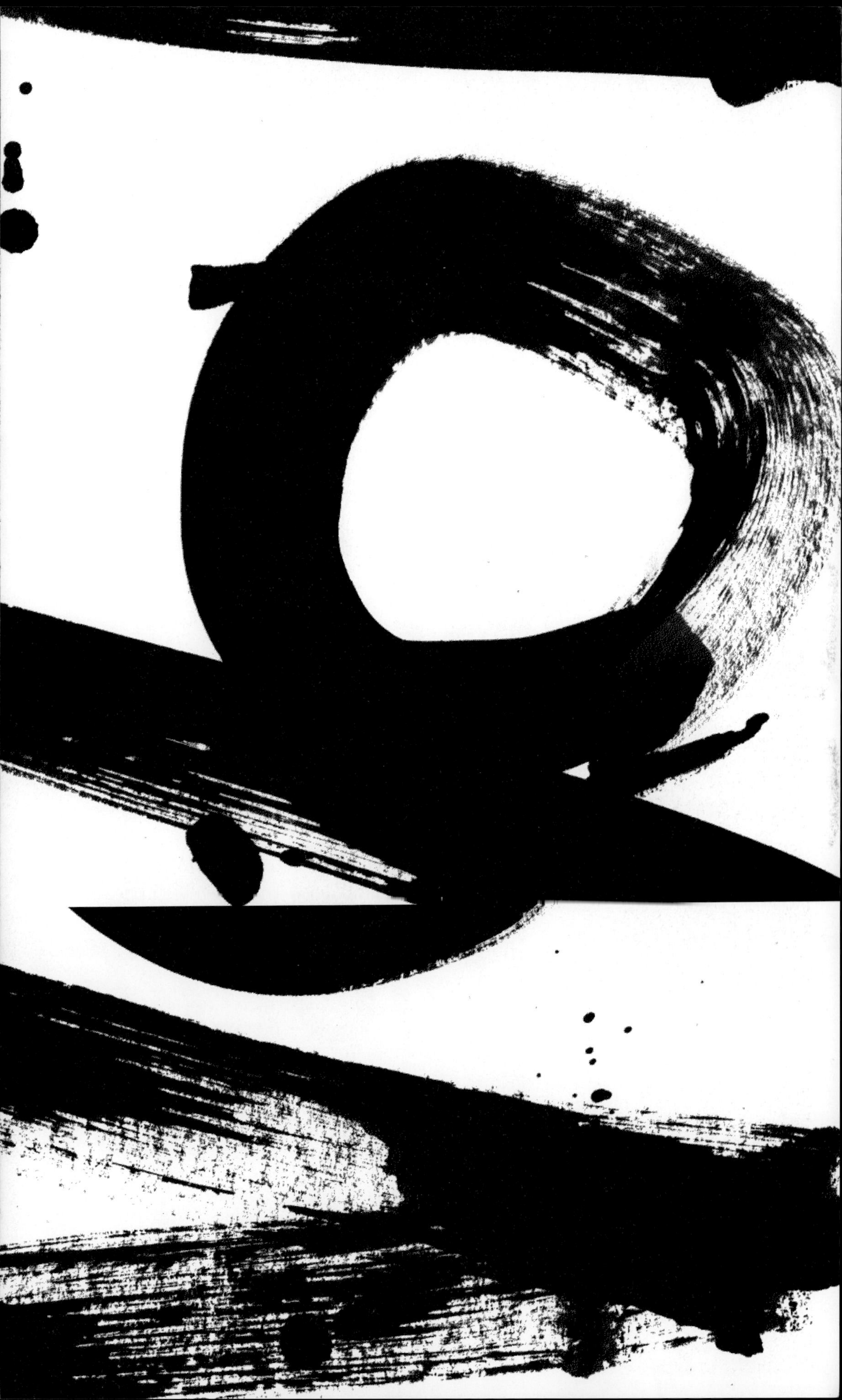

ORIGINAL WOLF #1–4 COVERS. ILLUSTRATED BY MATT TAYLOR AND DESIGNED BY TOM MULLER

Blood and magic.

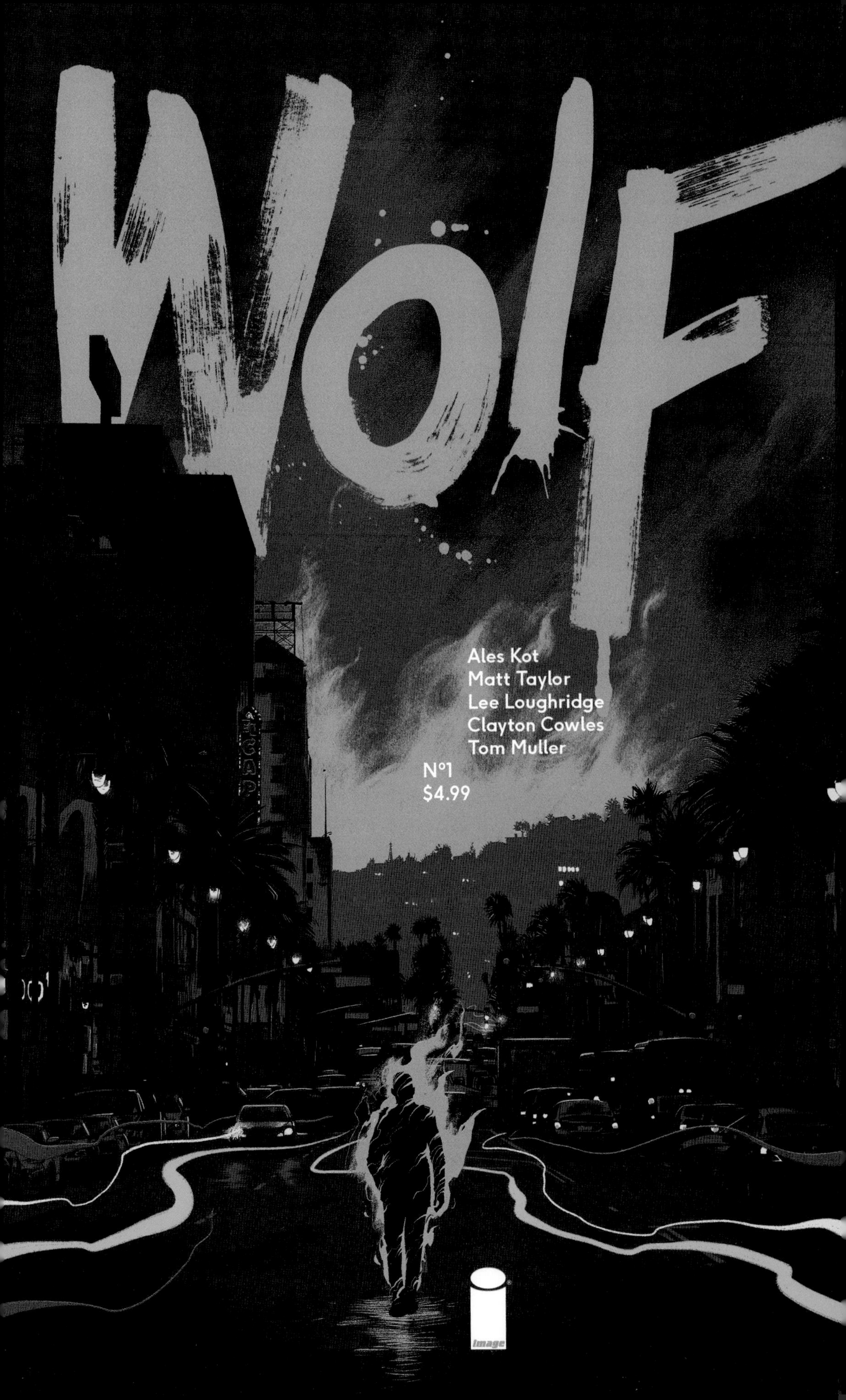
WOLF
Ales Kot
Matt Taylor
Lee Loughridge
Clayton Cowles
Tom Muller
N°1
$4.99

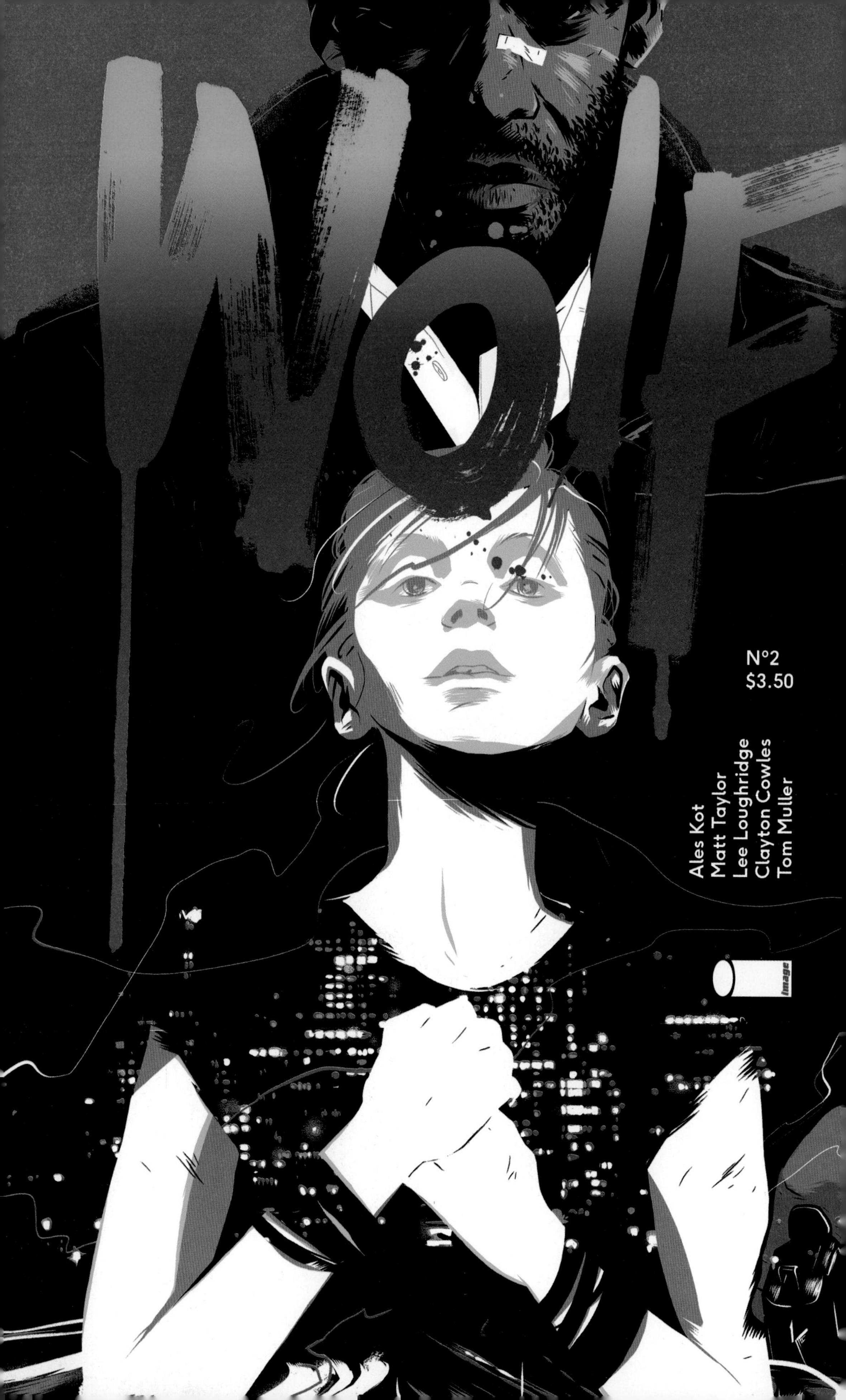

N°2
$3.50
Ales Kot
Matt Taylor
Lee Loughridge
Clayton Cowles
Tom Muller
image

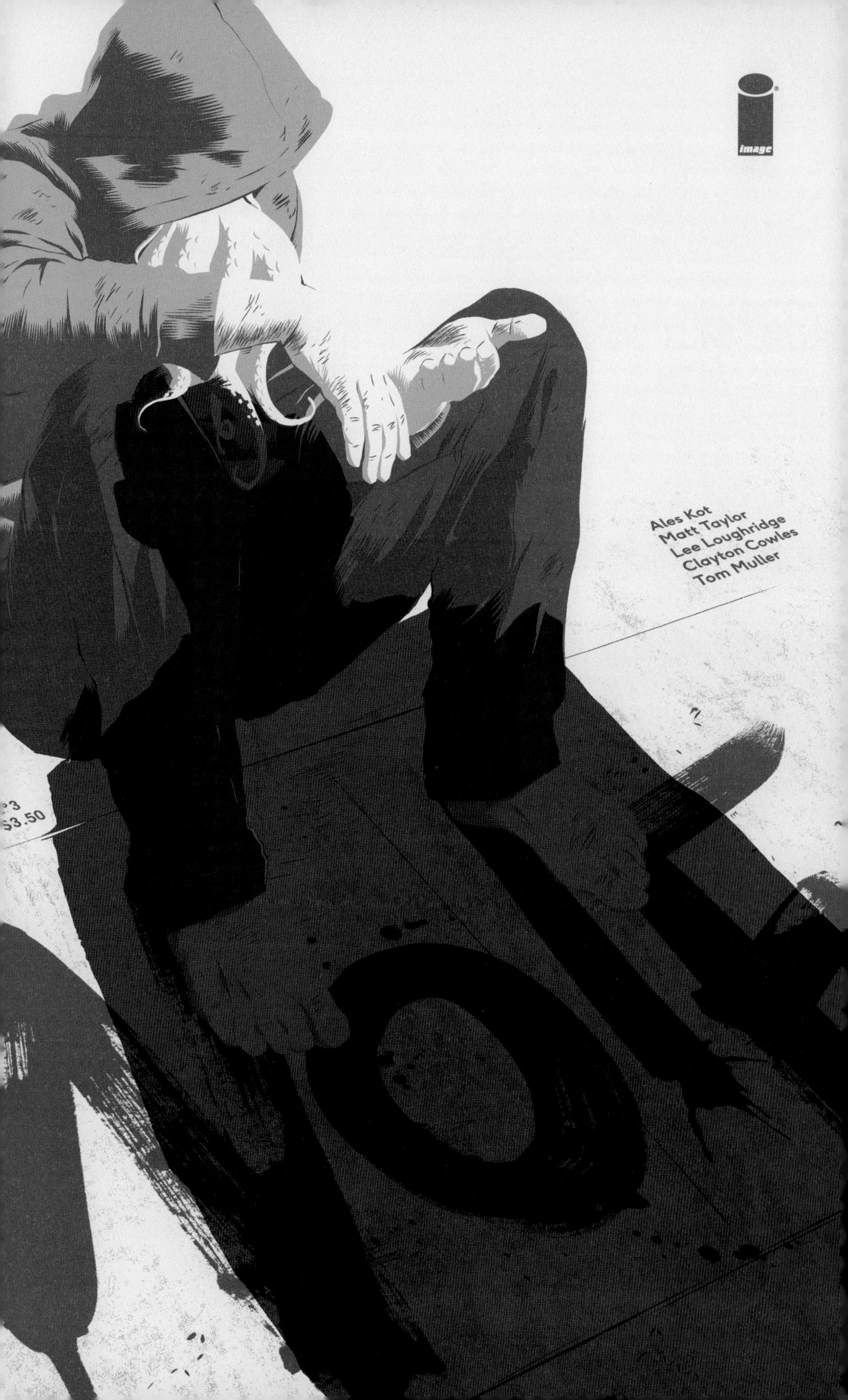

Ales Kot
Matt Taylor
Lee Loughridge
Clayton Cowles
Tom Muller
$3.50

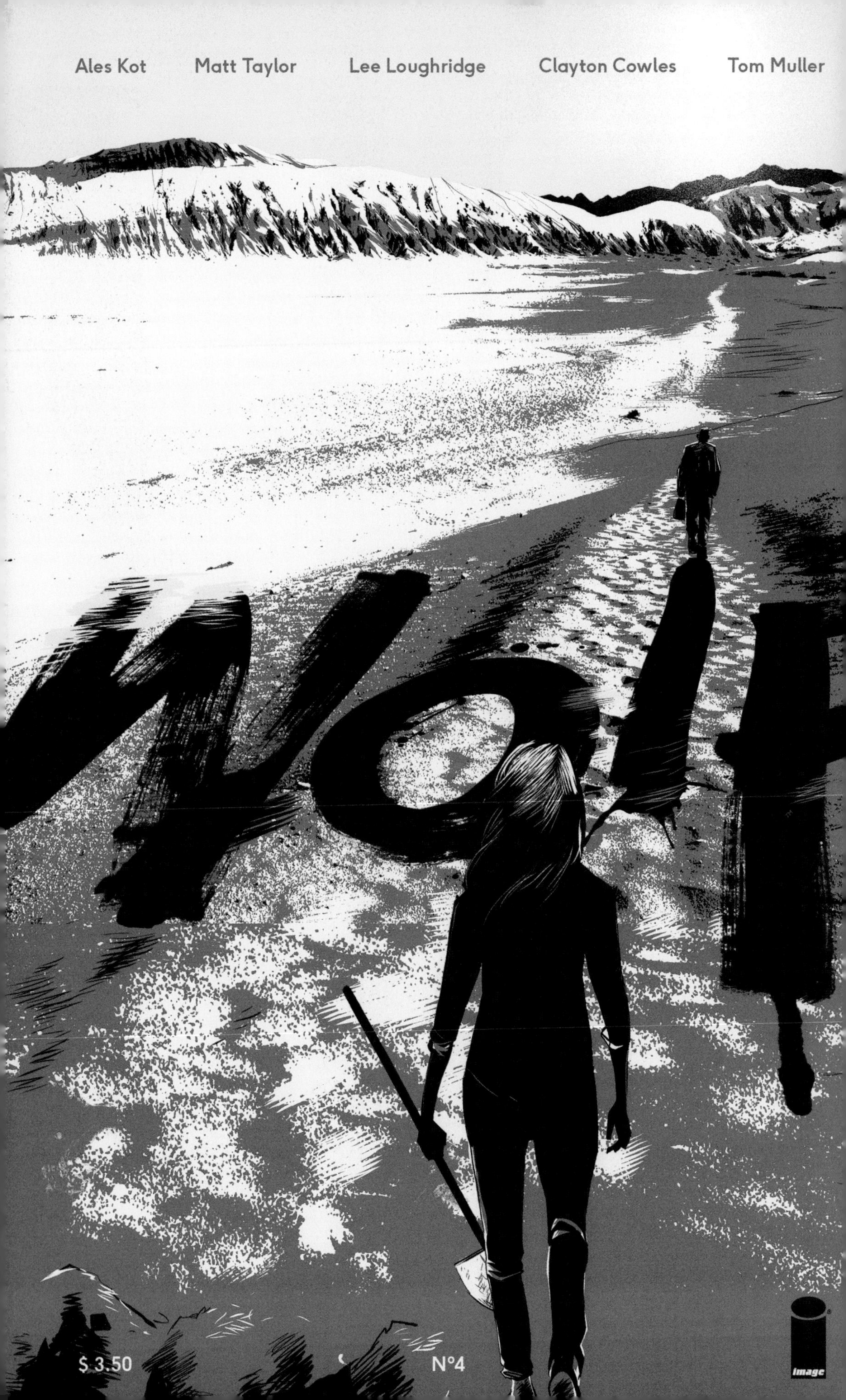
Ales Kot
Matt Taylor
Lee Loughridge
Clayton Cowles
Tom Muller
N°4
$ 3.50
N°4

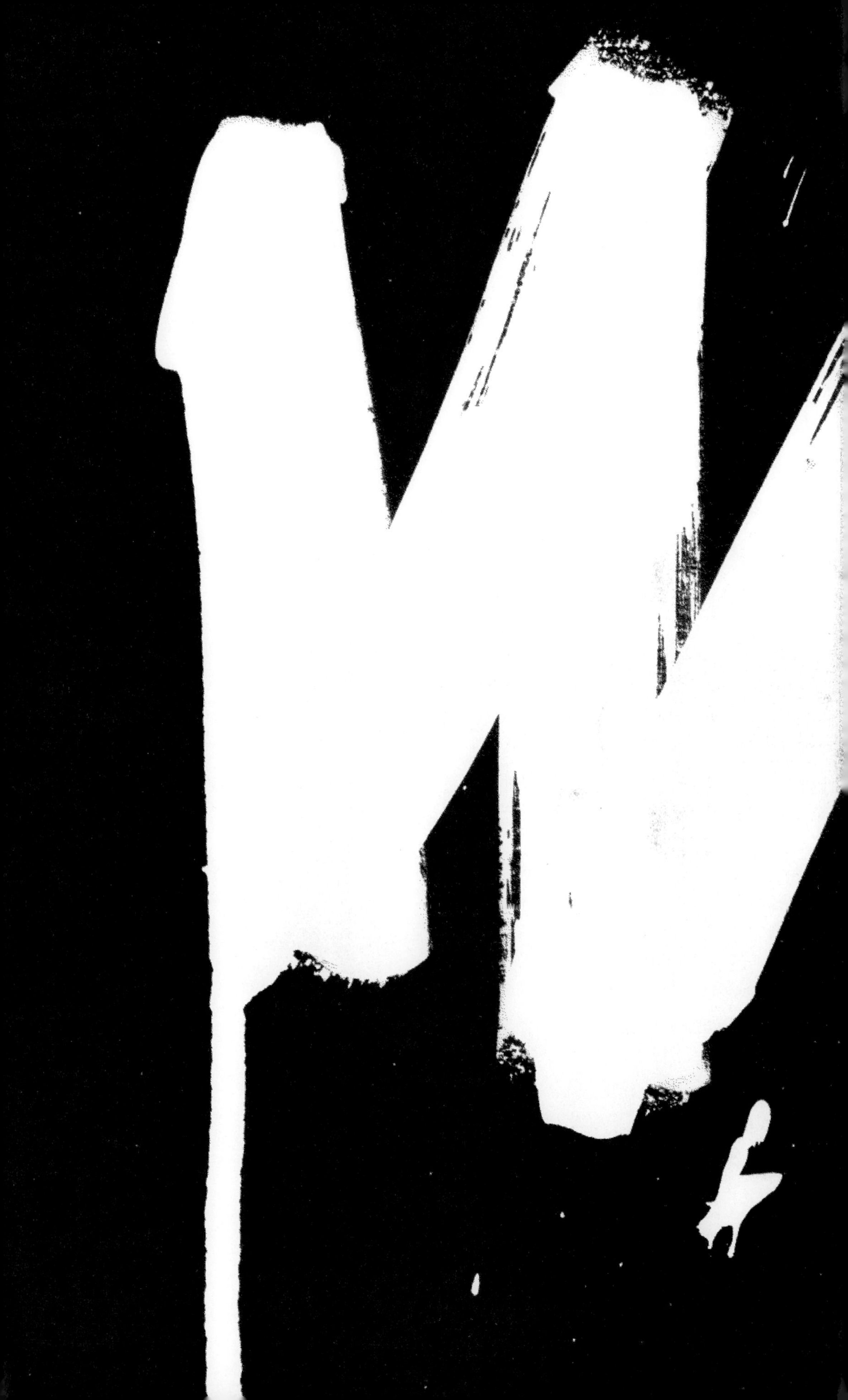

CREATORS:
ALES
KOT,
MATT
TAYLOR,
LEE
LOUGHRIDGE
CLAYTON
COWLES,
TOM
MULLER.

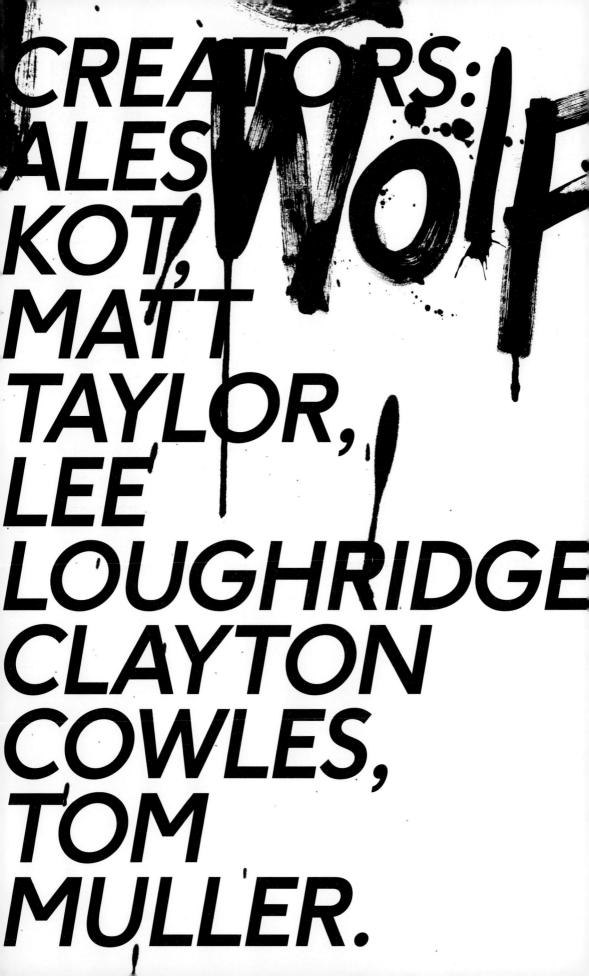

Photo by Clayton Cubitt

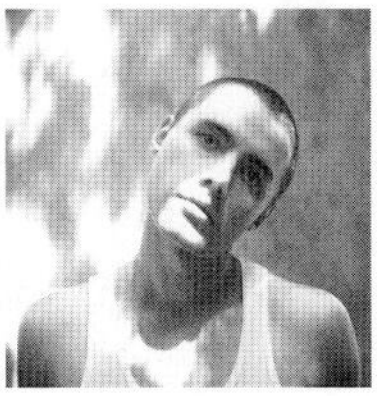

Ales Kot invents, writes & runs projects & stories for film, comics, television & more. He also wrote/still writes: *Change*, *Zero*, *Wolf*, *The Surface*, *Wild Children*. Current body born September 27, 1986 in Opava, Czech Republic. Resides in Los Angeles. Believes in poetry.

@ales_kot

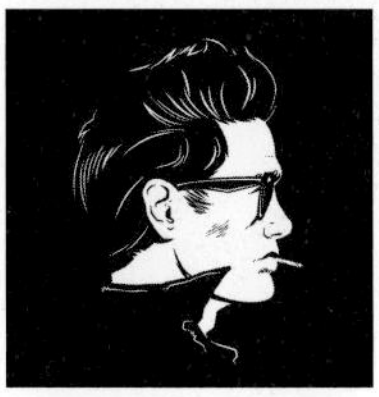

Matt Taylor is an illustrator and comic artist based in the Sussex countryside who spends his days crafting expansive, sometimes psychedelic, Americana inspired illustrations with a nod to classic comic book art of the fifties and sixties.

@matttaylordraws

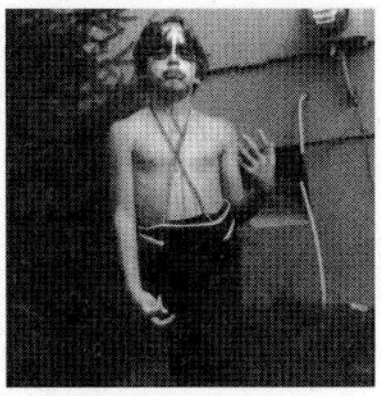

Lee Loughridge resides in Southern California.
He doesn't think a dog is just like a child and never takes photos of food.

@leeloughridge

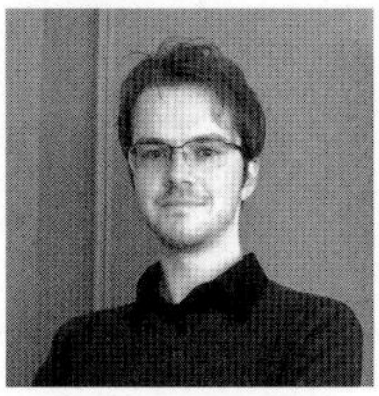

Clayton Cowles graduated from the Joe Kubert School of Cartoon and Graphic Art in 2009, and has been lettering for Image and Marvel Comics ever since. For Image, his credits include *Bitch Planet*, *Pretty Deadly*, *The Wicked + The Divine*, and less than ten others.
His Marvel credits include *Fantastic Four*, *Young Avengers*, *Secret Avengers*, *Bucky Barnes: Winter Soldier* and way more than ten others. He spends his real life in upstate New York with his cat.

@claytoncowles

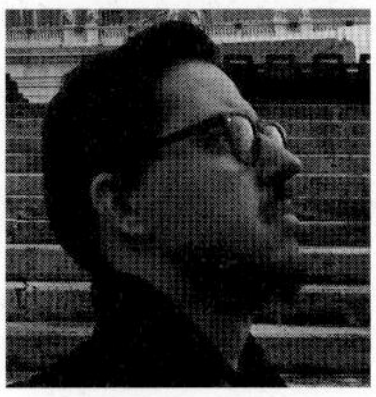

Tom Muller is an Eisner Award nominated Belgian graphic designer who works with technology startups, movie studios, publishers, media producers, ad agencies, and filmmakers. His recent comics design credits include Darren Aronofky's *NOAH*, *Zero*, *The Surface*, *Material*, and *Drifter* for Image Comics; *Constantine*, *Unfollow*, *Robin*, and *Survivors' Club* for DC/Vertigo Comics; *Divinity* and *Book of Death* for Valiant Entertainment.
He lives in London with his wife, and two cats.

@helloMuller

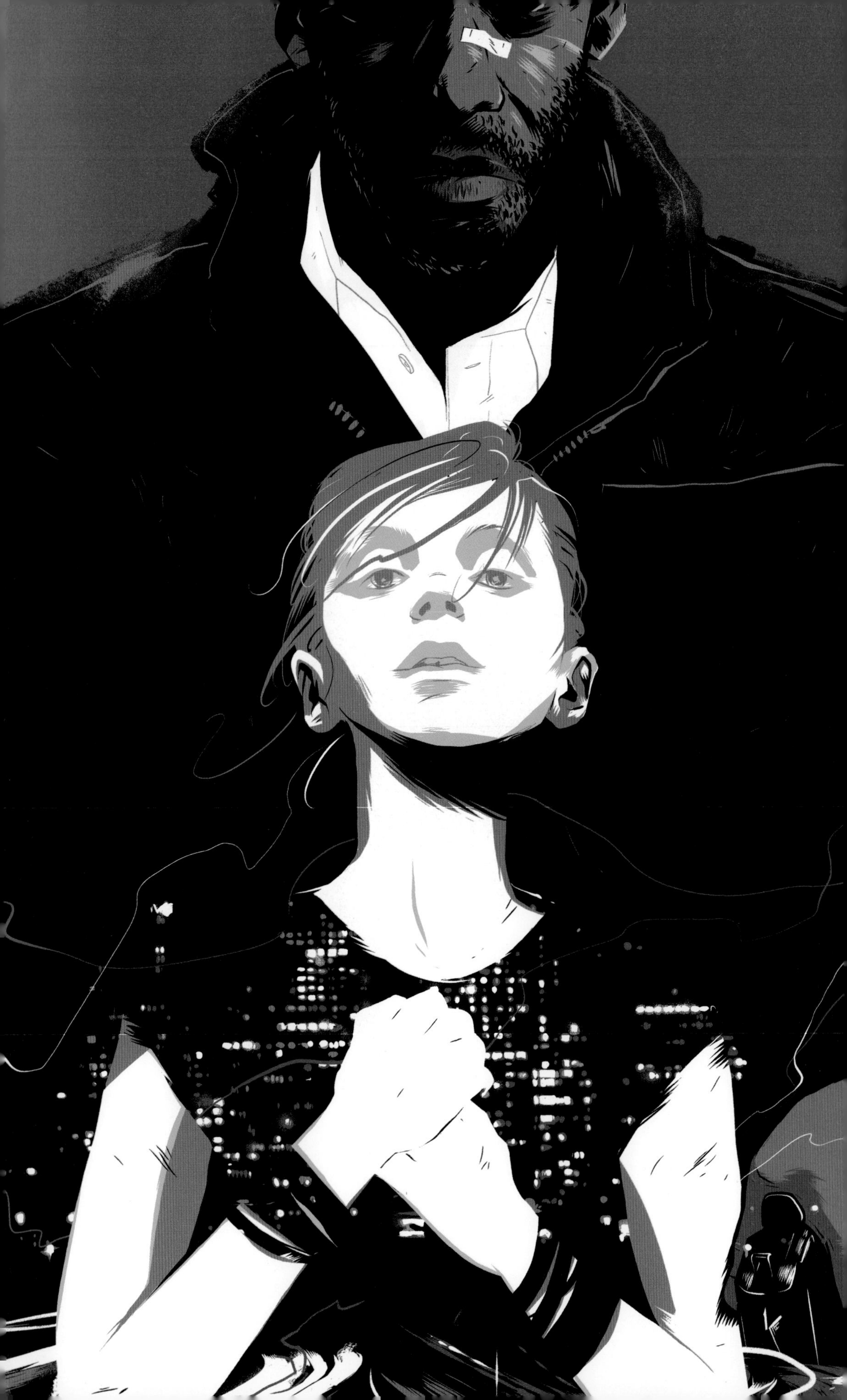

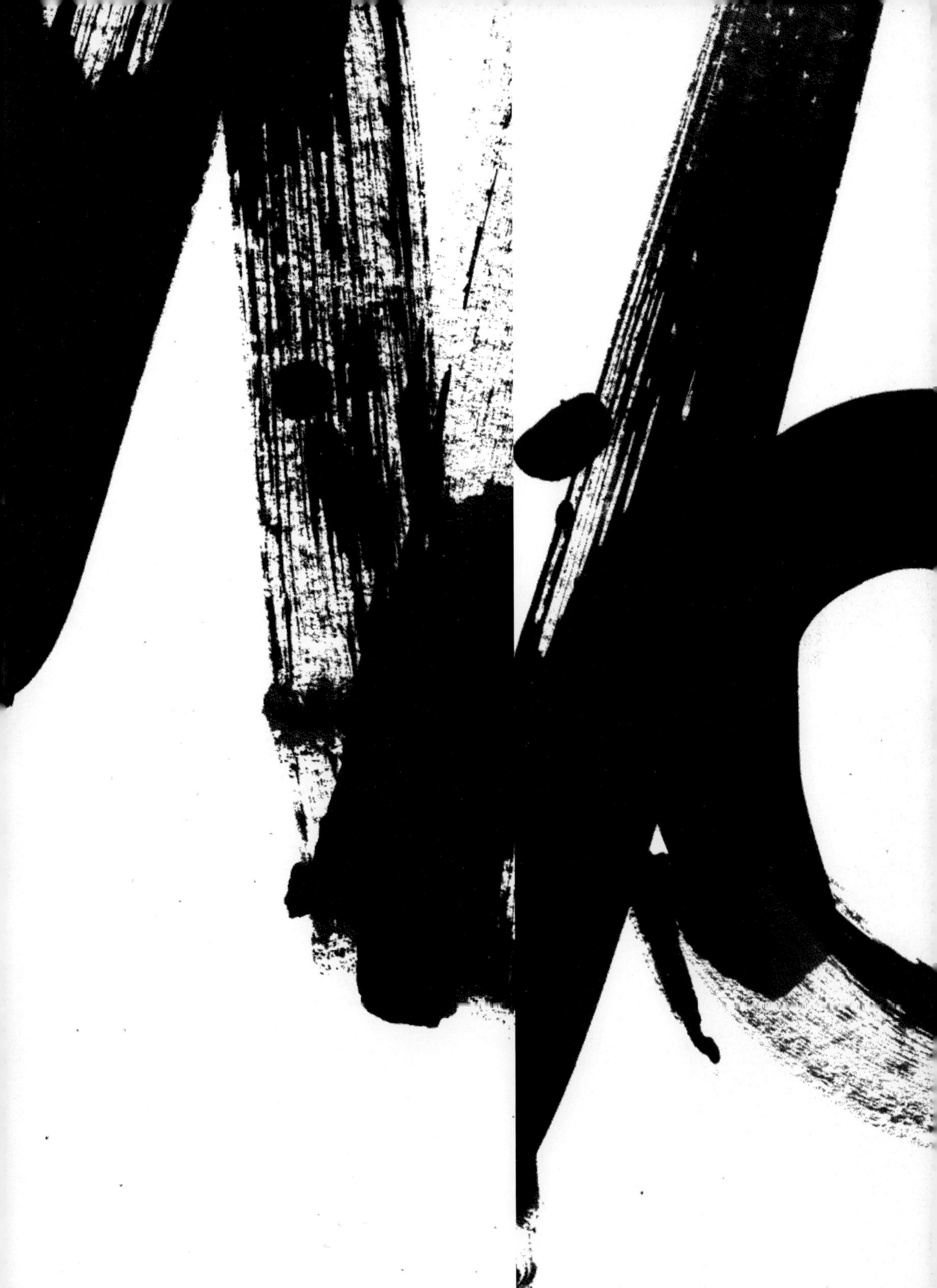

Media inquiries should be directed to Roger Green &
Phil D'Amecourt at WME Entertainment and Ari Lubet at 3 Arts Entertainment.

ISBN: 978-1-63215-502-3

Published by
Image Comics, Inc.

Volume 1

Blood and magic.